HITLER'S
WOMEN

HITLER'S
WOMEN

GUIDO KNOPP

TRANSLATED BY ANGUS MCGEOCH

SUTTON PUBLISHING

First published in 2001 by C. Bertelsmann Verlag GmbH, Munich,
under the title *Hitlers Frauen – und Marlene*.
This English translation first published in 2003 by
Sutton Publishing Limited · Phoenix Mill
Thrupp · Stroud · Gloucestershire · GL5 2BU

This paperback edition first published in 2006

In collaboration with Alexander Berkel, Stefan Brauburger,
Christian Deick, Friederike Dreykluft, Peter Hartl, Ricarda
Schlosshan.

Research: Alexander Berkel, Christine Kisler, Mario Sporn
Translation: Angus McGeoch

British Library Cataloguing in Publication Data
A catalogue record for this book is available from the British Library.

ISBN 0 7509 4438 2

Typeset in 10/12.5pt Galliard.
Typesetting and origination by
Sutton Publishing Limited.
Printed and bound in England by
J.H. Haynes & Co. Ltd, Sparkford.

CONTENTS

PICTURE CREDITS

LIST OF ILLUSTRATIONS

EVA BRAUN
1. Eva Braun
2. Eva Braun as a teenager
3. Eva Braun as Hitler's companion
4. 'A nice German girl . . .'
5. Hitler and his mistress

MAGDA GOEBBELS
6. Hitler and Magda Goebbels on an election tour in 1932
7. Joseph and Magda Goebbels
8. The Goebbels family
9. The bodies of the six Goebbels children, 1945

LENI RIEFENSTAHL
10. With Heinrich Himmler at the 1934 Nazi Party rally
11. Talking to Goebbels about her film *Festival of Nations*
12. With Hitler, her idol

WINIFRED WAGNER
13. With her husband Siegfried at Wahnfried
14. Winifred and Siegfried Wagner with their children
15. After a motor-trip with Hitler
16. Goering and Winifred Wagner leaving Bayreuth's Festspielhaus

ZARAH LEANDER
17. With Goebbels, the Minister of Propaganda
18. Collecting money for the Winter Welfare fund
19. Zarah Leander as a singer
20. With director Alfred Braun in 1953

MARLENE DIETRICH

INTRODUCTION

From the very beginning Hitler was helped by women. Yet up to now historical debate has focused on men – as perpetrators and guilty executives – while women have been assigned the role of mere auxiliaries, who mourned their dead and, at the end, contributed to the German catharsis as *Trümmerfrauen*, clearing the rubble of bombed cities. Yet although they did not fight at the battle-front, women often supported the dictator to just as great an extent as men. Like men, they voted the Nazis into power, played a part in the regime, averted their eyes from its crimes, and shouted '*Heil Hitler*' just as loudly. Some found the strength to withstand the allure of Nazi propaganda. This was true not only of the average woman in the street, but also for women who were prominent in Hitler's Reich. This book presents six life stories that vary from collaboration to dissent, from conformity to resistance. Here is Eva Braun, whose lifelong dream of marrying Hitler was only fulfilled in the face of death; Magda Goebbels, the woman more devoted to Hitler than to her own husband; the operatic muse Winifred Wagner, who even after 1945 refused to accept the truth about the monster she idolised; and the genius of propaganda cinema, Leni Riefenstahl who, at the age of 100 in 2002, weighed the achievements of her turbulent life against the errors she had committed. Then we meet the singer Zarah Leander who throughout her life faced the accusation of having been an opportunist, of profiting from the efforts of the regime to maintain a mood of national defiance in the face of constant bombing and inevitable defeat.

And what of Marlene Dietrich, Hitler's adversary? Is it permissible to mention her name in the same breath as 'Hitler's Women'? Yes it is, because her life symbolises those women who were able to break free from Hitler's spell. Despite the tempting offers to return to her film career in Germany, she resisted the Führer's blandishments – and fought him with all the means at her disposal.

What was it that made women follow Hitler? What was it about him that so fascinated them that they let themselves become the instruments of his will? And what enabled some to resist his frenzy?

What do these lives teach us? That it is often only a short step from conformity to dissent, from collaboration to resistance. None of these women were born with a predisposition to become attached to Hitler. In the end it was always their own conscious decision: from Eva Braun, who, while there was still time, could have refused to accept the bleak life that Hitler offered her – to Marlene Dietrich, who from the very beginning refused to have anything to do with him. Even if the particular turning-points that determined their life's path can sometimes only be recognised as such in retrospect, that moment of no return is always the product of their own will. History is not a black and white affair – it shimmers in many different shades of grey. The lives of 'Hitler's Women' are an example of this.

CHAPTER ONE

THE MISTRESS – EVA BRAUN

The one thing I long for is to be seriously ill and have nothing to do with him for at least a week. Why doesn't anything like that happen to me? Why do I have to go through all this?

He only needs me for certain purposes.

Why does he torture me so? Why doesn't he just end it right now?

Actually, it's quite obvious that he's not much interested in me, now that there's so much going on politically.

For the time being, love seems to have been dropped from his schedule.

Me, the mistress of the greatest man in Germany and on earth . . .

Eva Braun, diary entries 11 March–10 May 1935

The Führer himself has lost all faith in a successful outcome . . .

Any day and at any time it could be the end for us.

Eva Braun, letter dated 23 April 1945

She had a neat little figure, slim, very soignée. Of course, she had the time for that and the money too. Had a fantastic wardrobe and changed several times a day, for lunch, for dinner. Somehow you couldn't help liking her.

Herbert Döhring, Hitler's majordomo at the Berghof

Of course, she was vain. Otherwise she wouldn't have changed clothes so often. But she didn't do that to please others, only herself. She always wanted to see herself in a new pose, in a new dress.

Gertraud Weisker, Eva Braun's cousin

She never showed any feelings one way or the other about Hitler's politics or his brutal measures. None of that interested her. And as far as I know she never even said anything against the Jews. That was completely unknown territory to her. She never grasped the problems that drove Hitler to action, or the problems that he caused.

Otto Gritschneder, the Braun family's lawyer after 1945

She could have been a pleasant little sales-girl in a shoe-shop, who you might enjoy a chat with. She was just an average person – a nice German girl from a very ordinary background.

Reinhardt Spitzy, adviser to the Foreign Minister, Joachim von Ribbentrop

It was something no-one knew about. I think it was the best-kept secret of all; but no-one was *obliged* to keep quiet. The funny thing was, we just instinctively avoided talking or gossiping about it.

Traudl Junge, Hitler's secretary

The year when the Nazi regime paraded itself under false colours was 1936. It was the year when the nations of the world gathered in Berlin for the summer Olympic Games. For several weeks Hitler's Reich was on display to the world. The Party was asked to soft-pedal things, the SS and Gestapo were ordered to be on their best behaviour, anti-Semitic slogans disappeared from walls, and the smear-sheet, *Der Stürmer*, could only be sold under the counter. Suddenly, a wide selection of foreign publications could be seen on the news-stands. One morning a journalist, whom we shall call Alois W., found a copy of *Paris Soir* on his desk. This French tabloid was not normally very strong on foreign affairs – but that day's issue certainly was. On the back page was a sensational headline: 'Hitler and his women'. The story ended with the words: 'The clear favourite is now Eva Braun, the daughter of a Munich schoolteacher. It is obvious that Hitler has forgotten all other women and only has eyes for her.'

'It made me jump clean out of my chair!' Alois wrote later in a private memoir that he presented to a relative of Eva Braun. 'Our Eva? It can't be! Not the little girl I had helped, in my very inadequate way, when she was in despair over her arithmetic homework, the girl for whom I had rewritten so many essays, only to have them returned with the teacher's stern comment: "Strays from the subject!" – the girl who said her prayers every night, so deeply influenced was she by her pious grandmother.' But Uncle Alois, a cousin of Eva's mother, had not misread the item. Faced with information like that, what was he to do?

'I dashed to the phone and called my Cousin Fanny, to congratulate her on the fact that apparently she was soon going to be the Führer's mother-in-law.' Fanny certainly did not share her cousin's amusement: 'She told me not to talk such rubbish: the whole business had already given her enough trouble! And anyway, she did *not* want to discuss it on the telephone.'

Uncle Alois had touched a sensitive point in the Braun family – the 'sleazy' relationship between their Eva and the Reich Chancellor, Adolf Hitler. For years it had been a major headache for the family. For Hitler had no intention of making an honest woman of this Munich girl, twenty-three years his junior.

Things did not change for another nine years, when Hitler's Reich was on the brink of destruction. Eva's cousin Gertrude Weisker sums it up today with bitter irony: 'He no longer had any reason to hesitate. Until then, it was said that he was wedded to Germany. But now there no longer *was* a Germany. So he probably thought he *could* after all marry the woman he had strung along for sixteen years.'

*

Berlin, 28 April 1945. The bunker under the Reich Chancellery shuddered from direct hits by Soviet shells. Thirty feet beneath the earth the mood was apocalyptic. 'That day Eva Braun said something strange to me; she said, you will be shedding tears for me before today is over.' Hitler's secretary, Traudl Junge, believed the moment had come when Hitler and Eva Braun would take their own lives. But it was not that ultimate act that Eva was referring to. 'What she actually meant was her marriage to Hitler.' The rumour had been going round for several days. Certainly, some doubt was permissible. Throughout his political career the dictator had made strenuous efforts to appear as the legendary 'Führer', who was above all human needs and weaknesses. Only when his suicide became unavoidable could Hitler bring himself 'to take as my wife the girl who, after long years of loyal friendship, came of her own free will to this beleaguered city in order to link her destiny with mine'. In return for years of humiliation Eva Braun was finally to receive her reward – a wedding-ring. It had been acquired on the spur of the moment and was rather too large for the bride's finger. The ceremony was a grotesque charade and clearly only took place because the bridegroom had nothing more to lose.

Even under the hail of artillery-shells the marriage pedantically observed the formalities laid down by the registrar. Hitler's formal request, 'in view of the military situation to give oral notice of the intended matrimony', was no less macabre than the couple's written assurance that they were both of Aryan extraction and suffered from no hereditary diseases that would render the marriage invalid.

Eva Braun was nervous. A makeshift altar had been hastily assembled in the conference-room of the Reich Chancellor's bunker. A city official, one Walter Wagner, had been drafted in to speak the solemn words that Hitler's paramour had longed for so many years to hear: 'I now ask you, Fräulein Braun, whether you are willing to enter into matrimony with *mein Führer*, Adolf Hitler.' The 33-year-old Eva did not hesitate for a second before answering 'yes'. The strains of a song called 'Blood-red Roses' could be heard in the background. For the suburban girl from Munich a dream had come true. Wearing a dress of black silk taffeta, she became Frau Hitler. But just how long was this lifetime union to last? Less than a single day.

'I had the feeling', says Traudl Junge, 'that she remained in the shadows all her life and probably had no chance to do anything else. I expect she imagined she would at least go down in history as the heroic mistress.'

After the war, when the world became aware of Eva Braun for the first time, the questions came thick and fast: what kind of woman was it who stood at the dictator's side, who for more than a decade was so close to the Nazi war-lord, the greatest murderer of the century? What did she mean to Hitler? Was she just a mistress, or was she a partner in the fullest sense? Did she know nothing of the evil and misery that her lover plunged the world into? Was she a supporter or even an accomplice? Why did she follow the dictator, apparently without question, into death?

*

The story opens in a banal enough way. It is the childhood of a perfectly normal girl. Eva Anna Braun was born on 6 February 1912, the second daughter of a schoolteacher, Friedrich Braun, and his wife Franziska, née Kronburger – always known as 'Fanny' – who was a trained dressmaker. Eva's elder sister Ilse was then four years old; three years after Eva, Gretl was born. The girls grew up in a modest apartment on Isabellastrasse. They were raised as good Catholics, were confirmed and went to communion – all of which the Protestant father had to promise when he married the Catholic Franziska.

Conservative, monarchist and nationalist, the Brauns were a typical lower middle-class Munich family, and in 1925, with the economy recovering, they could afford to move to a more comfortable home. A small legacy enabled them to buy their first car, and a nursemaid looked after the three girls. Fritz Braun had wanted sons and there were times when he made his daughters aware of this. Certain authors like to advance the theory that this gave Eva a father-complex and may have made her search for a substitute father, which would explain her penchant for older men. But Eva never lay on any analyst's couch.

'The Braun girls were really just like us. There was nothing special about them. They played with us like anyone else', Anna Hiendlmeier, a childhood friend, recalls.

Eva was sent to a convent school in the country village of Beilngries. 'Eva was a difficult girl', one of the nuns said later, 'but clever enough to get where she wanted.' Some teachers found her unruly and lazy. As Eva's cousin Gertraud Weisker explains: 'She twisted everyone round her finger, so I think she got through school easily, without any great effort and without achieving very much. She had such charm that she didn't need to.' So, hardly a problem-child then. Pretty, good-natured, always ready for a lark, but reluctant to accept challenges. She was the darling of the family. 'No amount of scolding from her stern papa had the slightest effect on this curly-headed girl with her innocent gaze and studied smile', writes her Uncle Alois. Did she want to be the star in her family? 'No, not the star, but certainly the focus of attention', says her cousin Gertraud. 'She wanted to be at the centre of things.'

The nuns adored this radiant child.

I would say she was moderately intelligent, but not really clever, otherwise she would have done something else in life.
Gertraud Weisker, Eva Braun's cousin

At a boarding-school, the Convent of the English Sisters in Simbach, she completed her Catholic education. It must be one of the great ironies of history that one day she would be the woman at the side of the arch-enemy of the Church and of Christendom. At Simbach she learned typing, book-keeping, domestic science and French. However, young Eva was bored by the lessons in music and drawing that her father paid extra for. Sport and clothes were her lifelong passions. Later, albums of photos and home movies would provide vivid evidence of these predilections. Eva's journalist uncle, Alois, wrote in his memoir: 'Ilse, the elder sister, was superior to Eva academically, but Eva made up for this by her charm, which she consciously exploited. She lived her life in the world of emotions and shut herself off from the world of knowledge; this was what ultimately shaped the tragedy of her life.'

So was Eva Braun perhaps a little naïve? Her favourite writer was the cowboys-and-Indians novelist Karl May (who never set foot in America), and incidentally this was something she shared with the young Hitler. The difference was that when she was still reading *Winnetou*, Adolf was already planning a coup d'état. He wanted to destroy all vestiges of the democratic Weimar Republic, which he and many other Germans despised. When his amateurishly staged putsch failed in 1923, Eva Braun was eleven years old. However, until she met him for the first time, she knew almost nothing about the agitator and his brownshirt movement. Politics did not interest her. Instead she gave a high priority to movie magazines and trashy novelettes. Perhaps – as some of her biographers claim – this melodramatic reading-matter was filled with women who sacrificed themselves to their lovers with a burning passion, just as she would one day be destined to do. We will never know.

To what extent the young Eva dreamed of becoming an actress and dancer herself is debatable. She was certainly mad about film-stars and collected pictures of them. Perfecting her own appearance was definitely very important to her. 'Every morning before school she would kneel in front of a chair, combing her hair with one hand, while she did her English homework with the other', her mother later recalled. Eva loved to look chic. It was not so much that she had a particular yearning for luxury, she just wanted to put on a show and win approval. She could be lured with status-symbols. She once borrowed a friend's motor-cycle, but afterwards said: 'I prefer limousines' – and not just because of the comfort.

> She had to be best at everything. She had to swim the best, do the best gymnastics on the parallel bars. And in that way she was very, very ambitious. Apart from that I don't think she had much ambition. But in anything to do with sport she was certainly ambitious.
>
> *Gertraud Weisker*

People said that all her life she wanted to be a big film-star. At all events her first professional job had some connection with the world of film. Eva's father heard that there was an apprenticeship open at Hoffmann Photography, in Schellingstrasse. Herr Hoffmann had a particular preference for young women, whom he could exploit. But there was something else about him that would have a much greater influence on her future. He had worked his way into the position of 'house' photographer for the National Socialist German Workers Party, known to history as the Nazis, of which he was one of the earliest members. And he was on first-name terms with Hitler. The Nazi leader needed Hoffmann for photographs which would not merely confirm his existence, but would show him in dramatic poses, designed to make a deep impression and convey a sense of mission. Consequently Hitler was a frequent visitor to the studio. He always acted the gallant towards the lady employees, kissed their hands extravagantly and did not stint on small presents.

How did Eva first meet the man who was to become her lover? One evening in 1929 Hoffmann came into the shop with a 'Herr Wolf'. 'Wolf' was Hitler's *nom de guerre*. And like a wolf he intended to descend on the flock of his political opponents. Hitler's sister Paula, for as long as she received financial support from him, was obliged to take the name 'Wolf' as well – one more facet of the Hitler cult.

Eva later told her sister Gretl: 'My boss comes in and with him is a gentleman of a certain age with a funny moustache and a light-coloured English raincoat, and he's holding a big felt hat . . . I look from the corner of my eye, without turning round, and notice that this man is staring at my legs. That very day I'd shortened my skirt and wasn't very happy with it, because I wasn't sure I'd got the hem straight. I go over and Hoffmann introduces me to "Herr Wolf".'

Hitler (*alias* 'Wolf') paid Eva compliments, thus arousing her interest. But she clearly had no idea who she was talking to. After the meeting Hoffmann asked her: 'Haven't you guessed who Herr Wolf is? Don't you ever look at our photos?' 'No', said Eva. Nothing could be clearer proof of her political innocence. But now she had a reason to rummage through the drawers looking for pictures of this mysterious man.

At home, when Eva casually enquired who this Hitler person might be, her father replied: '. . . some young whippersnapper who thinks he knows it all. Better cross the road if you see him coming.' Eva did not breathe a word about her encounter with the 'young whippersnapper'. Their first dates were arranged in secret. Hitler invited the stylish Munich girl to the theatre and to restaurants; but his endless torrent of talk was a problem for her. As a friend of Eva's, Mizzi Joisten, remembers: 'She got frightfully bored with it.' Eva had to look words up in the dictionary just to understand his monologues. In spite of this, she knew she wanted to see him again.

Until the end of the 1920s there was no question of a liaison between Hitler and Eva. But Hitler liked Eva's natural gaiety and innocence, and she in turn was intrigued by the older man and his compliments.

Invitations to picnic outings in the Bavarian Alps alternated with visits to cafés and afternoons spent in the Osteria Bavaria, Hitler's favourite Munich restaurant. Hitler was always surrounded by a mob of Nazi party devotees, drivers and personal assistants. That made a big impression on her, as presumably did the Mercedes motorcade – paid for by wealthy supporters. Who else could claim such a high-profile admirer? It must have appealed to her vanity.

Even in the years 1930–1 the relationship was still strictly platonic. Not until the beginning of 1932, according to the housekeeper, Anni Winter, did Eva become Hitler's lover, in his apartment on Prinzregentenplatz. Eva also hinted at this to her sister Gretl.

Herbert Döhring and his wife Anna were in at the start of the relationship. Anna was in service with Hitler from the early 1930s, and when he moved to his palatial mountain retreat, the Berghof, Herbert became his house-manager. 'If Hoffmann had not paired the two off', says Döhring, 'they would never have got together. But Hoffmann never gave up; he kept on encouraging them, serving Eva up on a silver platter, so to speak, until Hitler finally took the hint.'

Hoffmann himself told a different story: '. . . neither I nor anyone else noticed Hitler's intense interest in her . . . Not so, Eva . . . she told her girl-friends that Hitler was in love with her, and that she would definitely succeed in getting him to the altar.' Even if Hitler's photographer denies his own calculated involvement, there is no doubt that the Hitler–Braun relationship suited him very well. It enhanced his business status, and that was to make him a rich man. The photographic shop grew into a major company.

> When I look at some of those old films of the female Hitler Youth, pigtails were the thing, and usually your hair piled up on your head. They were women who were supposed to be natural and unspoilt. Whether they *were* is another matter. We were told that German women don't smoke, German women don't drink, German women don't wear make-up. But Eva never fitted that stereotype.
>
> I think Hitler was attracted by her charm. And I think she was attracted by this man, too. He was 23 years older. And Eva was what we call a teenager today; in those days she was a 'flapper' who wanted to break away from her family environment.
>
> *Gertaud Weisker, Eva's cousin*

From the outset it was Hitler who set the pace in the relationship: when and where they should meet, how often, what they would do together. Discretion was all-important. His political objectives, and everything that seemed important in achieving them, took precedence – and that included contacts with 'society', with well-disposed and well-heeled ladies. He liked to surround himself with 'the rich and the beautiful', for only they could make him socially acceptable. Eva quivered with jealousy, since he quite obviously had time for other women. What was worse, she was no match for the likes of Winifred Wagner, the composer's daughter-in-law, Magda Goebbels, or the film-maker, Leni Riefenstahl. Those were the kind of women Hitler was seen with, while *she* was kept hidden.

Hitler wanted an undemanding, low-maintenance relationship. 'For "love" I just keep a girl in Munich', Hitler told his aide-de-camp, Felix Wiedemann. And of course the girl was carefully checked out. It was Martin Bormann, his devoted henchman, and later the Nazi Party chief, who investigated the Braun family tree for Aryan purity.

The 'doll' was never intended as a partner for Hitler. A man as autocratic as he was would never tolerate a female competitor. As he told his architect, Albert Speer, some years later: 'Highly intelligent men should take wives who are simple and stupid. Imagine if I had a wife who interfered in my work! In my free time I want peace and quiet . . . I could never marry!' Yet Eva Braun geared her life more and more towards Hitler, and her cousin Gertraud observed the humiliating spectacle: 'He had power over her. And he exploited that power. He could only do that because she let herself be exploited.' And that was how waiting for Hitler became the defining experience in the life of Eva Braun.

It began so harmlessly. And ended so catastrophically. The world came to an end, and with the destruction of the world, my cousin, who I was very fond of, was destroyed as well. With a man who brought the world to ruin. There really could be no greater tragedy.

Gertaud Weisker

In 1932 Eva was still living at home. She had telephone conversations with Hitler, ostensibly about Hoffmann business, and often under the bedclothes, so that her parents would not notice. But Hitler's calls became less and less frequent. He could scent power. Since the Reichstag elections of 1930 the Nazi Party had 107 seats in the German parliament. Now new elections had to be fought. The great seducer waged his campaign in the modern style, using aircraft to get around the country and expensive technology to transmit his propaganda. He wanted to give the German people the impression that he was omnipresent, floating down upon them like a Messiah from heaven. With all that rabble-rousing, there was not much time to spare for the little girl in Munich. In the final phase of the November election campaign she heard not a word from Hitler.

Eva's patience, strained to the limit, gave way to despair. In her self-pity she saw herself as a sacrificial victim. Increasingly she toyed with the idea of taking her own life. Why did it not occur to her to leave Hitler?

The fact that she would not let go of him, preferring ultimately to face death, is highly significant. We can only speculate about her motives. What is certain is that she was fascinated by the aura surrounding this strange individual, who came from nowhere and was making his way to the top. Furthermore, the sense of her own worth seemed to depend entirely on the success of this relationship. Being jealous and, in a certain sense, ambitious too, she probably did not want to let any other woman have him. As her uncle Alois wrote: 'Hitler was *the* great temptation for so many women. Who could blame poor Eva, or fail to understand if she fell victim to the fascination of this man? After all, women of far greater intellectual and personal stature fell for the man, one way or another!'

Of course she wanted him all to herself – whether out of pride, fascination, or the aphrodisiac of power. At all events, there was no going back. Her cousin tries to make sense of it in this way: 'There she was, a seventeen-year-old, meeting a man with a hypnotic gaze, twenty-three years her senior. He could have been her father. The man was interested in this cheerful, uncomplicated creature, and his admiration did not go unnoticed. What young girl is *not* proud to be admired by an older man . . . ? It was a very simple love-story, which was to lead to disaster. The man welcomes the secrecy, the fact that his young lady-friend keeps her family in the dark, and he backs her up in this as much as he can. But he can only make use of the girl at certain times, because of course he has this great goal: to become Reich Chancellor. He will stop at nothing to achieve this and the girl is often a hindrance. She gets in his way and so at times his attentiveness leaves a lot to be desired. He simply doesn't bother about her, and surrounds himself with the most beautiful women from the film world and high society. For Eva, under-age and led astray, it is sheer hell, particularly as she can't talk to a soul about it . . . She had to deal with the whole thing on her own, until eventually she tried to commit suicide.'

After three months had passed without any word from Hitler, Eva made up her mind to kill herself. On 1 November 1932 she wrote a farewell letter, then shot herself in the chest with her father's pistol. Her sisters found her covered in blood and with a near-fatal bullet-wound. Yet she survived.

> She wanted to be at the centre of things. And she did actually
> achieve that. Except that with Hitler – she wasn't really at the
> centre, but was standing on the sidelines. And strangely
> enough, there she stayed. Until shortly before her death.
> Then she placed herself at the centre of attention once again.
>
> *Gertraud Weisker*

Hitler immediately came to see her; if this was a genuine
suicide-attempt that had to be taken seriously, he was taking no
chances. 'She was aiming at her heart', the doctor assured him.
'We were only just in time to save her life.'

Eva managed to persuade her anxious parents that it was all an
accident. Even if the whole thing *had* been done for effect, Hitler
was at least flattered by such passionate devotion. He was also
relieved, because he did not want Eva to slip from his grasp and
suspected that her death could have been damaging to him. It was
not the first time that women had tried to take their life on
account of Hitler. One had died and a scandal had only narrowly
been avoided.

*

Hitler's preference was for young girls who idolised him and did
not answer back. 'There is nothing finer than to educate a young
thing as one wants: a girl of eighteen or twenty is as malleable as
wax.' Over some he cast such a spell that they believed they could
only escape him through suicide. 'That's little Mitzi', said Hitler
when he proudly showed Henrietta von Schirach (Hoffmann's
married daughter) a photograph of seventeen-year-old Maria
Reiter. That was in 1926, and for quite a time he had been
courting the pretty, blonde draper's assistant from Berchtesgaden.
They had even kissed. She busily knitted knee-socks and dreamed
of wedding-bells. But Hitler had not in his wildest dreams
considered a lasting relationship. Nevertheless, he wrote her these
emotion-filled words: 'My dear child . . . I wish I had your lovely
little face before me, and could tell you from my own lips what I,

you truest friend, can only write to you', and he ends: 'I would so love to be near you and be able to look into your sweet eyes and forget everything else . . . Your Wolf.' But Mitzi Reiter waited in vain for her 'Wolf', who sent her for her birthday the two volumes of his book *Mein Kampf* (My Struggle). The note that came with them said: 'Read these through and then I think you will understand me better.' She did not read them and did not understand. The lovelorn girl tried to hang herself from a door-post and her family only just stopped her in time.

'My bride is Germany', Hitler repeatedly declared with fervour. Germany was his life's work, and he often expressed concern that women might hinder his rise to supreme power. Moreover, he was conceited enough to fear that the people would never forgive him if he married; just as film-stars sacrifice their popularity when they opt for wedded bliss. A new passion had entered Hitler's life – sweet and only just seventeen. She was his niece, Geli Raubal, the daughter of his half-sister Angela. In 1929 Uncle Adolf, then aged forty, took Geli under his roof. In his strange mixture of fatherly affection and schoolboy infatuation, he cared for the guileless Austrian girl. Geli was quite unable to withstand Hitler. He encouraged her to take singing lessons, and took her out to the opera and to restaurants; but jealously watched her movements and controlled every minute of her day. When Hitler's chauffeur, Emil Maurice, once gave his pretty niece a warm kiss on the cheek, 'the boss' had a fit of rage: 'I was afraid he'd shoot me dead on the spot', the driver recalled later. Geli Raubal must have felt a virtual prisoner in the apartment on Prinzregentenplatz, and the constant supervision stifled her will to live. While Hitler was electioneering all over Germany, Geli waited in Munich, trapped and unsatisfied, for the uncle who scarcely ever showed his face at home. And when he did, he acted the tyrant. It was after a quarrel that Geli took her life.

'There was never any kind of intimacy between them' – Geli's friend Henrietta von Schirach was convinced of that. Yet it is a commonly held view that it was only towards Geli Raubal that the notoriously narcissistic Hitler was capable of deep and intense love. Geli's room in his apartment remained locked and no-one but he was allowed to enter it. It is a fact not known until now that there was even a 'Geli Room' in his Berghof residence.

With portraits and busts of his niece, Hitler created nothing less than a cult around the dead girl's memory. He built her up as the one great love of his life. The house-manager at the Berghof, Herbert Döhring, tells how his wife actually witnessed Hitler's own threatened suicide. 'Hitler was in total shock, completely distraught. He didn't eat a thing. Locked himself in Geli's room. With a loaded pistol on the table. "I'm going to kill myself", he said. "Life is over for me." My wife took the gun away from him. Later she regretted doing that.' That was the second time that a woman had held Hitler back from threatened suicide. But would he really have pulled the trigger?

When all was said and done, Hitler loved no-one but himself. The attention he had denied Geli in life he now gave her in death. And even then he was afraid that his niece's suicide would harm him politically; for all his grief, that was what his eye was on. Indeed, there were suspicions that he might have murdered her, though these later proved unfounded. In the very week that Geli Raubal had died, Hitler made a fanatical speech to 10,000 Nazi supporters. But, as Henrietta von Schirach believes, 'the element of tenderness' was missing from Hitler's life, as was the gentle scolding that he must have enjoyed being given by his niece. As his photographer, Heinrich Hoffmann, sensed: 'That was when the seeds of inhumanity began to grow inside Hitler.'

> He didn't want to spoil his chances with the German people. If he had been married, to Eva Braun or to any other woman, then his relationship with the people would have been quite different.
>
> *Karl Wilhelm Krause, Hitler's personal valet*

'I fear I bring women no happiness', Hitler, the object of so much female desire, declared in 1939, after yet another lady admirer had attempted to end her life. This time it was a well-known member of the British aristocracy. Unity Mitford (a sister of the authoress Nancy Mitford, and of the present Duchess of Devonshire) sought to follow every step the Führer took, and

Hitler thought of using her as a means of gaining access to the British upper class. Only a few hours after war had broken out, she sat on a park bench in Munich's Englischer Garten and put a bullet through her head. She survived this incident but died a few years later from its effects.

'I believe there are certain people who attract death', Henrietta von Schirach said, 'and Hitler was very definitely one of them.' Until Geli Raubal's suicide Eva Braun did not know that she had a rival, even though photos of Hitler's niece were not concealed from her. And it seems that from then on she wanted to imitate Geli's style. Did the dictator want this carbon-copy? This is how Eva's uncle, Alois, saw it: 'Hitler probably did not at first think of Eva as his great love, but as a substitute for Geli. And the unspoilt, easily influenced Eva did not think of Adolf Hitler as her ideal lover either, but as a challenge and a mark of her success as a person.'

Still working as a photographer's lab assistant, Eva was twenty years and eight months old when she tried for the first time to kill herself because of Hitler – on Halloween night, 1932. Hitler could not risk another scandal. 'I will have to take more care of her in future. If only to prevent her from doing something stupid again.' Some lover.

> He only ever loved one woman: his niece Geli Raubal. When she shot herself, he took up with Eva Braun. That was more toleration than love. He felt guilty towards her because she had twice attempted suicide on his account. I believe Hitler was incapable of love for a woman, because his sole obsession was Germany.
>
> *Leni Riefenstahl, film director*

On 30 January 1933 the aged Reich President, Paul von Hindenburg, appointed Hitler Chancellor of the German Reich. But the day brought no joy for Eva – what role could she play from now on? None of the politicians who had given their support to Hitler knew what kind of man they had levered into office.

They were unaware of his almost pathological weakness for under-age girls. They did not know that this man, personally isolated and utterly ruthless, would trample over corpses if necessary.

Hitler made his triumphal entry into Berlin as Chancellor of the Reich, while Eva had to stay in Munich. True, on her twenty-first birthday, 6 February 1933, he confessed his special affection for her, but this did not alter his attitude. In the capital Hitler met women admirers, from political or other circles, whenever he wanted to. Sophie Hoffmann, the photographer's second wife, apparently meant well when she tried to show Eva the pointlessness of her relationship, to prevent something worse happening – but in fact she was only rubbing salt in the wound: 'As Frau Hoffmann so kindly and so tactlessly told me, he now has a replacement for me . . .', Eva complained in her diary. And she went on waiting, for news, or a phone-call, or a meeting with her lover. Hitler knew just how much attention to give her, enough to keep her from any more acts of desperation.

At the Nazi party rally in Nuremberg in 1934, Eva was permitted to sit on the VIPs' podium, as a 'secretary'. But that itself was enough to cause a stir. Hitler's half-sister Angela Raubal, Geli's mother, was housekeeper in Hitler's Wachenfeld residence, which was later extended to become the Berghof, and from time to time she accompanied her brother. In Nuremberg she had words with him, as Herbert Döhring remembers: 'Frau Raubal, as well as Frau Goebbels and all those ministers' wives, knew all about Eva and were quite appalled that this young, sulky and dissatisfied-looking girl should be sitting with the VIPs. Frau Raubal gave Hitler a strong ticking-off about this and Hitler didn't like that at all. He wasn't having anyone tell him his business – and certainly not in that tone. He immediately banned his sister from living anywhere in the Obersalzberg area. She had to pack her bags the next day. That was a bombshell. And Eva was the cause of it.' It was clear that by now Hitler had allotted a permanent place in his life to Eva Braun. There she enjoyed his affection and his protection, particularly from the cutting remarks of arrogant society ladies. The party rally and everything else that was going on in the Reich – the nazification of state and society, the open discrimination against Jews and boycotting of Jewish shops and businesses, the grim charade of the 'Röhm putsch' which was a crime by any standards* – were all observed by Eva through the eyes of the Führer's 'official' mistress. Her diary entries give ample proof of this.

Only 22 pages of her diary have survived, covering the period from early February to the end of May 1935. Yet they are very revealing: 'All right, so his head is full of political problems at the moment, but what about a little relaxation? Look at last year. Didn't Röhm . . . give him a lot of trouble? And yet he found time for me.' World events were assessed according to whether her beloved had time for her or not. The diary fragments also reflect her mood-swings; between pride on the one hand ('Me, the mistress of the greatest man in Germany, and on earth') and on the other hand disappointment, bitterness and a longing to die.

On 11 March Eva noted in her diary: 'I am desperate . . .' and went on: 'He only needs me for certain purposes.' This is not the only evidence to show that there was physical intimacy between them. Yet Hitler kept her at arm's length. The eternal blowing hot and cold had worn Eva down. Later she wrote despairingly: 'Why does he torture me so? Why doesn't he end it right now?' And then: 'I've decided to take 35 of them. This time I'm going to make dead certain it works.' She was referring to Phanodorm sleeping-tablets. This second attempted suicide took place on the night of 28 May 1935. But again she survived, because her elder sister, Ilse, got to her just in time.

Did this mean the end of the Braun–Hitler liaison? No. Hitler made some concessions. With Geli's death still very much in his mind, he dreamed up a tantalising game: from this time forward he tried to stay in daily touch with Eva – even during the war, as his radio operator recalled. She was given certain privileges and was allowed to be present on some official occasions, if only as a 'secretary'. And she no longer had to work. Previously, when employed by Hoffmann, she complained that Hitler 'still has me bowing and scraping to strangers'. Now, she and her younger sister

---

* On 30 June 1934, after spurious rumours of a plot by the SA, the Nazi paramilitaries, to oust Hitler, he gave orders for the head of the SA, Ernst Röhm, and about a hundred others, to be shot.

Gretl moved into an apartment in Widenmayerstrasse, not least to escape the rebukes of her parents, who still could not come to terms with the 'sleazy relationship'. It was a comfortable, three-bedroom apartment with central heating and modern furnishings. The rent and the wages for their Hungarian maid were paid by Hoffmann, on Hitler's instructions.

> The upbringing at home was very, very strict, otherwise my uncle would not have written a letter to Hitler, asking him to return the two girls, Eva and Gretl, whom he had effectively abducted from their parental home.
>
> *Gertraud Weisker, cousin*

It was a disgrace for the family, thought their father, that his daughters should be removed from parental care in this way. Eva's uncle Alois gave an account of a noisy meeting he had with Fritz Braun. 'Fritz wanted to pour his heart out to me, but not at home. He thought the Hofbräuhaus would be just the place. We found an empty table in the saloon bar on the first floor. And then Fritz let rip, told me how for years he had been filled with dark suspicions, how he had tried to talk Eva out of this "idiotic" friendship, how furious he was at having to put up with snide remarks from his friends and how that "so-and-so" had destroyed his family life. Fritz became more and more irate, resorting to ever riper Bavarian vocabulary and when I tried to pacify him, he just got all the more vociferous. So much so that I seriously thought a plain-clothes Gestapo man would put an abrupt end to these impassioned outpourings. On that occasion Fritz also told me about a letter he had written to Hitler, asking him to keep his hands off Eva.'

It is the letter of an unsophisticated father concerned about his child. A draft of the letter has survived: 'Esteemed Herr Reich Chancellor! . . . You, the Führer of the German nation, have very different concerns, and certainly far greater ones . . . My family has now been torn apart because my two daughters, Eva and Gretl, have moved into an apartment provided by you, and I, as head of the family, have had no say in the matter. Furthermore, I stand by the perhaps old-fashioned moral principle, that children . . . are not removed from parental care until marriage. That is my idea of honour. Quite apart from that, I miss my children very much . . .'

Fritz Braun's rage became even more intense when he never received a reply. He had given the letter to Eva's former boss, Hoffmann, who had not passed it on to Hitler. Instead he handed it to Eva, who destroyed the embarrassing document. Hitler was now giving Eva greater freedom and a feeling of being appreciated. A year later, on Hitler's orders, Hoffmann purchased a respectable detached house in Munich's classy Bogenhausen district. Eva and her sister moved in on 30 March 1936. Built in 1925, the house cost 300,000 Reichsmarks. Though simple, it was decorated in a fashionable style, and Hitler himself had a hand in the detail. For instance, the dining-room furniture was made from exotic hardwoods to designs by Paul Ludwig Troost, the architect of the Nazi headquarters, the 'Brown House'. In the course of time, its rooms were filled with gifts from Hitler: an Aubusson tapestry, costly carpets, carefully chosen items of furniture and silverware. For Eva it was above all a sign of her recognition, a kind of status-symbol, but in fact it was a consolation-prize. Later the property was legally made over to the 'secretary', Eva Braun.

The first time I saw Eva Braun at the Berghof was in 1940. The guys said she was the housekeeper there.

Rochus Misch, Hitler's radio-operator

Actually I first heard about her shortly before travelling to Berchtesgaden. So I was prepared. 'At the Berghof you'll meet Fräulein Braun; she's the Führer's companion.' I was surprised by her: a natural young thing, very cheerful, who spoke with quite a strong Bavarian accent. A pretty girl, but not really what you would imagine as the wife of the supreme Führer.

Traudl Junge, Hitler's secretary

From the house on Wasser-burger Strasse it was only a short walk to Hitler's Prinzregentenplatz apartment. As Eva's maid, Margarete Mitlstrasser, tells us: 'Whenever he was in Munich, Eva went round there with a little overnight case.'

But he seldom did come to Munich and the Reich Chancellery in Berlin continued to be closed to Eva. Hitler offered her a substitute for this too. There was his other residence, the Berghof, near Berchtesgaden. Until 1928 the Nazi leader had rented 'Haus Wachenfeld' in the Obersalzberg mountains, close to the Austrian border. Then he bought the property, converted and extended it. While keeping the original groundplan, he erected a much larger building around the familiar interior. The result was a true monstrosity – a great blot on the idyllic alpine landscape, with huge picture-windows and massive furniture. At the same time, Swiss pine panelling, Germanic rune carvings and non-'decadent' paintings helped to provide a conventional country-house atmosphere. But it was not the visiting foreign statesmen nor the high and mighty men of the Reich who set the tone of daily life in Hitler's mountaintop home; that was provided by his substitute family. This was the closely restricted circle of the Führer's personal physicians, photographers, bodyguards, secretaries and aides. The dominant mode was a kind of impersonal familiarity. At the centre of the gathering storm there reigned the funereal calm of absolute servility.

> The domestic staff knew she was Hitler's girlfriend. But outsiders certainly didn't. Not a soul.
> *Herbert Döhring, Hitler's house-manager at the Berghof*

In 1936 Hitler brought Eva to the Berghof and made her a part of this fantasy-world. Only the innermost circle was allowed to know who she really was. Reinhardt Spitzy, then a young diplomat who was Foreign Minister Ribbentrop's liaison-man with Hitler, has these memories: 'In '37, when I went to the Obersalzberg for the first time and was standing there with Hitler and Ribbentrop, a quite young and pretty person came in and said: "We must go and eat now, if you don't mind." And I wondered who would dare to speak to the Führer like that. At the time I felt as though I had come to the Mount of the Holy Grail, but instead of a *grande dame* appearing, here was an ordinary little woman. So I went to Hitler's chief aide, *Obergruppenführer* Bruckner, and asked him who this woman was. And he said: "Listen, pal, you'll be coming here a lot, and you're often going to see this woman. But just forget you saw her, OK? The Führer has a right to a private life, and if you say a word about this to anyone, your family, your friends, anyone, you'll be in big trouble."'

> I'm sure she was the sort of woman who provided Hitler with a nice, cosy, middle-class life, with tea and cakes, and with whom he performed as necessary in bed. Nothing wrong with that.
>
> *Reinhardt Spitzy, adviser to the Foreign Minister, Ribbentrop*

In the years from 1936 to 1945 Eva Braun was to spend more than two-thirds of her time on the Obersalzberg. It was her own little empire. But to the outside world she remained the unseen and unmentioned mistress. Those staff who were directly responsible to her adored her, but from Hitler's aides and personal servants she received less than universal respect. 'She was a very ordinary girl, and I certainly didn't take orders from *her*', Hitler's former valet Krause is at pains to make clear even today. On one occasion he was expected to be up at 5 a.m. to get Eva's skis ready. He refused, saying he had to be at his master's service and therefore needed a full night's sleep – the mistress's complaint was to no avail; she came off second best in that trial of strength. Eva's personal maid, Margarete Mitlstrasser, tried to improve her mistress's status: 'All the ladies who came to the Berghof, we had to address as "Madam", but she was always just "Miss Braun". So I asked her if there was anything we could do about it. Then Eva asked Hitler and he agreed. So then I was given permission to start calling her "Madam" as well. Krause, Hitler's valet, thought at first that this did not apply to him. But then he had to toe the line too. And the fact that we had to address Eva as "Madam" gave her more status.'

Nonetheless, Hitler took delight in putting his mistress in her place from time to time, if necessary in the presence of servants. Once he was brooding over maps, late at night as was his habit – his majordomo, Döhring, had just laid out new ones for him – when Eva came into the room. 'Suddenly, there was a knock on the door between Hitler's bedroom and his study. But the Führer paid no attention. There was another knock, and again he appeared not to hear. All at once the door opened and Eva came in. She looked at me in amazement and said: "What? You still here too? What are you doing here?" Then she went up to Hitler and spoke to him. No answer. Tries again. Still no reaction. Suddenly he flips his lid. "You again! Can't you see I have to concentrate on this work? You always come in at the most impossible moments. I positively do not want you around just now." She was furious. Went very red in the face, threw her head back and stared at me. Out she goes, slams the door so hard it rattles. Then I saw the expression on Hitler's face. It was a cynical grin of pleasure . . .'

Hitler even seems to have distrusted his mistress. During the Führer's absences from the Berghof, Herbert Döhring had to be particularly watchful. 'Döhring', Hitler said to me, 'we must lock everything up. My bedroom, everything. And of course my study. Not a soul must come in. You'll lock up and keep the keys with you – and no matter who comes along, no-one gets in, not even the chamber-maids.' He meant Eva Braun, of course. He didn't trust her. Thought she might go in and snoop around, to see what papers and things he had lying about. That told you a lot.'

She always used to criticise him for his old uniforms and his old cap, and because he walked sort of crooked, with one shoulder drooping. 'Well', he replied, 'you've no idea what a tremendous burden I have on my shoulders.'

Herbert Döhring

There are reports which appear to give the lie to this. Again and again we hear of affectionate words and great courtesy. The Hitler–Braun relationship was nothing if not ambivalent, with a lot of 'carrot and stick'. It was a case of 'can't be with you and can't be without you'. If Eva took too much for granted, he humiliated her. If he thought he had gone too far, he flattered her.

One of Hitler's film cameramen, Walter Frentz, remembers: 'We were out walking together and I suddenly said to her almost provocatively: "Miss Braun, you're the most envied woman in Germany", because she was now with Hitler. And she said: "Oh, I'm just a prisoner in a golden cage."' Hitler knew exactly how he had to treat Eva, to keep her from complete despair: 'He had a very affectionate way of talking to her', says Hitler's secretary, Traudl Junge. We can see from rare photos of their private life, kept strictly secret until now, how Hitler would extravagantly kiss her hand, how they mounted the steps of the Berghof side by side, snuggling close to each other. But most of the pictures show a distance between them; we see two people from two apparently quite different worlds. And this was very symptomatic of their relationship: 'In the presence of others they never showed any tenderness to each other', Traudl Junge remembers.

He always called her 'bumpkin'.* In the presence of other people he was always rather distant, never affectionate.

Herbert Döhring

Eva Braun, formally employed as a secretary at a monthly salary of 450 Reichsmarks until the end of the war, had her part to play on the Obersalzberg. The daily round in the Berghof was strictly regulated – and monotonous. Hitler slept late. The day began shortly before lunch, then followed receptions, motor excursions, meetings, trips – whatever the Führer felt like. For those who were

* Hitler used a Bavarian dialect word, '*Tschapperl*', which is untranslatable, but suggests gawkiness and rustic unsophistication. 'Bumpkin' is the nearest I can get. *Tr.*

present, the evenings often left 'a memory of strange emptiness' – three to four hours of films: some entertaining, some sentimental, some flat and banal. The staff, being part of the substitute family, were allowed to watch as well. If a film was shown that was banned in Germany, or had been imported from the USA, the entire entourage foregathered. Hitler always sat with Eva in the front row. Even during his endless monologues, Eva scarcely ever left his side. As Alois W. wrote: 'She would give the signal for the party to break up, when those around Hitler were no longer able to suppress their yawns. She also claimed the right to speak her mind to Hitler on personal matters, criticised his uniform and his suits, and defended her two Scotch terriers with furious determination against Hitler's Alsatians. She aired her natural wit in many a sharp-tongued remark about the weaknesses and pomposity of Hitler's closest associates. Eva liked jazz and occasionally would put on a record in Hitler's presence. Apparently, Hitler once said: "That's nice, what you're playing." To which she retorted: "Your friend Goebbels has just banned it."' Contrary to the Nazi ethos, Eva smoked the occasional cigarette, though never when Hitler was around. Being critical on unimportant matters, imposing her style in trivial areas – that was the extent of Eva Braun's power in her little empire.

There was strict separation between the private and the official domain. In the latter half of the 1930s the Obersalzberg increasingly became the political centre of the Reich. Here foreign heads of state were received, ambassadors were summoned to make their reports, generals were instructed to come and receive their orders. As her uncle Alois explained: 'On such occasions Eva retreated behind the scenes, as much guided by her own instinct as in obedience to Hitler's request. To those guests Eva remained the more or less invisible, unsophisticated,

> The Eva that people saw did not have much to offer, since she was completely unpolitical. And she had no influence either. She couldn't have had, since in Nazi circles she was clearly not accepted.
>
> *Gertraud Weisker*

unpolitical girl, who had no time for the grubby business of politics, but all the more time for the finer things of life, for socialising, music, swimming, skiing and the never-failing feminine interests of clothes and flowers.'

Looking elegant was important to her; she had suits and dresses made for her by the top couturiers in Berlin and Paris. She bought her shoes personally from Ferragamo in Florence. Sometimes this passion for clothes prompted her to change as many as seven times in a single day. Her personal hairdresser was constantly giving her new styles. Eva frequently felt a longing for novelty. Hitler, on the other hand, thought she should always wear the clothes that appealed to *him* and 'best of all, have a thousand of the same in your wardrobe'. This was a reflection of his own attitude, of always wanting to look the same. The psychopathic Hitler hated anything new. Unlike Eva he distrusted change and variety.

> She was always elegantly dressed. Before the war, we all were. She was very soignée and made sure her make-up was always at hand. Other women did too, or tried to.
>
> *Gertraud Weisker*

The hidden mistress seldom had the opportunity to show off her couture in public. She was not invited to official receptions, and during political or military meetings she was not allowed to enter the main hall. When important people were visiting, she had to go to her room. If their stay was a lengthy one, she had to move out altogether. During the 1930s there were a great many VIP visits, by men like Admiral Horthy, the ruler of Hungary, Britain's premier Neville Chamberlain, King Boris of Bulgaria, the Aga Khan and the Papal Nunzio, Cardinal Pacelli. However, what was most hurtful to Eva Braun was not being presented to the Duke and Duchess of Windsor. It was their tragic love-story that interested her most of all. On the few occasions when she was permitted to attend a reception, she had to address Hitler in front of the guests with the formal pronoun '*Sie*', rather than the intimate '*Du*'. That was only allowed when among his innermost cirle, and even then she called him '*Mein Führer*'.

> She was always obliged to keep at a certain distance. She was definitely not allowed to behave as she wanted, like a girl or an adoring lover, when they had guests.
>
> *Herbert Döhring*

As a distraction from the boredom and monotony of the Berghof, Eva busied herself not only with fashion, music and sport, but also with photography and home movies. The four-and-a-half hours of material that she called 'Eva's Variety Film-show', and some twenty private photograph albums, give an insight into life at the Berghof. Some of the pictures portray stiff and awkward rituals. But they also illustrate how Eva adapted to the life that was her destiny. The captions to the pictures sometimes display irony, even self-assurance. On 12 August 1939 some revealing sequences were filmed. With her hand-held 16mm camera, Eva first filmed from her window the arrival of Count Galeazzo Ciano, the Italian foreign minister. Ciano noticed her and asked who she was. Hitler immediately ordered her to shut the window. But she went on filming with a telephoto lens – from behind a curtain. The commentary runs: 'Windows shut! That's an order! Make of that what you will.' Another snapshot, taken by Hoffmann, shows Count Ciano from the side, looking up at her. This picture, too, has been stuck into the album – with the triumphant caption: 'There's something forbidden to be seen up there – me!': a small secret victory in the confined world of Eva Braun.

> She wasn't very keen on children. She only played with children when there was a photographer around.
>
> *Margarete Mitlstrasser, Eva's maid*
>
> They were never seen in a loving pose, not even one of deep friendship.
>
> *Herbert Döhringm*

Other prominent residents of the Obersalzberg were equally unclear about her role. Hitler's henchmen, Göring, Bormann and Speer, had acquired properties of their own in the same alpine setting. As Herbert Döhring tells us: 'Once, while Hitler was away, Frau Göring happened to invite all the ladies for coffee – including Eva Braun, the 'secretary', because at that time she did not know any different. When Hitler heard about this he was furious and forbade it immediately.' It is true that, outwardly, Eva Braun had to act the part of a secretary but, on the other hand, Hitler was too conceited to want other people to regard her as such – an absurd charade. His behaviour was similar on a trip to Italy. Eva loved visiting the country that was now Germany's ally, if only because of the fashionable shoes she could buy there. Sometimes her mother joined the party. In 1938, for the first and only time, Eva accompanied the Führer on a state visit to Italy – albeit among his retinue of secretaries. This meant she was excluded from the official ladies' programme, a fact that she was unwilling to accept. So she was admitted to the official review of the fleet in the Bay of Naples, but not as Hitler's lady-friend, only as a member of his staff.

Back home the same game went on. Outside the Berghof, scarcely anyone knew the truth. In the nearby town of Berchtesgaden only a few people learned of the liaison. And those who did kept their mouths shut, so great was their fear of being hauled off by the Gestapo. True, a number of local people got to know Eva, but had no idea who she really was. One of them, Josef Grösswang, the son of a Berchtesgaden hotelier, was a teenager at the time. 'I often used to cross the Königsee lake with my father in what we called a Landauer; it was a long boat, like a Venetian gondola. We went to the Königsbach waterfall and beached on a spit of land running out into the lake. There was a lady there, lying on a rug, sunning herself. We said hello and exchanged a few words about the weather and the temperature of the water. Then the lady went swimming, came back and lay down again. I fetched my accordion from the boat and played it. The next day we rowed over to the waterfall again, and the same lady was there. And she said: "Well, well. Here you are again." And we chatted, and I played the accordion again. Altogether, we went to that waterfall five or six times and kept on seeing the same lady.'

The next time he 'saw' her was not until after the war had ended. Early in May 1945 the victors marched into Berchtesgaden; first the French, followed a few hours later by the Americans. 'They came to our hotel and moved in. That evening a French soldier – he must have been about my age, nineteen – chucked a whole lot of photos on to the table and said: "Look at these! Lovely girls, eh?" And I said: "Oh, I know that one." "No", he says, "you can't know *her*." So I say: "Why not?" He says: "Well, you can't know her because she's Eva Braun, Hitler's girlfriend, the one he later married." So of course I didn't say any more. At that moment I realised that the lady I'd met that time by the waterfall, who I'd played the accordion to, was the wife of Adolf Hitler. And I didn't know how the soldier would react if I told him any more.'

The occupying powers tried to discover as much as possible about Hitler and Eva Braun. The Berghof staff described in detail the layout of the rooms in the residence, which by now had been destroyed by bombing. The 'Hitler' and 'Braun' apartments on the first floor were only separated by a small landing. A photograph exists that shows the door from Eva's bedroom on to the landing. Next to it stands a chest-of-drawers, on which is a gloomy portrait of Hitler, which his mistress had obviously taken a liking to. Hitler's bedroom was across the corridor. Beside the door a couch was positioned. Here the two could rendezvous – away from prying eyes.

> On the Obersalzberg there were certain rules which just had to be respected. You had to respect the fact that she was Hitler's 'companion', and that was all there was to be said. No further comment. Period.
> *Reinhardt Spitzy, adviser to the Foreign Minister, Ribbentrop*

Debate continues over the question of whether Adolf Hitler and Eva Braun were lovers in the fullest sense of the word. There is hardly a chapter in the dictator's life that is more riddled with grotesque and elaborate mythology. Certain authors consider it a proven fact that Hitler must have been as perverted sexually as he was in other ways, and offer some dubious evidence for this. Others believe he was impotent – but that is not provable either. Yet other 'Hitler-ologists' hold the view that he was little short of being a true Casanova. He is said to have had sexual relations 'regularly and over a long period' with his mistress, Eva Braun, and his half-niece, Geli Raubal, and 'probably occasionally' with two dozen other women. The sexual partners who have been named include other men's wives, princesses, and actresses. It is claimed that Hitler's intimacies also took place on an international level, among others with Martha Dodd, daughter of the US ambassador in Berlin, and Lady Unity Mitford. The essence of this 'Hitler research' is that numerous women, 'who expected to encounter a ranting boor, left him charmed and very taken with him'. Much of this is sheer fantasy. The only solid indications we have concern his relationship with Eva Braun. There is some evidence to suggest that, particularly in the Munich years, the two were physically intimate. Eva's maid, Margarete Mitlstrasser, tells how Eva would repeatedly set off for the Hitler apartment on Prinzregentenplatz carrying a special little suitcase, which was nicknamed the '*BuKo*' – short for *Beischlaf-Utensilien-Koffer* (in crude English, the 'screwing-kit'). But what went on in the Berghof?

'It was a proper relationship between man and wife, and if anyone imagines that they lived together and didn't have it off, then they're crazy. Anyway, to us they were man and wife', says the Berghof employee, Willi Mitlstrasser. On the other hand, house-manager Herbert Döhring tells us: 'My wife was very inquisitive, and always took a peek in the laundry before washing it. Nothing. Zilch. She didn't find a thing. Not a hint. Nix.' Hitler's valet, Krause, adds: 'Whether they spent the nights together, I don't know. It was all sealed off. If anyone claims they know what exactly went on, they're wrong.'

Margarete Mitlstrasser was probably Eva's closest confidante. She is clear in her own mind: 'I know very well that they were a couple, because when he came to her and she had her period, she got something from the doctor to get rid of her period. And it was usually me who fetched it from the doctor. I went myself. So it was obvious that something was going on.'

When the war was on, it is clear that the sex-drive of the rapidly ageing warlord was drastically reduced. Hitler's personal physician, Dr Morell, gave evidence to an American Commission of Inquiry. He told them that in the final years Eva Braun pestered him to give Hitler something that would stimulate his waning libido.

*

As early as 1938 the atmosphere at the Berghof was transformed. More than before, Hitler's residence became the centre of political decision-making. It was the time of the so-called 'wars of the flowers'; the *Anschluss* or annexation of Austria in March 1938 was followed by the march into the Sudeten region of Czechoslovakia – both without a shot being fired. In the build-up to the real war, Hitler was at the peak of his popularity. Was Eva Braun able to follow the huge political changes that were taking place? 'She didn't wanna know about politics', says Willi Mitlstrasser. 'She wanted to be loved, that's all. And she loved *him*. End of story.' Nothing could shake her in her attitude, which was to observe the world first and foremost from the perspective of her relationship with Hitler. When the dictator blackmailed the Austrian prime minister into allowing his country to be brought 'home to the Reich' this was seen by Eva chiefly as having certain logistical advantages, as Herbert Döhring tells us: 'Basically, she wasn't particularly impressed. What she was thinking about as usual were clothes, fashion, elegant shoes. And now Salzburg, being just across the border, offered a good chance to shop in super boutiques and buy chic clothes.' The incorporation of Austria into 'Greater Germany' was to Eva Braun initially no more than a foretaste of the single European market. And while Hitler was occupying the Sudetenland, he gave a thought to her in his first private will, which provided her with a monthly pension of 1,000 Reichsmarks from Nazi party funds. This made her the principal beneficiary, ahead of Hitler's sister Paula, his half-sister Angela and other relatives. This was the first official document written by Hitler in which the name Braun appears at all – whereas in the complete internal telephone directory of the Berghof, which has no less than 140 entries, Eva's name is nowhere to be found.

Nonetheless, should the worst happen, her financial security was now guaranteed. Furthermore, in the summer of 1938, in the cellar of her house in Munich's Wasserburger Strasse, an air-raid shelter was installed, complete with a ventilator and 'iron rations'.

Yet Eva Braun saw the man she loved, not as a warmonger, but as a peacemaker, who did everything possible to protect his people from the worst that might happen. She avoided thinking too much about it. Only rarely was she present when political decisions were being made. While Germany's Foreign Minister, Ribbentrop, was still in Moscow with his Soviet counterpart, Molotov, putting the finishing touches to the Non-Aggression Pact, Hitler was on tenterhooks, awaiting news from the Russian capital. Eva devoted a short series of photos to this historic event, to which she added the naïve comment that her beloved wanted to prevent war 'by every means possible'. But others at the time, far better informed than she, had also been taken in by the dictator's devious stratagems.

> Eva had a pretty bad time in the years before the war, when Hitler gave big receptions at the Reich Chancellery for celebrities from the arts world. Up to a thousand at a time, from the theatre, films, music, art – everyone who was anyone got invited. And on these occasions he used to love surrounding himself with extremely elegant, exciting and mysterious women. She was just eaten up with jealousy.
>
> *Herbert Döhring*

Eva was among the guests on 1 September 1939, when Hitler gave his speech at Berlin's Kroll Opera House, and once more lied to the world – by portraying the attack on Poland as an act of self-defence. However, Eva's presence in the German capital was not so much a matter of political commitment as an opportunity to show herself in the territory of those she presumed to be her most serious female rivals. Since the beginning of 1939 Eva had had her own apartment in the Reich Chancellery; by a nice irony it included the room that had once been President Hindenburg's bedroom. Yet even there Eva was no more than the mistress in hiding. She had to use the staff entrance and take her meals alone in her room. Clearly Hitler did not consider her place to be at the seat of government, but was never at a loss for a mollifying word: 'Evi, you aren't made for this sophisticated kind of life . . . You're too precious to me . . . I must protect your purity . . . Berlin is a city of vice . . . The world outside is dirty and nasty.'

The war revealed the gulf between their two worlds more than ever. As Herbert Döhring recalls: 'Hitler often ignored her completely. Just didn't see her. Well, there was a war on, and questions were going through his mind: What do we do now? Where do we go from here? The whole women's side of things disappeared with the start of the war. Until the first victories, when things got back to normal a little.'

> She loved to be entertained, and that was something Hitler didn't share with her at all. She had to give it all up. At best he would tease her about all that kind of thing.
>
> *Herbert Döhring*

The invasion of Poland brought with it a new military concept: '*Blitzkrieg*' – 'lightning war'. Then, when the French campaign came to a successful conclusion – for Germany – within a matter of weeks, it put Hitler into a mood of euphoria. With his victory over the old 'arch-enemy' in June 1940, Hitler's status and reputation reached their peak. General Keitel, chief-of-staff of the armed forces, lauded him as 'the greatest military commander of all time'. It was not long before the German phrase '*grösster Feldherr aller Zeiten*', was mockingly abbreviated to '*Gröfaz*' (roughly pronounced 'grow-fats'). Nevertheless, for the moment a surprising number of his former opponents could be counted as 'converts', if only in recognition of his undeniable success in the field. Many Germans who were not Nazis seemed to ignore Hitler's amoral nature in their – sometimes grudging – admiration for his leadership. And what of Eva Braun? She may well have been proud of him, but according to people who knew her, she longed for the moment when she could be at his side, sharing in the glory. Alone on the Obersalzberg she painted a future in terms of a Hollywood epic, in which Germany would finally triumph over its enemies (including the USA, of course), and her hidden love-affair would be revealed to the gaze of world history. It was a flight into a world of fantasy.

In the weeks when the campaign in western Europe was raging, Eva was not in fact the woman on whom Hitler's thoughts dwelt first and foremost. In June 1940 there was an odd little transaction in the Berghof, as Herbert Döhring confesses: 'Hitler sent for my wife and said something to her. She then rushed to our quarters and came back immediately with a large, grey envelope. I had no idea what was in it. Then we went up together to his rooms, and I said: "You wanted to see us, *Mein Führer*." And he seemed overjoyed. Went up to my wife and said: "I tell you, Anna, I'll never forget what you've done for me." Then my wife gives him the envelope and he pulls out a very rare and beautiful photo of Geli [Raubal]. Geli had given it to my wife as a present before she died. She's sitting on a stool, wearing a superb fur stole; very elegant and sophisticated. And Hitler knew that my wife had kept the picture. So he said: "Would you be very kind and lend me this photo for a while? I want to take it with me to my headquarters. And when this whole damn business is over, you'll get it back again." But she never did.'

The scene took place in Hitler's study. 'And next door, no more than 30 yards as the crow flies, sits Eva Braun – his passionately loved, or merely tolerated mistress. I don't know which. And he still worshipped Geli. Eva never found out. We kept quiet.' If we are to believe Döhring, Geli Raubal remained the one Hitler was really in love with.

> Well, what she liked was popular music. Operettas too, but her favourite dance was the tango. The racier it was, the wilder she became. She loved it. She was in seventh heaven.
>
> *Herbert Döhring*

The day when Hitler's 'war within a war' began was 22 June 1941. This was 'Operation Barbarossa', the invasion of the Soviet

Union. While the warlord issued orders from the Obersalzberg for an unparalleled campaign of annihilation, in which millions of men, women and children were slaughtered, little changed in Eva's daily routine amid the alpine scenery. But no sooner had Hitler set off for his headquarters on the Eastern Front than Eva invited friends over. Among them was often her sister Gretl. As Hitler's telephonist and radio-operator, Rochus Misch, remembers: 'Once he was away for six days. And Eva was a different person. Happy, light-hearted and free. She immediately gave a party; all the domestic staff were invited and there was even dancing. This was the other, exuberant Eva. But then, when the boss came back, she withdrew into herself again.' At the outbreak of war Hitler had banned any form of luxury on the Obersalzberg, and even introduced food coupons. 'But she obviously didn't want to go without anything', adds Herbert Döhring. 'She wanted oranges, like before – and not even to eat, just for squeezing. And of course, turtle soup – that was her favourite late-night supper, with all kinds of exotic snacks. My wife had to order them specially.' For Eva the comfort of the Berghof was a compensation, albeit a small one, for everything she lacked in her relationship with Hitler. Why should she be deprived? It took her some time to come to terms with this.

> At first Eva's lifestyle went on as before, as long as supplies lasted. You see, when the war started we had plenty of provisions, enough to keep us going for months.
>
> *Herbert Döhring*

A photograph album with the initials E. B. inscribed on the cover in a clover-leaf pattern has recently come to light in the United States. It is one of three personal albums that Eva Braun put together only for her best friends. It has a signed dedication and is dated Christmas 1941, the third Christmas of the war. More than 100 photos have been stuck into it, many of them hitherto unknown. This particular find shows Eva's life story in a selection of beautiful pictures, mostly in immaculate poses, either fashionably dressed, or playing some sport or other, or else bathing in one of Bavaria's beautiful lakes. Hitler himself is scarcely to be seen in this album. And what is striking is the date when the album was created. It was in the late autumn of 1941, when Hitler's war of annihilation against the Soviet Union had been in progress for several months, and hundreds of thousands of civilians, mainly Jews, had been murdered behind the battle-lines. We cannot be certain how much Eva knew about all this at the time. She had learned some time ago to close her ears.

> Eva Braun is a bright girl, who means a great deal to the Führer.
>
> *Josef Goebbels, diary, 10 August 1942*

Eva enjoyed making home movies and taking photos, and particularly liked being photographed herself. The pictures taken by a photographer named Ernst Baumann were among her favourites. His son-in-law, Rudolf Baumann-Schicht, tells us: 'She expressed the wish to have more pictures taken of herself. The shots that my father-in-law took of her were a purely private commission.'

However, the photographer got dangerously close to Hitler's mistress. Some of his shots found their way into the gift-albums – but many did not. Those too have been discovered in Baumann's archive. They show Eva in the late summer of 1941, relaxing in the sun, doing gymnastics, or bathing in the Königssee. The collection includes photos of her sister Gretl: on a lounger with a glass of wine in her hand, or posing with a boyfriend. 'The photos were never intended for anyone else to see', says Baumann-Schicht. But somehow they *were* seen by Martin Bormann, Hitler's secretary and chief factotum on the Obersalzberg. 'Towards the end of '41, my father-in-law was suddenly posted to the front, without a word of warning. After the war he found out from a former superior officer that he should actually have been sent on a mission from which he was not meant to come back alive.' But the photographer survived – and so did his pictures.

Ernst Baumann was not the only person in Eva's entourage to fall foul of *Reichsleiter* Bormann. Her chambermaid, Anni Plaim, was obliged to leave the Berghof, amid quite a stir. 'Bormann sent word that I had to get out of the Berghof', Anni relates. Herbert Döhring is still incensed about it today. 'What's all this about, I said. She was hired by my wife; and she's not going to be fired.' Anni takes up the story again: 'Then Eva Braun said: "I won't have that. You're *my* employee. I'll phone the Führer right away."' Eva's personal maid, Margarete Mitlstrasse, tells what happened next: 'Eva then talked to Hitler. And he said that if Bormann had settled the matter, there was nowt 'e could do.' The grounds for Anni's dismissal were her Catholicism. 'She was sent packing because her parents were dyed-in-the-wool Catholics, and often contributed money to the church.' Eva had to back down. In any matter remotely connected with politics, she had no say at all. And she did not really make an issue of it. Her meek protest fell silent.

> She had to suppress a lot. Especially her own will. She could not get what she wanted out of Hitler.
>
> *Herbert Döhring*

Bormann did not like her – and it was mutual. He considered Eva 'a layabout, a time-waster, a freeloader, who's not good enough for Hitler', and she thought him an insensitive 'lout'. But she used him. She found Hitler's financial manager to be generous enough when it came to extending credit. With his guarantees behind her, she could go into a jeweller's shop and take her pick, without asking the price. She was aware that with Hitler Bormann's word counted for more than hers, and made allowances for that – by fitting in with him. Willi Mitlstrasser recalls a telling occurrence: 'I'd come back from Munich, where there'd been an air-raid, about 250 people killed. I told my wife about it and she told Eva, "such and such a number dead". Eva then told Hitler. The next day Hitler had words with Eva, who then said to my wife: "You were wrong; there were only 25 killed. Reichsleiter Bormann says so." This time Eva may actually have been grateful to Bormann, since he was helping her to suppress the terror of war, something which was becoming more and more essential for her own peace of mind. She was after all the mistress of a man who had talked only of victory and who bore the responsibility for what was now happening.

> After Stalingrad, from 1943 on, it was clear to anyone that it was all over. But obviously he couldn't say so publicly. She knew it too. And she exploited that knowledge. From then on she noticed that he was apathetic about a lot of things and so she was able to get her own way more often.
>
> *Herbert Döhring*

Perhaps she could even sense that by now Hitler himself secretly believed the war was lost. There is some evidence for this. 'We sometimes talked together, just the two of us', says Herbert Döhring. 'Eva kept on asking "d'you think it'll be all right, d'you think it'll be all right in the end?" That was in 1942. And I didn't give a definite answer. I once told her: "We've failed to reach another military objective." She got very depressed. Then came Stalingrad, and she completely went to pieces.'

Ultimately, it was a matter of loyalty to her lover to believe in all the slogans about 'keeping up the fight'. It was said that she once even boxed her sister's ears for being rash enough to remark that the war was lost anyway. A couple with whom Eva was friendly asked her to pass on a request to Hitler for their two sons to be given leave from their front-line posting. Her reply was: 'You should be proud that your boys are fighting for the Fatherland!' A relative of the two young soldiers is still furious about that. 'From then on, we had no time for Eva', she says.

> By doing what she did, she wanted to prove to him: 'Maybe I'm worth more than you thought. I'm the kind of person who sees things through. And now perhaps you'll see me as I really am.'
>
> *Gertraud Weisker*

What did Eva Braun know about the crime of the century – of any century – the murder of the Jews? Herbert Döhring makes this much clear: 'Whether people want to believe me or not, I can tell you that working for Herr Hitler on the Obersalzberg, we heard nothing, not the slightest thing, about those atrocities. The whole staff, everyone – none of us ever knew a thing. I dare say people knew about the Dachau concentration-camp [near Munich], but other than that, nothing . . .'

We can probably assume that, until 1944, Eva Braun knew nothing of the genocide of Jews in the death-camps and the mass shootings behind the front line. But she certainly knew about the anti-Jewish discrimination and the deportations. Nor can the fact have escaped her that Hitler had people killed on a whim, and 'when necessary' committed mass murder. Perhaps she even knew enough to know very well that she did not want to know more.

> She was simply a young woman who got into a love-relationship and who really did maintain that relationship right up to her death. But she can't be blamed for that. If my partner is guilty of something and I love that partner, that doesn't automatically make me guilty as well.
>
> *Gertraud Weisker*

On one occasion all hell broke out at the Berghof. Hitler's secretary, Traudl Junge, tells of the time when Henrietta von Schirach – the daughter of Eva's former boss, Hoffmann, now married to the head of the Hitler Youth, Baldur von Schirach – mentioned in an after-dinner conversation how barbarically the Jews in Holland were being treated. She deplored the terrible fate of those poor people. Hitler immediately leaped to his feet and with a face of stone retorted: 'Humanitarian claptrap!' Then he strode out of the room. Frau von Schirach was never invited again. She had broken a taboo by allowing politics to invade the private sphere. Woe betide anyone who exposed the lie at the heart of the dictator's two separate worlds.

The lie was that Hitler, the private man, was anything but a monster. In his 'free time', in the idyll of the Berghof, there was no trace of his ruthless inhumanity. Even today, Hitler's former secretaries speak warmly of their boss's 'friendliness', his hand-kissing charm. That was the Janus-face of the dictator: relaxing on the Berghof terrace with his loyal retainers and his favourite Alsatian dog, under a blue Bavarian sky, and with a backdrop of Alpine peaks – while not far away people were being tortured or beaten to death in concentration camps. He could watch *Gone with the Wind* in his private cinema while German cities were being flattened by bombs. He would kiss the hand of a lady, and the next moment sign a death-warrant. To the delight of his womenfolk he would show a passionate aversion to the mistreatment of animals, but thought nothing of the fact that millions of German men were dying on the battlefields of his devastating war. He could show compassion for animals, but not for human beings. Murder, charm and banality – all were a part of his daily life.

Was his conscience clear? Why should it not be? After all, everything was for a 'higher cause'. Hitler had not visited a single concentration camp, had never used personal violence. He never allowed the horrors to come near him. Perhaps the idyllic alpine surroundings actually made many of his brutal decisions easier for him. To that extent Eva Braun was an element in his carefully constructed fantasy-world.

She respected the taboo areas. Eye-witnesses say that if staff or guests at the Berghof began talking to her about political events, she would often give evasive answers or even put a finger to her lips to discourage further questions. The fragile façade was not to be further disturbed.

> She was always true to herself, through and through. And from time to time she brought trouble on herself because of her family. Not only my own father, but also Eva's father, and our grandfather, were all critical of the Nazi regime. But she stayed loyal to that man, just as she stayed true to herself.
>
> *Gertraud Weisker, Eva's cousin*

In the end, even the Braun family, who had previously kept their distance, fell under the Berghof spell. They objected less and less to their daughter's 'immoral lifestyle'. They ultimately displayed a kind of pride in their 'quasi-son-in-law', and anyway the relationship brought the family many enjoyable benefits. A cousin of Eva's mother described it like this: 'Eva's contacts with her relatives varied in their frequency during the period when she was lady of the house at the Berghof. Once it was clear that her parents' attempts to bring her back into the family fold had failed, they resigned themselves to the role of uninvolved spectators, without influence. Opportunities to visit Eva were few, though the occasional invitation to afternoon tea with Hitler on the Obersalzberg could not be turned down. It's possible that Hitler intended these invitations as a gesture of friendship – but he was so obsessed with himself that it's doubtful.'

Uncle Alois has stated that Eva's father, Fritz, kept his distance politically from the Nazi regime. That can only be partly true. Even on Eva's home movies, his party badge can be seen. Fritz Braun had joined the Nazi Party in the late 1930s. In November 1939 a clock-maker named Georg Elser planted a bomb in the Bürgerbräu beer-cellar, which exploded moments after the Führer had left the hall, but killed several others. One author maintains that Fritz Braun was in the audience at the time, and that his escape was enough to make him acceptable to Hitler.

However, the most telling evidence comes from the lawyer Otto Gritschneder, who defended Braun in a denazification hearing after the war. He quotes his client as saying: 'I have never accepted or promoted Nazi ideology, but I was impressed by Hitler because of his successes. He built the autobahns, got rid of unemployment, and defeated France, which was a considerable military achievement.' According to Gritschneder, it was these things that turned Braun's initial aversion into eventual respect. His was by no means an isolated case among his contemporaries.

*

However, that was far from the only appearance of the Brauns in this story. It is a macabre fact that a splendid wedding-reception was held at the Berghof, at the very moment when the end of the war unleashed by Hitler was looming more clearly than ever before. It was June 1944 and the Allies were preparing to open the Second Front, with their massive landing on the Normandy beaches. On 3 June, three days before D-Day, Eva's younger sister Gretl was married on the Obersalzberg to SS-*Gruppenführer* Hermann Fegelein. In March 1944 Heinrich Himmler, the head of the SS, had called on Hitler on the Obersalzberg, and introduced the new 'Waffen-SS liaison-officer to the Führer' – the same Hermann Fegelein. He was probably one of the most repellent careerists among the Nazi elite, and was jointly responsible for the murder of tens of thousands of women and children behind the Eastern Front in 1941. However, among the ladies of Hitler's entourage he made quite an impression. In many respects the marriage was an arranged one. By linking himself with Eva's sister, and thus with Hitler's mistress, Fegelein saw an opportunity to rise still further.

> I think it was an arranged marriage. Because in my view Gretl was not the sort of person to deliberately cause a rift with Eva. Who was really behind it, whether it was Hitler, or Bormann, or even Fegelein himself, I don't know.
>
> *Gertraud Weisker*

Eva herself is said to have told women-friends that, as a man, Fegelein appealed to her very much. 'If I'd met Fegelein ten years sooner, I would have asked the Boss for my freedom', she told her friend Marion Schönmann later. The fact that Eva had resigned herself to her own fate is shown by how she smoothed the way for her sister's marriage. One of Hitler's secretaries, Christa Schroeder, takes up the story: 'After failing several times to marry her sister off to men in Hitler's entourage, Eva now steered her towards a new target: Gretl had to marry Fegelein.' Finally, under Eva's direction, the wedding took place. 'I'd like everything to be just as if it were my own wedding', hinted the Führer's mistress. Her cousin, Gertraud Weisker, interprets her real meaning: 'My little sister, who was always just an appendage, is now going to be a wife, and here am I, after sixteen years, still the girl-friend, the mistress.' Was Eva trying to make clear to her lover what she herself was being deprived of?

It is doubtful whether the message ever got to Hitler,

especially not at this stage of the war, when he had his back to the wall. A week after the Braun–Fegelein wedding the coast of Normandy was in the hands of Allied forces. The advance on the Reich had begun. It was not the only thing that made Hitler stop in his tracks that summer. At 7 o'clock on the morning of 20 July an aircraft took off from Rangsdorf military airfield in Berlin. On board were Colonel Count Klaus von Stauffenberg and his adjutant, Lt.-Colonel Werner von Haeften. Stauffenberg's briefcase contained two bombs, each packed with nearly a kilo of plastic explosive. At 10.30 the guards on duty at Hitler's headquarters in East Prussia, known as the 'Wolf's Lair', let the two officers in immediately. They had no idea that they had just admitted the leader of the military resistance group, which had decided that Hitler must be removed. At 12.42 exactly the silence was broken by a deafening explosion. The bomb that Stauffenberg had placed under the map-table in the conference-room had detonated. Assuming that their bid to kill Hitler had been successful, von Stauffenberg and von Haeften made their way hurriedly back to Berlin.

At the same moment Eva Braun was bathing with friends in the Königssee. Margarete Mitlstrasser tells us what happened that afternoon: 'All of a sudden the driver, Zechmeister, comes up in a great hurry, and I say: "Why are you back so soon?" And he says: "Something terrible's happened. Someone's tried to assassinate the Boss!" Then Eva must have noticed that we'd suddenly turned pale. So of course she asked what the matter was, and Zechmeister told her. "We're driving straight home", she said. So we drove back to the Obersalzberg, and we'd hardly got out of the car when she said: "Margret, pack my things. I'm going to Berlin." So I said: Madam, you can't do that. The Führer told us specially that whatever happens you're to stay at the Berghof.'"

Eva immediately wrote to Hitler, no doubt expecting that he would be particularly in need of her now: 'Beloved, I am beside myself. I am dying of fear and feel I'm nearly going mad. The weather here is so lovely and everything seems so peaceful that I am ashamed of myself . . . You know that I live only for your love. Your Eva.'

> Well, our Eva was not a political animal. It just wasn't part of her nature. She would never have got deeply involved in anything, wouldn't have had any organised commitment to politics. And she never did, whether about politics or anything else. She never showed any great involvement.
>
> *Gertraud Weisker*

The failed attempt on Hitler's life may indeed have marked a turning-point in the relationship between Hitler and Eva. Hitler's tone did in fact become friendlier. After the events of 20 July 1944, Eva's biographer, Nerin Gun, claims that Hitler wrote: 'My dear bumpkin, Don't worry, I'm fine, just a bit tired perhaps. I hope to be home soon and then to be able to relax in your arms. I have a great need of rest, but my duty towards the German people must come first . . . I am sending you the uniform I was wearing on that unfortunate day. It is proof that Providence protected me and we have nothing more to fear from our enemies. With all my heart, your A.H.'

*

Where Eva spent the next few months can no longer be pieced together in detail. Sometimes she was in Berlin, sometimes Munich, sometimes on the Obersalzberg.

In January 1945 the Soviets began their final offensive, with Berlin in their sights. The Reich capital had long been in ruins. Allied bombers were dropping their deadly load on the metropolis nearly every day. And nearly every day Hitler telephoned Eva. He advised her not to come to Berlin.

At the beginning of March she decided nevertheless to make the journey, as her confidante, Margarete Mitlstrasse, describes: 'On 7 March 1945 she travelled of her own free will by special train to Berlin, which was now under siege. And she stayed up there – although Hitler was appalled and tried to send her back straight away. But there was no shifting her. To think that she stayed for the sake of such a dreadful man, and then went to her death with him . . .'

Was this self-destructive foolishness or the final proof of her love? In the view of her Uncle Alois, 'we can now see that Eva's friendship with Hitler was more than the opportunistic, fair-weather friendship of a young woman with an appetite for life; and we can also see that Eva was more to Hitler than a plaything, to amuse him for the odd hour.' What she wanted was the recognition she had so long yearned for, even at the cost of her life. She had abandoned herself to her fate.

Hitler's architect and armaments minister, Albert Speer, has described at length his parting visit to Hitler in late April 1945: 'Eva Braun and I were able to talk in peace, as Hitler had retired to bed. Indeed Eva was now the prominent personality in that bunker, awaiting her death with an admirable and proud tranquillity. All the others were either putting on heroics like Goebbels, planning their escape like Bormann, burnt out like Hitler or in a state of collapse like Frau Goebbels, yet Eva Braun exhibited an almost cheerful composure . . . "How about a farewell bottle of champagne? And some canapés? I'm sure you haven't eaten for ages." After my long hours in the bunker, she was the first person who had worried that I might be hungry. I was touched by her concern. The steward brought us a bottle of Moët et Chandon, and some cakes and biscuits.'

*

The final hours in the 'Führer-Bunker' degenerated into a melodramatic swan-song in the manner of a Wagner opera – with betrayal, marriage, a will, suicide and immolation. In the last days in the 'catacomb' the dictator's state of mind swung between attacks of blind rage and moments of profound depression. After periods of lucidity he plunged once more into the depths of obsessive fantasy. This apocalyptic mood was shattered on 23 April by a telegram from Reich Marshal Göring announcing, in the form of an ultimatum, his intention to assume power. Hitler was beside himself with fury. It was unheard of that one of his paladins should 'betray and abandon both myself and the Fatherland! Now I am left with nothing, no more loyalty, no more honour. There is no disappointment that I have not endured!' Hitler elevated himself to the role of sacrificial victim. Even those men who had accompanied him on his political path from the very beginning were now no longer his friends. On the night of 28 April there came a second blow. The Reuters news service reported that Himmler was engaged in peace negotiations with Sweden's Count Bernadotte. Another betrayal! And this time, the 'faithful Heinrich', of all people. 'He stormed about like a madman', recalls the wartime ferry-pilot Hanna Reitsch.

The death of Hitler's good friend Mussolini increased his mood of panic. Italian partisans had shot *Il Duce*, along with his mistress, Clara Petacci, and hung them upside down from street-lamps in Milan. It was a severe shock for Hitler. The grim fate of the man he had once modelled himself on must have seemed like the writing on the wall. Did Eva see it like that as well? 'All I can say is that Hitler was lucky to have her', thinks Reinhardt Spitzy, a visitor to the Berghof in the years 1937 to 1939. 'Because she remained true to him to the end, when all the generals were trying to make their getaway, and even the top men in the Party were falling apart. But in spite of all, she stuck by him and went to her death with him in a very noble manner, just as Petacci did with Mussolini.'

Eva Braun sensed that, faced with obliteration, she could take on the role she had always longed for. She wanted to be closer to him than anyone else. 'Poor Adolf, they've all abandoned you! They've all betrayed you!' she accused the world and fate. She just wanted to show that she was the only one who still stood by him. She did not realise that this promise merely reinforced his paranoid delusion that he was the real victim, and thus gave him an escape into imaginary worlds.

She was still fixated on Hitler, and showed no particular sympathy when Gretel's husband, SS-*Obergruppenführer* Fegelein, was caught trying to escape with a suitcase full of jewellery and banknotes, and then executed for alleged complicity in Himmler's treason. The fact that Fegelein was Eva's brother-in-law did nothing to mollify Hitler, and there is no evidence that Eva herself put in a plea for the man.

The continuous bombardment of Berlin's government district by Red Army artillery could clearly be heard when Hitler asked his secretary, Traudl Junge, to follow him into his office in the bunker. It was the evening of 28 April 1945. Hitler dictated two wills – without once pausing or correcting himself. In his 'political' testament, the dictator gave final evidence of the kind of paranoid world he inhabited. Frau Junge took down in shorthand his torrent of words, filled with hate and accusation. With hackneyed phrases he attempted to justify his bestial acts. He attributed blame for the war to 'international Jewry'.

In his much shorter personal will he announced what would take place a few hours later, his nuptial union with Eva Braun: 'Although during the years of struggle I considered myself unable to take on the responsibilities of marriage, I have now decided, shortly before the end of my life, to wed the woman who, after many years of true friendship, freely came to the beleaguered city of Berlin, in order to share my destiny. As my wife, at her own request, she will join me in death.' The rest of the document contains details of the disposal of his possessions. Then follow the final, decisive words: 'My wife and I are voluntarily choosing death, in order to escape the disgrace of usurpation or capitulation. It is our wish that our bodies be immediately incinerated in the place where, for the last twelve years of service to my people, I carried out the greater part of my daily work.'

> That day, Eva Braun said something very odd to me. She said: 'You'll be shedding tears for me before today is over.' So I thought, that's it then. Because she'd always said the Führer would tell her when the time had come for him to do away with himself. But then she said: 'No, no. I don't mean that.' She meant she would be married that day,
>
> *Traudl Junge, Hitler's secretary in the bunker*

Hitler's statement on the subject of matrimony was given modest effect in an unadorned and improvised wedding ceremony. The registrar, a city official named Wagner, had been drafted in from a *Volkssturm* militia unit, fighting close to the Reich Chancellery. Apart from him, the only others present were the two witnesses: Bormann and Goebbels. It was all over in a few minutes. The bride was so excited that she started signing the wrong name on the marriage certificate. When she realised her mistake, she crossed out the 'B' for Braun and appended her new name to the document: 'Eva Hitler née Braun.' The ceremony was rounded off with drinks in Hitler's private rooms. The few guests included Hitler's secretaries and his cook. It was an eerie wedding celebration, at which the bridegroom, after accepting congratulations all round, talked of suicide. Even after the marriage, no-one in the bunker dared to call Eva 'Frau Hitler'.

However, in the eyes of history Eva Braun had now achieved what she had always wanted. As Traudl Junge says: 'I had the feeling that all her life she remained in the shadows and probably had no chance of changing that. I expect she imagined she would at least go down in history as the heroic mistress, the wife of the Führer. I believe it was that hope that gave her strength.'

Only in that way could Eva have finally made sense of things. Some people give her credit for having sacrificed herself for love, others only see her death as the logical outcome of that self-destructive relationship that she had originally entered into voluntarily, from which she had repeated opportunities to break away, but which out of blindness she refused ever to abandon.

However, I am very fortunate to be close to him, especially at this time.

Eva Braun, letter of 19 April 1945

I die as I have lived. I do not find it difficult.

Eva Braun, letter of 22 April 1945

The Red Army had occupied the zoo district in Berlin and was now in Potsdamer Platz, at the heart of the city. Stalin's troops were only a matter of yards from the Reich Chancellery and its bunker, when Hitler and Eva Braun said goodbye to the last of the faithful. On 30 April at about 3.30 p.m. a single shot rang out in the bunker, scarcely audible amid the thunder of the Russian artillery. In his private room Hitler sat slumped on the blood-spattered sofa, Eva Braun beside him. The former Reich Youth Leader, Artur Axmann, described what he saw in the room: 'Adolf Hitler was sitting on the right-hand side of the sofa, his upper body leaning slightly to one side, his head tilted back. His forehead and face were remarkably white, and blood was trickling from his temple. I saw Eva Braun collapsed on the sofa beside Hitler; her eyes were closed. I could see no external signs of what killed her. She had taken poison and looked like someone asleep.'

There was never any doubt about the cause of Eva Hitler's death. She had poisoned herself with potassium cyanide. In Adolf Hitler's case there was a long dispute as to whether he had died from the shot to the head alone, or from a combination of the bullet and poison. Today we know that he first bit on a cyanide capsule and then shot himself in the right temple.

SS men and stewards carried the bodies wrapped in blankets up the narrow staircase of the bunker and into the small garden. A block of reinforced concrete with a small door separated the catacomb from the outside world, where Soviet shells were exploding relentlessly. An adjutant named Günsche carried Eva's body to a spot some 15 feet from the entrance. There petrol was poured over the two corpses; there was as much as 300 litres available for the task. Some crumpled paper was lit and thrown on to the pyre, which at first refused to catch fire. 'The Boss isn't burning!' Hitler's chauffeur, Kempka, is said to have shouted.

From the doorway of the bunker Martin Bormann and Joseph Goebbels watched in silence as the two bodies went up in flames – the corpse of the man who had brought million-fold misery to the world, and whom the German people had followed in blind obedience to the end; and the mortal remains of his secret mistress, who only when facing death became a dictator's wife.

On 1 May 'Greater German Radio' broadcast its version of these events. Adolf Hitler had 'died in his command-post in the Reich Chancellery, fighting to his last breath for Germany'. It was the final lie of the regime. No mention was made of a woman at Hitler's side.

> Eva Braun is not a factor in history. No-one would have been
> interested in her, if she had not got married to Hitler in the
> final days, and gone to her death with him.
>
> *Gertraud Weisker*

Gertrud Weisker first heard about her cousin's death in June
1945, and reached her own conclusion: 'For her it was the logical
outcome. She had finally done what she had been working
towards all her life. It had been her objective to marry that man at
any price. And since she no longer had the chance to do it while
alive, she did it in death. It seemed the only logical ending to the
love-story that had begun when she was a seventeen-year-old.'

The verdict of historians is an anti-climax. Hugh Trevor-Roper
once wrote: 'Eva Braun is one of the great disappointments of
history.' She certainly played no part in the decisions that led to
the most terrible crimes of the twentieth century. Hitler was too
self-obsessed, too immersed in his own paranoia, to let a young
lass from Munich tell him what to do. Yet she was a part of his
private world, the deceptive idyll in which he found respite and
ease. Perhaps that merely enabled him to pursue his horrific
programme with even greater ruthlessness.

CHAPTER TWO
THE DEVOTEE –
MAGDA GOEBBELS

If Germany today is arising once more from despair and adversity towards faith and hope, then it is German mothers who are playing an important and momentous part in this.

I personally find it unpleasant and intolerable to be suspected of wearing clothes from a Jewish couturier.

Of course I love my husband, but my love for Hitler is stronger; I would be willing to lay down my life for him . . . Once I realised that, apart from his niece Geli, Hitler is unable to love any woman, but, as he has always said, can love only Germany, then and only then did I agree to marry Dr Goebbels, because it meant I could be near the Führer.

I am trying to make German women more beautiful.

. . . Should we lose the war, my life will be over anyway. I hope to continue to bear the burdens of this war with him. Then that will be the end . . . for me there is no way out.

Magda Goebbels

She was known as the 'First Lady' of the regime and rightly so, since she was not just the only lady, but the only woman of any kind to play a public role alongside one of the world's greatest and most influential men. Hitler did not of course have any females in recognised or official positions in his circle.

Anneliese Uhlig, actress

She became in a way the other half of Hitler's personality, held together . . . on her side by a sacred will to serve and by the sense of a higher duty.

Otto Wagener, SA chief-of-staff and economic adviser to Hitler, 1931

She didn't actually come from a Nazi background; on the contrary, she had a strict Catholic upbringing. In no way was she a Nazi 'bitch', as we used to say. Absolutely not.

Wilfried von Oven, personal adviser to Joseph Goebbels

She was very beautiful and very elegant. She had the first Elizabeth Arden cosmetic-case to come on the market. She got it from Elizabeth Arden with all the little boxes, pots and flacons . . .

Ariane Sheppard (née Ritschel), Magda Goebbels' half-sister

. . . I was unable to share Magda's enthusiasm in any way. From the start, Magda's unshakeable faith in the mission of Adolf Hitler was a complete mystery to me.

Auguste Behrend, Magda's mother

She'd had a difficult marriage; she was divorced and the son from her first marriage was often with her. Life wasn't easy for her. And probably for the sake of the children, she tried to keep this marriage going as long as possible.

Birgitta Wolf, a neighbour of Magda and Joseph Goebbels in Berlin

I have never before seen a woman with such ice-cold eyes.

André François-Poncet, pre-war French Ambassador to Germany (in a 1932 interview with journalist Bella Fromm)

The game of patience is a time-honoured way of passing time and calming the nerves. People can spend hours making well-ordered rows from piles of shuffled cards according to predetermined rules. Some people read the cards as an oracle that foretells the future. Patience does not require excessive mental agility, but is a pleasant distraction and enables one to take one's mind off other things when alone.

It is doubtful whether playing-cards have ever been laid out under such eerie circumstances as on the evening of 1 May 1945, in a room in the 'Führer-Bunker' beneath Hitler's Reich Chancellery. Stony-faced, a 43-year-old woman plays one game after another on the heavy, rectangular table, while her husband wanders around aimlessly, occasionally gazing over her shoulder into a void. The couple do not exchange a word, and avoid any physical contact. The sound of the cards being slapped down on the table is all that can be heard – apart from the woman's sobs. She weeps a great deal. She has just killed her children.

Magda Goebbels loved her children above everything. She had given up several years of her life to them, made many a sacrifice, endured illness and deprivation. Her offspring had repaid her generously. Everyone who met them was impressed by how well brought up and delightful they were. Each of the six children had their own distinct personality.

Magda Goebbels had always gone to great lengths to make a good impression as a mother. Not only that, she was in some ways the 'super-mum' of the Third Reich. In the picture-magazines of the day, you could often see the elegant lady with the gracious smile surrounded by her smartly dressed children. The wife of the Minister of Propaganda and her family circle were themselves a jewel in the propaganda crown. The blessing of many children, brought up by their mother to be the new generation carrying Hitler's Reich forward into the future: that was how every good National Socialist household should be. Magda devoted a lot of energy to living up to the ideal. In the end her children were forced to believe in it too.

Before she began delaying her own suicide with absurd card-games, she had bidden an orderly farewell to her children. Each one was dressed in a snow-white nightdress, and the girls wore white ribbons in their hair. They were cloaked in the image of childish innocence before being sent unsuspectingly to their deaths. It was a final pitiful attempt to dress up the act of murder as a 'clean solution'. As a betrayal of herself and others, it was entirely in keeping with the past twelve years under the swastika.

Magda Goebbels wanted to be a perfect, idealistic National Socialist, and ended up a murderess – there was no contradiction between the two.

Like Joseph Goebbels, she had given herself over body and soul to Hitler. Both held rigidly to their faith, even when the coming collapse of Nazism was clear to see. Both were wrapped up in the deranged and mystical belief that their whole existence was linked to the rise and now to the destruction of Hitler's Reich. Even when all the signs were still pointing to a victory for Germany, Magda Goebbels and her husband had decided to depart this life together, if and when the page of history were ineluctably to turn. Both knew only too well what terrible crimes the regime was guilty of, and how deeply Joseph Goebbels himself was implicated in them. Trapped in her absurd ideology, the 'model woman' of the Third Reich feared that after the collapse of the dictatorship she would be left to the mercies of 'Jewish vengeance'. Behind this gloomy prophecy was a panic-stricken fear of ultimately being held to account for her participation in all the madness, for which so many had been made to pay with their lives. Once the terror was over, she did not wish to languish as a guilt-ridden footnote to history, without influence or privilege, without even the comfort of self-delusion.

Magda did not want to go on living in that after-world, stripped of all pretensions. She had attached herself indissolubly to the regime to which she was completely devoted and to which she owed much.

But why did she also condemn her children to death, even though they were free from their parents' guilt? 'We will take them with us, because they are too beautiful and too good for the world that is coming.' That is what, some weeks earlier, she had confided to her sister-in-law from her first marriage, who later repeated the words in evidence. 'The world that is coming will regard Joseph as one of the greatest criminals that Germany has ever produced. His children would have to hear that every day, they would be tormented, despised and humiliated. They would be burdened with everything he did. People would take revenge on them . . .'

Did she really kill her children in order to safeguard them? In reality, this surge of maternal protectiveness cloaked a large degree of self-interest. It is true that the settling of accounts with tyranny would also bring shame and loss of status to the children of top Nazis, but there were no grounds for expecting anything comparable to the Nazi custom of *Sippenhaft* – the imprisonment, or worse, of the families of offenders against the regime. The chimaera of children being maltreated and humiliated in place of their guilty parents in truth concealed a much more mundane motive: the one thing that Magda Goebbels could not bear to think of was that her children would go on living without her; that they would gradually come to see, in the shattered fragments of a once glittering façade, the lie their parents had been living. She wanted to draw a line under everything she had built up and which was part of her. In the end there should be no heirs or legacy left behind, no witnesses or testimony, only a myth of steadfastness and loyalty unto the grave.

For herself, death held no great terror. Influenced by Buddhist philosophy, Magda Goebbels was convinced that her death would open the way to a new life. Her half-sister Ariane Ritschel describes how once, on the island of Capri with her father, Magda stood at the edge of a sheer cliff and shouted to him: 'You see, father, this is what my life will be like: when I've reached the very summit, I shall fall and cease to exist, because I'll have had everything I ever wanted!'

To climb so high that the downward plunge loses its terror: this was a kind of recurring *motif* in the life of Johanna Maria Magdalena, whose succession of surnames marks her upward progress: Behrend, Ritschel, Friedländer, Quandt and finally Goebbels. In the course of this life we see her adopt various personalities. Her rise could have culminated in achievements of a totally different kind, but always there was that urge to climb, an urge that defined Magda's career.

*

It began in Berlin on 1 November 1901. Her mother, Auguste Behrend, was anxious to leave her humble origins as a housemaid behind her as quickly as possible. The story she herself told was that, after Magda's birth, she persuaded the baby's father, an engineer from the Rhineland named Oskar Ritschel, to legitimise the child by marriage. Although this was a pure formality, and the couple were divorced in 1903, the well-off father continued, until his death in 1941, to ensure that his daughter wanted for nothing. At Ritschel's behest, Magda was sent at the age of five to Belgium, where he was working at the time. There he arranged for Magda to receive a strictly Catholic education from the venerable Ursuline nuns in the convent schools of Thild and Vilvoorde, near Brussels. It was from this draconian schooling that Magda acquired not only her knowledge of French, but also her enduring self-control and self-discipline. Here the hard-working schoolgirl received the foundations of a considerable fund of knowledge, which she acquired over the years without great effort.

All this would certainly have been approved of by her less intellectually gifted mother, who followed her to Brussels in 1908. By this time Auguste Behrend was already involved with another man, a Jew named Richard Friedländer, who travelled from Berlin specially to take the marriage-vows. This was apparently a popular move all round, since the man who gave her away at the wedding was none other than her former husband, Oskar Ritschel.

To Magda, Richard Friedländer was more than her mother's new husband. He was the father-figure of her youth, with whom she forged a close bond. Although Friedländer was not a deeply religious man, through him the Catholic girl gained access to the world of assimilated Jewish society. This familiarity with Jewish life was deepened by a momentous meeting, for which the turmoil of the First World War was indirectly responsible. When war was declared, the Friedländers, as Germans in Belgium, turned from neighbours into enemies overnight. In August 1914, the family had to set off back to Berlin – from the border of neutral Holland in a cattle-truck.

A similar journey – though under different circumstances – was made by a Russian-Jewish family, who had fled from the pogroms in their native Ukraine and found refuge in the East Prussian city of Königsberg. Germany had declared war on Russia as well as France and Britain, and as subjects of the Tsar the Arlosoroffs were expelled from the fortress city near the Russian frontier.

The result was that both the thirteen-year-old Magda and Victor, the fifteen-year old son of the Arlosoroffs, were beginning a new stage of their lives in Berlin. As refugees they felt equally strange in their new home, and this would influence their later life. Magda continued her education in a high school for young ladies. There she formed a close friendship with a classmate, Victor's sister, Lisa Arlosoroff – the kind of friendship that only girls of that age are capable of. In the cosmopolitan and liberal household of the Russian emigrés Magda found a substitute home and the family security she had never experienced before.

Meanwhile Victor was attending the prestigious Werner von Siemens high school, which was known for its progressive teaching methods and had a high proportion of Jewish pupils. Although German was not his mother-tongue, Victor collected excellent grades and made his name as pupils' representative and editor of the monthly *Werner von Siemens* magazine. His exuberant German patriotism in the general euphoria of early victories was replaced, in the course of the war, by a new self-awareness, which the eighteen-year-old achieved through examining his own origins: 'I am a Jew', Victor wrote to his German literature teacher in 1917, 'and I feel strong and proud to be a Jew. I feel my nature to be different to that of true Germans and I never try to conceal it. I sense how much of the Levant lives in me, how much divided loyalty, how much longing for wholeness – things which native-born Germans do not experience.'

The high-school boy devoted himself with fervour to the study of Hebrew, and immersed himself in the ideas and history of Zionism. As a result, Victor came to the conclusion that the future of the Jewish people, scattered around the world, could only be found in 'Eretz Israel', the national homeland in Palestine. He was no zealot or sectarian, he forced no-one to accept his own convictions. But he derived enjoyment from preparing himself, in theory and practice, for a future life as a settler in the 'Promised Land', even though he felt quite at home in Berlin. As he had charisma and a sociable nature, he had soon gathered around him quite a crowd of young people – Jews and non-Jews – who shared his views, and who discussed German literature as often as questions of Zionism and Judaism. However, meetings of 'Tikvath Zion', as the group called itself, were also notable for their enthusiastic singing and partying.

Thus it was almost inevitable that the exuberance and *joie de vivre* of these young people would also infect Lisa Arlosoroff's friend Magda. The gentile girl eagerly took part in the debates about the future of Palestine. Soon she was even wearing a Star of David on a chain around her neck and seemed determined one day to emigrate to the Zionist homeland. That at least is the account given decades later by Lisa Arlosoroff; and she also suggested a significant motive: Magda had fallen in love with 'Chaim', as Victor now called himself. Magda found in the self-confident young intellectual the strong, purposeful determination that attracted her in men throughout her life. As an only child, who had grown up without a permanent father-figure, she was always searching for decisive personalities, who were cloaked in a special kind of aura.

*

The youthful love remained no more than an episode. Their ways parted. Magda turned to such other diversions as come and go in the changing moods of youth. Chaim found a Jewish partner, with whom he had a daughter, and in 1924, after completing his studies, he moved to Palestine. From his new home in Tel Aviv the 25-year-old embarked on a tireless programme of travel on behalf of the Zionist movement. He represented the Jewish National Homeland at the League of Nations in Geneva, attended congresses, conferences, and meetings, and published numerous essays and articles. He talked to politicians, diplomats and benefactors, and was the founder and leader of the socialist Mapai Party. Finally, he acted as the overseas representative of the Zionist Jewish Agency. Despite his youth, Arlosoroff was one of the most brilliant and effective of the Zionist leaders.

Magda's life took her in a different direction. After passing her school-leaving examination, the *Abitur*, she began the training in domestic science that was obligatory for all middle-class girls, and went to a select finishing-school for girls near Goslar, in the Harz mountains of Lower Saxony. However, she only stayed for the autumn term, because a chance meeting on a train was to settle all questions about the future of this ambitious young woman. On the train from Berlin to Goslar, another passenger in the overcrowded compartment offered her his seat. He appeared immediately attracted to the charming young woman. With the single-mindedness of the entrepreneur that he was, the passenger embarked on his conquest. During the journey through the snow-covered mountains, he engaged her in courteous conversation, and on arrival he took care of her luggage. Three days later he was standing outside Magda's hall of residence, with a bunch of flowers for the house-mother. The suitor did not possess the obvious attributes that usually make a girl's heart beat faster. At the age of thirty-eight, he could have been Magda's father, and an almost bald head reinforced the paternal image. His manner was stiff, he was awkward with people and finicky in matters of detail. However, this attentive admirer did possess one crucial advantage: he was one of the richest industrialists in Germany.

Thanks to the world war, inflation and his entrepreneurial skill, Günther Quandt was in the process of turning his family textile business in Mecklenburg into a far-flung industrial empire. His wife had died of influenza in October 1918 and he was now a single father of two sons, Hellmut, aged ten, and the eight-year-old Herbert. So it was that Magda, the fresh-faced and alert boarding-school girl, with her charm and her thoroughly respectable education, seemed to him the salvation he never dared hope for, someone who could restore to him the happiness of a full family life.

Nor did the widower's wooing leave his ideal candidate unmoved. The prospect of a luxurious lifestyle, the absence of material worries and the chance of motherhood, all had a stronger attraction than boarding-school life. Despite many reservations and warning voices, Magda agreed to a wedding at the beginning of 1921. True, for his part Quandt imposed certain conditions: Magda had to give up her Catholicism in favour of the Protestant church and to adopt her father's name, Ritschel, rather than the Jewish surname of Friedländer. These were the requirements for a socially acceptable alliance in Quandt's stolid, provincial home town, and Magda accommodated herself to them. Around this time her mother separated from her Jewish husband, who was scraping a living as a head waiter in Berlin.

*

Magda now began a new phase of her life, both stimulating and adventurous, with a husband almost twenty years older than herself, and two stepsons scarcely ten years her junior. The almost feudal way of life in a country house, idyllically situated beside a lake in the outer Berlin suburb of Neubabelsberg, promised Magda a swift and glittering ascent up the social ladder. There were long trips to Italy, Switzerland, Britain, France, the USA and Latin America, which, for those days, provided an almost unparalleled opportunity to widen her horizons. For a while Magda found her happiness in running the household and being a mother. In November 1921, much to Quandt's delight, she gave birth to a son, whom they named Harald. Four years later, the family was further enlarged by three foster-children, orphaned by the sudden death of their parents, with whom Quandt had business connections.

The alliance also proved lucrative for Magda's mother, now alone once again. Her wealthy son-in-law set her up with her own chemist's shop on Berlin's Borsigsteig. In 1927 Quandt acquired an additional property, a spacious city-centre apartment for the winter months. His young wife could now call on the services of a housekeeper, a private tutor, a cook, a chambermaid, a gardener and a chauffeur. With so much free time she could devote herself to bringing up her children, playing the piano and fulfilling her social obligations. It was life in a golden cage. But the truth was that no amount of luxury could bridge the predictable gulf between the spouses, who were separated by more than just age. As a businessman, Günther Quandt was constantly travelling, and even when he returned home his mind was fully occupied with business matters. Discussion of deeper things was not on the agenda. At best, Quandt was not known for his conversation or wit, and sometimes, due to the rigours of work, he would simply fall asleep, occasionally during one of their infrequent visits to the theatre. Only with difficulty could Magda persuade her spouse to attend social functions. Furthermore, in financial matters the multi-millionaire was decidedly tight-fisted. Then their family life became overshadowed by the death of Magda's beloved stepson, Hellmut, who died in Paris in 1927, as the result of an operation that went wrong.

Not even their shared grief could bring the estranged couple together again. By 1929 a separation had become inevitable. Quandt found grounds for divorce, when Magda had a brief affair with a young student with whom she had sought consolation. But seeing her status threatened, Magda was clever enough to extract herself from this predicament. She produced a collection of letters from former female admirers of Quandt in his bachelor years, which she had discovered in a drawer. In a court of law, such relics of youthful passions would have carried no weight. Nonetheless, the mere public knowledge of these amours from the distant past would attract attention in the industrialist's home town, and that was something he preferred to avoid. Thus the cuckolded husband agreed without demur to a settlement that was extremely favourable to his wife. Magda received a princely alimony of 4,000 Reichsmarks per month, a spacious apartment on the Reichskanzlerplatz in Berlin, and custody of their son Harald until he reached the age of fourteen. This meant that as a divorcée she had no need to worry about her financial future.

Still only in her late twenties, and an attractive woman, she had no lack of attention from the opposite sex. The most prominent and wealthiest in a series of admirers was Herbert Hoover, nephew of the then President of the United States, whom she had got to know during one of her trips to America with Günther Quandt. In 1930 Hoover visited Berlin specially to make her a proposal of marriage.

When she refused, her suitor was apparently so upset that he turned his car over, driving too fast. Magda, who was in the passenger-seat, was taken to hospital with several broken bones and a fractured skull. The much sought-after young woman decided that in future she would not accept the role of trophy-wife to a millionaire.

Magda was now independent in every respect – yet she was not happy. In saying goodbye to the world of a respected lady of the house, she had forfeited the central focus of her life. In place of the accustomed combination of luxury and surfeit, she felt only an inner emptiness. Her golden cage was open, but at the same time the ground had been cut from under her feet. After the war, Magda's mother described, with thinly veiled reproach, the impression her daughter made on her at that time: '"Oh hell, everything's so *dull*", she would moan. And then with bitter irony she would say: "Oh, aren't we just madly happy today! Waiter, another guest please . . ." Then I suddenly knew what was tormenting that spoilt young woman, who was admittedly my daughter but who was often more of a mystery to me than if she had been a complete stranger: she was bored. She didn't know what to do with herself. Most people would have been more than happy with just a fraction of what she possessed. But she went around yawning and doing nothing, constantly in danger of becoming a good-for-nothing "young lady", throwing her life away.'

She was twenty-nine years old, with one marriage behind her, and her life ahead of her. But that inner emptiness must have been the driving force that made her seek a new purpose in the field of politics. The fact that, of all people, this affluent woman of the world should fall into the clutches of a plebeian like Hitler is less curious than it might appear. It was the blend of reactionary philosophy and radical, dynamic posturing represented by Nazism that aroused the curiosity of Berlin's sensation-seeking smart set. Not a few of the titled, decorated or fur-coated denizens of the capital, though worlds apart in lifestyle from the lower-middle-class brownshirts, were in sympathy with what they took to be the uncompromising nationalism embodied by Hitler. So it was no coincidence that Magda's first contact with the Nazi Party took place in the 'Nordic Circle', an exclusive club, which was instrumental in making extreme right-wing views acceptable in the drawing-rooms of Berlin's high society. Later, on 1 September 1930, she joined her local NSDAP branch in Berlin's West End district, as member number 297442. It was a step that cannot simply be explained away as the result of boredom, desperation or naivety. She was a well-educated citizen and knew only too well what the swastika stood for.

She believed in Hitler. In her eyes he could do no wrong. It was plain to see that she swooned over him like a teenager.
Ariane Sheppard, Magda's half-sister

With typical thoroughness and consistency, she plunged herself into the realm of Nazi ideology. She read Hitler's seminal book, *Mein Kampf* (My Struggle), to the very last page. She studied Rosenburg's *Myth of the Twentieth Century*, the ideological 'bible' of National Socialism. She subscribed to a Nazi newspaper, read party tracts and followed Hitler's speeches in the press. With the same passion that she had devoted to planning her future in a Zionist homeland, she was now convinced of the superiority of the 'Germanic race', of the underhand dealings of Jewish conspirators, and of the heinous crime of the 'dictated peace of Versailles'.

The 'Movement' attracted her, not because it offered distraction or a change of scene, but because in it she found fulfilment for her yearning to believe in something. She was given something to occupy her time and to aim for, something that seemed to rescue her from her feeling of disorientation. And in this she was not alone. With increasing success at the polls, the sermons of salvation preached by the Nazi prophets drew in a growing number of disciples among the seekers after truth as well as the converted, the hopeful as well as the desperate. The swastika was very much the symbol of its time.

Admittedly, in her first Party role, Magda proved a miserable failure. The *Blockleiter*, or Nazi Party representative in her street, was only too eager to put the wealthy 'party colleague' in charge of the women's section of the local branch. Up to that time few people in the classy West End district of Berlin shared Magda's interest in the Nazis; those that did wander into the extreme right-wing party were mostly clerical workers or janitors. The arrival of a grand and exotic lady in this petty-bourgeois milieu caused a sensation – and provoked a reaction. For the feelings among the women she addressed were aroused more by her freewheeling divorced lifestyle and her wickedly expensive wardrobe than by the lectures she gave.

After this unsuccessful debut the ex-Frau Quandt reconsidered her position in society and decided to present herself at party head-quarters, where she offered her services. Thanks to her ideological preparation and knowledge of languages she was immediately given a job in the records section of the office of the *Gauleiter*, the head of the party and Hitler's representative in Berlin, to whom she soon gained an introduction.

Four years earlier Hitler had given the Rhineland-born Joseph Goebbels the task of storming the 'red bastion' of the capital, which had always been very difficult territory for the Nazi Party. To begin with, his unscrupulous campaign of agitation garnered few votes for the demagogue, but at least it made headlines and attracted attention. With his parades, torchlight processions, meeting-hall brawls and tirades of hatred, Goebbels quickly raised his own profile in a capital that was hungry for sensation. Driven by curiosity, Magda herself had already attended one of his electioneering appearances in the Palace of Sport. After the audience had been warmed up with brash marching music and waving banners, the bright hope of the Party mounted the stage. He looked like a living caricature of the scrawny demagogue that he was – an undersized runt of a man, with a disproportionately large head, ill-fitting jacket and a shirt-collar too large for his neck. When he walked, he visibly dragged one stunted foot behind him – the result of osteomyelitis contracted in childhood. Yet as soon as the orator raised his sonorous, hypnotic voice, with his precise and telling phrases, uninhibited pugnacity, biting sarcasm and populist sideswipes, he was able to hold an audience spellbound. The elegant woman listening to him might have seemed out of place in this fairground hurly-burly, but she could not deny the impact of his words. The bravura performance of this stentorian preacher had very little in common with the stiffly formal speeches of the leading politicians of the Weimar Republic. Goebbels employed a sophisticated arsenal of mimicry and gesticulation, modulation and crescendos, elaborate choreography and rhetorical punch-lines. He mastered his audiences by appealing less to their sober intelligence than to their sensuality, and swept a suggestive public up in a heady blend of collective resentment and enthusiasm. It was Goebbels' enticing election speeches that had reinforced Magda's decision to join his party.

Magda become a more and more enthusiastic propagandist for the new cause. She gave herself to it heart and soul.

Memoirs of Günther Quandt, Hans-Otto Meissner, 1978

Now she was sitting opposite him in his office. The Gauleiter had not let the opportunity slip. As soon as he had noticed this distinguished-looking woman in the corridors of his headquarters, with her fine features, graceful figure and elegant clothes, he sent for her. The new employee was happy to oblige.

In his office Goebbels showed no outward sign of emotion as he explained to the party novice that he had selected her for the job of setting up a private archive for him. The Gauleiter knew the value of knowledge in the game of political intrigue. Detailed dossiers on the background to national and international events, on political opponents and especially about his own colleagues within the party, could become effective ammunition in the battle for power. And Goebbels wanted to hand the job of assembling this material over to this attractive party member who – unlike her boss – was capable of extracting information from foreign-language newspapers. In this way Magda came under the direct orders of her new superior and also into his personal orbit. Thus, from the outset, she was privy to the shady manoeuvres by which he jockeyed for power.

'Apart from that, not a word of warmth fell from his lips', Magda's mother said, looking back on that first encounter between Goebbels and her daughter. 'Not a compliment, scarcely even a personal remark. It was just his eyes that seemed to consume Magda. "I thought I would burn under that arresting, almost devouring gaze", she once told me much later.'

When it came to ladies' company, our agitator was no shrinking violet. In his diaries from those years a dizzying sequence of female acquaintances are presented like the trophies of a conqueror. 'Every woman gets my pulse racing', the would-be Casanova confided to his diary in 1926. 'I dash around like a hungry wolf. And at the same time I'm as shy as a kid.' Though not exactly blessed with the attributes of a ladies' man, he was driven by an almost manic urge to put his masculinity to the test. Every affair, whether real or imagined, was balm to a wounded soul, which he felt had been exposed since childhood to the taunts and contempt of his physically normal classmates.

Thus we can read his diary entries that recount this new acquaintance like the chronicle of a campaign of conquest. 'A beautiful woman named Quandt is putting together a new personal archive for me', he noted on 7 November 1930 and added a week later: 'Yesterday afternoon the lovely Frau Quandt came to my office and helped me sort out some photos.' The entry for 28 January 1931 already bears witness to greater familiarity: 'Frau Quandt came to do some archive work at home (!). She is a beautiful woman.' Then on 15 February he reports his mission accomplished: 'Magda Quandt came this evening. And stayed for a very long time. She is blossoming into an enchanting, blonde sweetie. What a queen you are to me!' At this point the diarist felt obliged to enlighten posterity as to the nature of this first intimate encounter, with a Don Juan-style figure '1'. 'A lovely, lovely woman! I will probably fall deeply in love with her. I'm walking around today almost in a dream. I'm so sated with happiness. It's so wonderful to love a beautiful woman and to be loved by her.' Four days later her lover gushes: 'Magda Quandt came and we had a perfectly marvellous evening. She is a gorgeous woman. She calms me and gets me out of myself. Lovely Magda!' A week later the Gauleiter invited his chosen one to accompany him to a party rally in Weimar. 'Sat alone with Magda till deep into the night', his diary records. 'She is a captivatingly beautiful and kind-hearted woman, and she loves me beyond measure.'

> My father often used to wonder how anyone could throw away their life so, being married to a tearaway. To the end of his life my father was baffled by it.
>
> *Ariane Sheppard, Magda's half-sister*

Yet this certainty soon began to teeter. For it turned out that the woman he had set his heart on was very different from the office affaires and flirtations in Nazi circles which had occupied the Gauleiter up till then. Magda certainly returned his turbulent affection, and she consciously sought a closer relationship with the man in whom her sure instinct had sensed charisma and the aura of power, but she was much too sure of herself to yield rashly to his courtship. She wanted to be more than just an air-headed trophy. She had a mind of her own. 'At home we had our first quarrel over something thoughtless I said', we read in the diary for 26 February. 'She wrote me a farewell note and went away in tears. Always the same old story! Now I see how beautiful she is and how very much I love her.'

It was to be the overture to an endless series of passionate declarations of love, dramatic fallings-out and theatrical reconciliations. The tension between the two had been predictable – a self-confident woman of the world, who had no doubt calculated her 'market value', coming up against a hot-blooded male chauvinist, who made no secret of his crude disdain for the opposite sex. 'It is a woman's job to be beautiful and bring children into the world', was how Goebbels had once summed up his attitude.

The jealous lover watched carefully for the appearance of any rivals likely to challenge his conquest. Once, having heard nothing from Magda for several days, Goebbels learned that one of his predecessors had, for his part, gone mad with jealousy and was plaguing his beloved. Goebbels' diary shows him close to madness himself: 'There I was, all alone with my fear and torment. Magda doesn't call. I phone her a good thirty times. I rage, I despair. The craziest nightmares fill my head . . . Why doesn't she give me a signal? This uncertainty is killing me. I have to speak to her, come what may. I'll do anything to make her see me today. The whole night was one long screaming pain. I feel like yelling. My heart is being ripped apart in my breast . . .'

Admittedly, in moments like this the fiery Lothario continued to seek solace with other women, though on 22 March he wrote in his diary what seems like a declaration of surrender: 'There is only one woman I love now.'

> I shall now stop fooling around with women, and devote myself to one alone . . . She has an intelligent, realistic attitude to life, and at the same time a generous way of thinking and behaving. A little more training for both of us and we'll make a fabulous match.
>
> *Joseph Goebbels, diary, 10 March 1931*

Despite all the emotional schisms, a relationship developed between the Beauty and the Beast, which seized them both more strongly than any of the affaires either had previously had, or were still having. The bond between them was their shared faith in a pseudo-religious doctrine of salvation under the sign of the swastika. This also involved disposing of a past that now could no longer be reconciled with the image of the world and of the enemies of Germany created by this abstruse ideology. During a holiday together on the North Sea coast in July 1932, Magda revealed to her companion the details of her earlier life. In Goebbels' diary we find only cryptic allusions to what his mistress confessed to him. But it appears to have genuinely frightened him, as can be seen from one entry: 'Serious battles with Magda about our happiness. In her earlier life she was very irresponsible and thoughtless. And now we shall both have to pay for this. Our fate hangs on a slender thread. God grant that we are not both destroyed by her undoing.'

What was it about Magda's story that so disturbed the ambitious Nazi? Had it only been her description of youthful indiscretions, this would hardly have provoked such massive rhetorical fire-power from Goebbels. More probably it was Magda's confessions of her former enthusiasm for Zionist ideas and her romantic attachment to one of Zionism's foremost champions. Goebbels' mistress, of all people, once inhabited the world that was demonised by his party. Did he now fear the 'undoing' that would follow, if her early history should come to light? As soon as he had been given his job with the Nazi Party in Berlin Goebbels had not hesitated for a moment in giving the heave-ho to his own former partner, Anka Stalherm, whose mother was Jewish. With his new companion he was by no means sure he could be so ruthless. 'A bit of a row with Magda. She's sometimes so heartless when she talks about her past. She hasn't yet completely broken with it.'

Yet Goebbels did everything he could to force this break. The apartment on Reichskanzlerplatz, which Magda's ex-husband Günther Quandt continue to maintain, increasingly became a new home for Goebbels. Until then, he had led a nomadic existence in a series of student-like lodgings, grabbing meals in cheap restaurants. For the ambitious Goebbels, coming from a lower-middle-class background (his father had been a book-keeper), Magda's grand lifestyle meant a gain in prestige that he noted with pride. For the first time the bachelor had a woman at his side who not only brought him recognition, but provided him with some basic instruction in manners, etiquette and dress-sense. The live-in lover repaid her by showering her with expensive presents, but maliciously passed the bills on to Magda's father, Oskar Ritschel, for payment.

> This woman could play a big part in my life, even if I weren't married to her. In my work she could provide the female counterweight to my exclusively male instincts. Pity she isn't married.
>
> *Hitler to Otto Wagener, SA chief-of-staff and Hitler's economic adviser, 1931*

The palatial Quandt residence soon became a rendezvous for Nazis and their sympathisers in high society. So it was only a matter of time before Hitler himself appeared in Magda's salon, during one of his stays in the capital. The party leader was thoroughly impressed by the plush surroundings and even more so by his hostess. With her junoesque figure and halo of blonde hair, not only did she seem to embody the typical 'Germanic' wife and mother, as portrayed in the propaganda *kitsch* of the day, but she herself displayed a convinced belief in the 'Führer' and his doctrine. What is more, she combined this faith with intelligence and spirit. The master soon let it be known in his immediate circle that, as far as status was concerned, this model of National Socialist womanhood would actually be a more suitable consort for him than for his underling, Goebbels. However, as the future leader of the nation, Hitler had, he said, taken a vow of celibacy and would allow his lieutenant in Berlin to marry her in his place, as it were, in order to ensure that in future the fair muse would never be far away. Leaving aside all the legends that arose from these rituals of masculinity and power, there could be no mistaking that Magda exerted a strong attraction over Hitler, since she was one of the few women in his circle who not only radiated charm, but at the same time was a loyal devotee of his and a gifted and intelligent conversationalist.

> It was a certain intellectual sympathy that Hitler admired in Magda and that is why, at Hitler's urging, so as to keep her close to him, she got married to Goebbels.
> *Wilfried von Oven, personal adviser to Joseph Goebbels*

For her part, Magda found in Hitler a father-figure, something she had lacked since her early childhood. She was overjoyed to have reached the place in the Party to which she had always aspired: the very top. Coolly appraising the situation, she told her mother she was convinced there were only two alternatives: a communist takeover, or the victory of Nazism. 'And if Hitler's movement comes to power, I'll be one of the top women in Germany.'

> Goebbels had picked up on the fact that this Frau Quandt was very keen on Hitler and Hitler was very keen on her. And that was the reason he married her. That's how Frau Goebbels became dependent on him and in the end paid for it with her life. Frau Goebbels was a cultured woman.
> *Herbert Döhring, Hitler's house-manager at the Berghof*

However, she needed no command from Hitler to make her decide on marriage to Goebbels. Despite urgent warnings against it by those close to her, including her natural father Oskar Ritschel, Magda was convinced that in the Berlin Gauleiter she had, with Hitler's blessing, found the man of her life. Goebbels was also being forced to legalise the liaison, so as to quell the pointed gossip within the party. His political rivals had begun to discredit the relationship between the self-confessed social revolutionary and the former wife of an industrial tycoon, a woman who, to make matters worse, had once borne the Jewish name of Friedländer.

> In Father's eyes Goebbels was an extremely dangerous man. But Father was powerless, of course. There was nothing he could do, either about the persecution of the Jews or about the wedding.
>
> *Ariane Sheppard, Magda Goebbels' half-sister*

Curiously, the couple chose, of all places, the Quandts' feudal estate near the town of Severin in Mecklenburg as the venue for their wedding ceremony. Thanks to a friendly estate-manager, the ex-Frau Quandt still had access to this remote country house, where the two felt safe from pursuit by political opponents. On 19 December 1931 the bride and groom walked past a guard-of-honour with arms upraised in the Nazi salute. They were accompanied by Magda's son Harald in an improvised Hitler Youth uniform, and Hitler himself was their witness. In a little church on the estate, a trusted Nazi pastor officiated at the union of the Catholic-born church-hater and the Protestant woman, who had been raised in Catholic convents. A swastika flag served as the altar-cloth.

> Hitler was the witness at their wedding. He had set up the whole thing and thereby arranged that, through his close contact with his propaganda minister, the contact with her would also be practically uninterrupted. He had a very, very close relationship with her, and precisely because Goebbels went on having flings with other women, Hitler had more influence over her. There was more opportunity for contact and more openness between them. Hitler was a man she revered, and her husband was being unfaithful to her.
>
> *Wilfried von Oven, personal adviser to Joseph Goebbels*

True, the honeymoon had to be sacrificed for party reasons. The marathon series of elections in the dying months of the Weimar Republic sent the newly wed Gauleiter off on an exhausting round of rallies, speeches, processions and meetings. Magda's apartment, in which the couple settled permanently, acted as a kind of headquarters for all this. It was on Reichskanzlerplatz that the top echelons worked out their political strategy. Here, Hitler's foreign press chief, 'Putzi' Hanfstaengl, and Magda too, spent long evenings at the piano. And here Hitler was served vegetarian delicacies by the lady of the house.

Magda, who had suffered several miscarriages in her previous marriage, was now full of hope again. Despite all the inconveniences of life at the centre of the political struggle, the future looked promising. Ten months after the wedding, on 1 September 1932, she brought a daughter, Helga, into the world. Although the traditionally minded father would naturally have liked a son to carry on his name, he was nonetheless delighted that the foundation of a happy family had been laid.

> They behaved very sensibly together. It was not a rapturous, seventh-heaven kind of love, but a perfectly sensible husband-and-wife relationship.
>
> *Frieda Smyrek, Goebbels' family housekeeper*

Whenever this healthy family image came under attack, for example through press criticism of the new-found wealth and patrician lifestyle of the former 'champion of the people', the good doctor had his own way of springing to the defence of his honour. 'The editor of a tabloid rag has made a disgraceful attack on my wife's honour', he fumed in his diary, then went on to boast that 'an SS man paid him a call, and beat him with a horsewhip until he sank to the floor, covered in blood. My man then placed his visiting-card on the desk and left the office without any of the creeps at the newspaper trying to stop him. That's the only way to deal with those scandalmongers.'

Violence was part of the agitator's armoury. He used every

imaginable means to get into the public eye. As head of propaganda for the party, Magda's husband played a large part in increasing the number of Nazi deputies to become the largest party in the Reich parliament – which they were only there to destroy. Yet now every shot in the locker seemed to have been fired. In November 1932, in the second national election within six months, the Nazi Party's share of the popular vote dropped back for the first time. Hitler's party was threatened by a split between rival wings and was practically out of funds. The serious economic slump, which the extreme right had exploited to their advantage, had turned the corner and prosperity was returning. The prospect of breaking through to seize the levers of power by democratic means was dwindling fast.

The gruelling reversals of fortune had their effect on Goebbels' spouse. On Christmas Eve Magda was taken to hospital with severe pains. 'The year 1932 has been one long run of bad luck', her despairing husband wrote in his diary. There was worse to come. While Goebbels was at his master's side in the tense poker-game for power behind the scenes of the Weimar Republic, his wife was in hospital, fighting for her life following yet another miscarriage. 'We're going to battle on, to victory or death!' Goebbels wrote grimly in his diary. 'I shook Hitler firmly by the hand and said "I want to see you in power!"'

The following day he was once again gripped by blind panic: 'I'm between life and death. And 600 kilometres away, trapped in my hotel room. This fear has taught me for the first time how much I love that woman and how infinitely I need her . . . I did nothing but shiver and pray all night long: may God preserve this woman for me. I can't live without her. I arrive in the early dawn. Go straight to the hospital. Everyone looking very serious. I have the most terrible anxieties.'

After an operation the patient regained her strength. At the same time Hitler succeeded in his final bid for power, thanks to some influential backers in the retinue of the aged President Hindeburg, who were more than willing to give him a leg up. On 30 January 1933 Hindenburg appointed Hitler as his Reich Chancellor. Two days later Magda Goebbels was able to leave hospital. But the moment that saw both her recovery and the political triumph of Nazism also brought bitter disappointment. Her party might now be in a position of power, but her husband was not. For despite Hitler's 'solemn promise', the new government, adorned as it was with reactionary grandees, had no room for the rabble-rouser. And that meant that his wife was also banished from the front rank. 'Magda very miserable', Goebbels noted. 'I'm being squeezed out. Hitler's hardly any help. I've lost heart.'

But the doughty propagandist was soon to find it again. Hitler disposed of his conservative coalition partners as soon as they had voted him sole authority. The hour had struck for Goebbels too. As 'Reich Minister for National Enlightenment and Propaganda', he was able to mount his frontal attack on the consciousness of the German people.

> Goebbels knew how to manipulate people. And he managed to do that to Magda time and again. In spite of that, she stayed with him.
>
> *Ariane Sheppard, Magda's half-sister*

The *Frau Minister* also benefited from this increase in status. Although women were in the majority among those who had voted for Hitler, within the party they had, from the very beginning, been of no interest to him. The Nazi movement had been largely presented as a male organisation, entirely in line with Hitler's views, as he often liked to make clear in private discussions. 'A woman's world is her man', he opined; or 'Where women are concerned, intellect doesn't come into it'. Thus it is no surprise that the Nazis, once in power, were initially without any suitable female representatives. The head of state himself considered it appropriate that no woman should be allowed to stand at his side, so that in quasi-celibacy he might embody his claim to be devoting his creative powers exclusively to his 'bride', the German nation.

So it was that the sophisticated and presentable minister's wife, now the object of the dictator's favour, was given the task of filling this gap in his life. Official engagements and state visits, such as that to the fascist ally, Italy, were enhanced by Magda's grace and elegance. As the 'First Lady of the Reich' she was playing the role of a lifetime.

> But I can well imagine that later on Frau Goebbels would have gladly married Hitler, instead of Goebbels. In her own mind that possibility was always there.
> *Herbert Döhring, Hitler's house-manager at the Berghof*
>
> It's my personal opinion that Hitler and Magda were strongly attracted to each other. And that they had many points of contact, albeit not physical. There is no doubt at all that Hitler was mad about Magda Goebbels.
> *Wilfried von Oven, personal adviser to Joseph Goebbels*

As the regime's unofficial female leader, she was allowed to proclaim the new paradigm for women, in a radio broadcast on Mothers' Day, 14 May 1933. In the spirit of the now prevailing ideology she wove a laurel-wreath for German mothers, before launching an attack on the tentative steps towards women's emancipation under the Weimar Republic: 'The most sacred treasures of the German people were falling into ruin. Morality, honour and patriotism were forced to give way to the subversive and destructive power of a base and impious mentality. In this way even the value of motherhood was degraded. The idiocy of a frivolous age dragged mothers down from their exalted position as upholders and guardians of the family and put them on a par with their husbands, whom they wanted to match or even exceed in politics, work and morality. It is no wonder then, when one man rose up from the people, the pioneer of a new age, battling for a new morality and a new honour, that our womenfolk, and especially mothers, instinctively rallied to his side and that, having embraced his high intellectual and moral goals, they became his enthusiastic supporters and fanatical campaigners.'

However, apart from her radiant presence at official receptions, Magda's 'fanatical struggle' was chiefly limited to an honorary position in the Nazi welfare organisation, *Nationalsozialistische Volkswohlfahrt* (NSV), and acting as unpaid chairwoman of the newly created 'German Office of Fashion'. The elegant Magda was made for this position, if only because of her extensive and well-chosen collection of dresses and hats. From her chair she fought valiantly against the rampant tendency towards standardisation, and here too she captured the mood of the times: 'I consider it my duty to look as attractive as I can. In this way I hope to influence German women. They ought to look as attractive and elegant as possible. I have been put in charge of the German Office of Fashion, and in this capacity I will try through my own example to make German women into true representatives of their race.'

Her role as 'First lady' of the German Reich was one she fulfilled to the hilt. For her the most important thing was that she was doing what Hitler required, because he didn't have a wife. The Eva Braun woman had no authority at all.
                                    Ariane Sheppard, Magda's half-sister

Even Magda Goebbels could not fail to notice the terrible impact on her country of the frenzy that had now been elevated to official doctrine. German citizens, now ostracised as Jews, were robbed of their rights and often of their profession and livelihood as well. Goebbels himself stoked the racial hatred with crude and inflammatory tirades that led to the boycotting of Jewish shops and businesses, and the burning of important works of German literature. His wife obediently gave her support to this disgraceful desecration of culture. The Third Reich was simply anti-Jewish, she explained to her former sister-in-law, Ello Quandt, and as Minister of Propaganda it was her husband's job to attack the Jews in the press and on radio: 'That is what the Führer wants, and Joseph has to obey.'

But Goebbels was acting out of conviction, not just obeying orders, and anyway his wife knew how much she owed to his position. For the 'First Lady of the Reich' any ties of family or friendship with Jews were totally impermissible. As she wrote to an official of the German Labour Front (DAF), a compulsory union, it was 'intolerable' for her 'even to be suspected of having my dresses made by a Jewish couturier'. This was the pretext she gave for getting the DAF to close down a fashion-house on Berlin's Kurfürstendamm and force the Jewish owner of the business to emigrate.

What must have been even more 'intolerable' for Magda was the thought of her name being linked with that of Chaim Arlosoroff, the friend of her teenage years, who by now was one of the leading representatives of the Jewish Homeland in Palestine. In his capacity as head of foreign affairs in the Jewish Agency, in May 1933 he risked a return visit to his old home city of Berlin. Under the swastika, this was like Daniel entering the Lion's Den. He was on a tricky political mission into hostile territory: in negotiations with Nazi officials, some of whom he remembered from his student days, the emissary attempted to alleviate the conditions for Jewish emigrants and to enable them to rescue their assets.

On his way through the familiar streets, as his sister later recounted, Arlosoroff noticed a glossy photo in the window-display of a photography shop; it was of the propaganda minister with his wife and child. The love of his youth, Magda, was now married to the fast-rising persecutor of the Jews! It took Arlosoroff quite some time to get over the shock. But then he thought about the opportunities that his earlier acquaintance with the Reich's leading lady promised to open up for him in his negotiations. Brushing aside all objections from friends and colleagues, he got in touch with Magda in order to gain access through her to her husband and thus to the Nazi government. However, his one-time sweetheart cut him off abruptly on the phone, with an urgent warning that any further contact could bring great danger to both of them. According to his sister, Arlosoroff afterwards described his approach as a grave mistake.

On 16 June 1933, two days after his return to Palestine, the Zionist leader dined at a secluded Tel Aviv hotel with his new wife Sima; then the couple took a stroll along the beach. Suddenly two men came towards him; one asked him for the time and what his name was; then the other pulled out a pistol and fired twice. Help came too late for the 34-year-old politician. He died the same night

in the nearby Hadassah hospital. Meanwhile his murderers had
melted into the darkness. The killing of Arlosoroff robbed Jewish
politics of one of its most promising talents in Palestine. Even at that
young age, he had played a crucial part in the development of a
Jewish homeland, and had every prospect of a leading position in
the future state of Israel.

The settlers in Palestine were plunged into deep shock, the effects
of which are still being felt today. This was fratricide: Jewish assassins
had laid low one of the ablest figures in their own ranks. Or was
there another explanation? Did the order for the young politician to
be shot in fact come from outside? Had Goebbels himself had a
hand in the business? Did the power-hungry and unscrupulous
minister want to make sure that Arlosoroff took his knowledge of
Magda's former life to the grave? Were Magda's warnings on the
telephone to her old flame inspired by tangible fears? Despite much
rumour and speculation, there is no real proof that the propaganda
minister was behind it. Most of the clues support another theory:
that Arlosoroff's killers came from the extremist wing of the Zionist
movement, which took a dim view of the young diplomat's dealings
with the Hitler regime. In the subsequent court hearing, this was
the view also expressed by his widow, Sima.

In the end, no-one was ever convicted of the murder. Due to
lack of evidence the precise background to this episode remains
unclear to this day. However, what is beyond dispute is that the
early death of her one-time lover protected Magda Goebbels for
the rest of her life from the embarrassing revelation of her youthful
Zionist leanings. Even the murdered man's sister, out of fear
of repercussions, kept this knowledge to herself until shortly before
her death.

*

Although the German media, under Goebbels' control,
maintained a conscientious silence about the assassination in
Palestine, echoes of the event spread as far as Arlosoroff's former
homeland. The *Jüdische Rundschau* (Jewish Review) in Berlin,
whose publication was still allowed under strict supervision,
published a lengthy obituary of the Zionist leader. On 26 June

1933 his friends and supporters held a memorial ceremony for him at the Philharmonie hall in Berlin. This silent demonstration of sympathy was still possible, despite the sound of anti-Semitic chanting that could be heard all around.

We do not know whether Magda Goebbels was given details of the murder or even learned of it all. Far removed from these turbulent events, the young mother was at that time enjoying the summer air at the North Sea resort of Heiligendamm. With her eleven-year-old son Harald and nine-month-old Helga, the model mum was treating herself to a holiday break after the first six stressful months of the 'Thousand Year Reich'. 'Quiet, blessedly tranquil evening', Goebbels noted, on a visit to his family by the sea on 18 June 1933. 'All this work and a good deal of strain had made us to some extent strangers to each other. We must get back to how we were before. We have promised ourselves this.'

Yet this resolution remained rather an empty one. Once his wife had come home from the seaside Goebbels never intended to let her return to the public stage, on which she had found increasing confidence. In his desperate hankering after recognition Goebbels clearly feared he might be outshone by the radiance of his wife. At his official engagements the minister was in the habit of banishing his spouse to a vehicle at the back of his motorcade. Now he obliged Magda to withdraw from all her public-relations functions, which were beginning to earn her respect and popularity. Without any real leverage against his domineering behaviour, Magda responded by defiantly turning cold on him. 'Another row with Magda last night about her Fashion Office, which has caused me God knows how much trouble', Goebbels wrote in his diary for 20 July 1933. 'Noisy scenes. Magda must keep herself to herself more. Things can't go on like this. As far as this is concerned I have nothing but problems with her. She goes to bed in a huff. This morning she makes silly excuses. Doesn't want to come with me. Well, that's women for you. At least I'm glad we're off to Bayreuth soon.'

However, this time the supreme guardian of Nazi culture had to make his pilgrimage to the Wagnerian shrine without the company of his wife. Magda stayed at home in a sulk. If her husband wanted to cut her out of being the regime's female representative, then she would leave him alone to face the audience that gathered for the annual Wagner festival at Bayreuth. However, when Hitler's loyal assistant confessed to him how he had been humiliated in a marital tiff, the Führer had no sympathy with Magda's ostentatious strike-action. He immediately had his treasured muse summoned to Bayreuth.

The slighted spouse bowed gladly to the Führer's will. After the first act of *Die Meistersinger*, Magda made her belated entrance in the opera house, and Goebbels was once more lost in admiration for his master: 'He has made peace between Magda and me. He is a true friend. But says I am right: women have no business in political life. Then the row blows up again violently. Much misery back at the hotel. Everything hanging by a thread. Then we make it up . . . Magda is sweet and good. She can be so lovable. But in matters of principle there is no reprieve.'

*

The ambitious wife did indeed bend to these masculine principles. For a considerable time Magda Goebbels disappeared from the public stage and devoted herself to the role that she had been so keen on promoting. She protected hearth and home and devoted herself to the duty of presenting the Führer with numerous children. By this time the family had left the city apartment, which Günther Quandt had stopped paying for once his ex-wife had remarried, and moved into a home of their own in the quiet Berlin suburb of Kladow. Magda was now allowed to decorate it with her own good taste. On schedule a second child by Goebbels had been added to the family. But this led to renewed marital squabbles. 'Let's hope it'll be a boy', the proud father-to-be had prayed in his diary. But contrary to the indications it was another girl, Hilda, to whom Magda gave birth on 13 April 1934. The father sulked, refusing to send flowers or even visit the hospital. But when Hitler and his entourage arrived there to offer their congratulations, Goebbels could not avoid at least acknowledging his undesirable offspring. Nevertheless, at the end of his visit he hissed at Magda through clenched teeth: 'Next time it's going to be a boy!'

This challenge was promptly met by the prolific mother. Some eighteen months later, on 2 October 1935 she produced a male heir, whom the parents – apparently stuck on the initial 'H' – christened Helmut. 'There the little chap lies: he looks like a Goebbels', the proud father exulted in his diary. 'I'm happier than I could imagine. I could go round smashing things out of sheer joy. A boy!'

But the son was followed by yet more daughters: Holde, on 19 February 1937, Hedda on 5 May 1938 and finally Heide on 20 October 1940.

> Woman was created to be a mother, and man to support and protect the family. Just as the man finds his greatest happiness in successful creativity, ambition and work, and in achieving his goals in life, so does the woman find this happiness solely in fulfilling her life's purpose, in motherhood!
> *Magda Goebbels, quoted in* The Joy of the Cradle, *by Hannes Schmalfuss, 1941*

By now the growing family had moved again, this time to a red-brick period house on the picturesque Schwanenwerder peninsula in lake Wannsee, not far from Berlin. The previous owner had been Jewish. The idyllically situated property provided the perfect backdrop for the model National Socialist family with well-behaved little children and a caring mother. A movie of them at home was made in 1937 by the Ufa film company, as a birthday present to the top man in the German media. On Goebbels' instructions a shortened version was shown on cinema screens all over Germany – though parading the grand lifestyle enjoyed by his family earned him a good deal of criticism.

When Goebbels produced the repugnant propaganda documentary film, *Victims of the Past*, which was intended to give spurious respectability to the inhuman discrimination against the mentally ill and disabled, he had no hesitation in presenting his own numerous offspring as a prototypical, hereditarily healthy and 'racially pure' generation. And whenever 'Uncle Führer' put on his favourite act as a lover of children, the propaganda boss's cute little brood, all dressed in white, always had a walk-on part. Contrary to the accepted story, the children were not to be spared from donning the uniform of the Hitler Youth as soon as they reached the entry age. Both Harald and Helga became members of the official Nazi youth organisation and were 'tremendously excited' about it, as their father noted proudly.

> The public thought it marvellous when Frau Goebbels appeared with her pretty children, so neatly dressed. The couple were all smiles. It made a big impression. It was just a lovely picture . . . The children were quite simply dressed and they behaved like perfectly ordinary children, not stuck up at all . . .
> *Brunhilde Pomsel, secretary in the Ministry of Propaganda*

To add a finishing touch to the *nouveau riche* lifestyle, the ambitious Goebbels surrounded himself with a collection of status symbols, including a fleet of expensive cars, a motor-launch named *Baldur*, and a large sailing-yacht. Magda ran the household with a practised hand. She took on the job of redecorating the rooms with style and taste, and discussed conversion plans with architects, one of whom was Albert Speer, then Hitler's personal architect. As a hostess she kept a close eye on all the arrangements. Even though cooking was not one of her natural skills, she confidently gave orders to her staff and was thus never embarrassed by the unexpected arrival, often at very short notice, of her husband's guests. As she was fond of saying: 'You can tell a true lady by the fact that she can go on entertaining her guests without batting an eyelid, even when the gas-cooker explodes in the kitchen.'

The hostess also paid great attention to her own appearance. Several times a day she would apply new make-up and change into a different outfit, always one that had been made for her by a select fashion-house. She made sure she was always to be seen well manicured and with her hair perfectly coiffured. The elegant Magda was happy to leave other German women to follow the Nazi Party's exhortation that they should be non-drinking, non-smoking,

unmade-up Gretchen types. Where that was concerned Magda
Goebbels stood above the crowd.

> Magda Goebbels was a clever, superior woman, who knew what
> she was doing. It got to the point where she asked Hitler to
> agree to her separation. He was very upset, because he was very,
> very fond of the children. Then somehow Goebbels managed
> to tone down his escapades a little. But she was above the
> situation. She was an intellectual woman with many interests.
>   *Birgitta Wolf, neighbour of Magda and Joseph Goebbels in Berlin*

Later, the family estates were expanded still further with the
acquisition of a country house by the Bogensee lake, north of Berlin.
The minister had it converted at a cost of 3.26 million Reichsmarks –
and sent the bill to the film industry. As if that were not enough, he
then had an official residence near his ministry remodelled to suit his
own and his wife's taste. This time the extravagant 3.2 million
reichsmark cost was met by the government. The crowning glory of
his rapid social ascent was to be a glittering ball to celebrate the 1936
Olympic Games in Berlin. The minister and his lady invited 3,000
guests from all over the world to the magnificently appointed
Peacock Island in the Wannsee. However, due to the presence
among them of some hard-drinking ruffians from the 'campaigning
days', who started brawling, the elegant reception deteriorated into a
social disaster.

*

Meanwhile, the ladies of Nazi high society were secretly looking
down on a rival who seemed to them to be quite beyond the pale:
the former photographer's assistant, Eva Braun, was the constant
object of snide remarks and disrespectful mockery from the
moment she appeared in Hitler's entourage. The wife of the
Minister of Propaganda herself considered it beneath her dignity
to invite to her coffee-circle a rival whom she classed – not
without justification – as a 'blonde airhead'. However, the Führer
was not at all amused when his indignant mistress came to him

with the woeful story of her social ostracism. For a long time Magda suffered the disapproval of the almighty leader. Hitler, who normally enjoyed spending time with the Goebbels family, stayed away from Magda's door.

She was very hurt at being rejected by her fatherly friend but, as was her custom, she did not show it. Stoic self-control was the sterling quality of Hitler's devotee. With the same iron discipline with which she subjected her daily life to a detailed and meticulously maintained schedule, Magda Goebbels went on showing the world a façade of unblemished family life, long after this had begun to crumble. Without displaying the slightest emotion, she courteously welcomed an unknown female visitor to her breakfast-table, before calmly sending her off to the railway station. Yet there was no mistaking the fact that the young lady had spent the previous night with the master of the house.

Even as the father of a family, Goebbels was unable to rid himself of the burning urge to prove his power over women – on the contrary: his position in charge of the entire film industry of the Third Reich also gave him privileged access to the casting-couch. A series of Ufa's stars and starlets were prepared, more or less willingly, to lend their lustre to the minister's reputation as an irresistible seducer. For what most concerned the complex-ridden would-be Casanova was the outward impression he made. 'Louis XIV of France, England's Charles II, and the victorious Napoleon took as many women as they wanted, and the people idolised them nonetheless', he announced with a conceit that was all his own.

As far as success with women was concerned, the latter-day imitator failed to match the achievements of his historical exemplars; nevertheless, the public openly discussed the amours of the 'Babelsberg Buck', an allusion to the famous Berlin film studios. And his own wife, who, as popular gossip would have it, was the only person to remain unaware of his many adulterous escapades, more probably chose to look the other way. It was far more important to her to preserve the appearance of a happy home life.

Well, I had the feeling that she was totally convinced she had a faithful husband. The public were not so sure.

Frieda Smyrek, the Goebbels' housekeeper

Rumours went round that Goebbels couldn't let a skirt go past without taking a closer look. And he reserved the right at least to look over the cast-lists for films. How much influence he had over them, I don't know. But of course people said, aha, he's got some new girl-friend.

Brunhilde Pomsel, secretary in the Ministry of Propaganda

It should be mentioned that, for her part, Magda was capable of arousing jealousy in her wayward husband. On 1 August 1936 Goebbels recorded another 'row with Magda' in his diary. 'Rosenberg has told me an unpleasant story involving Lüdecke. I talk to Magda about it. But the business has not yet been clarified.' Kurt Georg Wilhelm Lüdecke, then aged forty-six, had in the 1920s been among Hitler's closest associates and at that time had handled contacts with Nazi activists in the USA. In 1930, after Magda's divorce from Quandt, Lüdecke had a liaison with her for a time. According to some reports, it was he who first brought Magda into the Nazi Party. However, in the web of intrigue between the rival party factions he soon fell out of favour and in 1934 was even held for a time in Sachsenhausen concentration camp, until a friend in the party helped him get out. Meanwhile it seems that he stayed in touch with Magda, in the hope of enjoying her protection.

According to Lüdecke's own version, which he wrote while in exile in America as a way of getting his own back on the Nazis, he visited his former mistress several times, the last occasion being in 1936: 'I was just telling Frau Goebbels about my disappointment over the undignified squabbling within the Party at that critical time. We were sitting on a wide, comfortable sofa, with a low coffee-table in front of us. I was speaking with emphasis and Magda laid her hand on my arm, in a friendly, sympathetic gesture . . . Suddenly the door opened and there stood the little Doctor.

'He stopped for a moment, with his hand on the door-knob, and stared at us wide-eyed, his face pale and tired. For a moment there was an awkward silence. I stood up slowly and carefully removed Magda's hand from my arm. Goebbels approached with a glowering face . . . Clearly he was not best pleased to see me there. His wife asked me to stay for dinner, but I made my excuses and left hurriedly.'

Was all this an unfortunate misunderstanding? At all events we find signs of a genuine marital crisis in Goebbels' diary: 'First a row with Magda. About her visitor. She cries and then I feel sorry for her. It's wretched. But this thing with Lüdecke is not clear at all. Is she telling me the truth? I just don't know.' By the next day he knew a bit more. 'Last night Magda admitted it was true about Lüdecke. I'm very depressed about it. She has been persistently lying to me. This is a big loss of trust. It's all so horrible. One can't get through life without making compromises. That's the terrible thing! It'll take me a long time to get over this.'

Plagued with jealousy, the husband, quite unscrupulously, sought to 'get over it' through amorous distractions. But in one instance the Lothario was not immune to more profound feelings. A fling with the 22-year-old Czech actress, Lida Baarova, turned into an affaire that was to have dire consequences. Whenever he had the chance, the minister took the young woman with him to his country property by the Bogensee where, undisturbed, the two could abandon

It was the picture of a happy family, even later, when the rumours about Baarova were going around. They were thrust so much into the public eye that people thought it was really beastly of him. Especially as Frau Goebbels was a mother of children, having to put up with it all. But afterwards, of course, they made it up and were a happy family again.

Brunhilde Pomsel, secretary in the Ministry of Propaganda

themselves to their Hollywood-style romance. The lovers began brazenly attending film premières and receptions together in the full glare of publicity, until the liaison became the talk not only of the town, but of the whole country, and finally came to the ears of Magda herself.

Even in this case, in order to maintain appearances, the distraught wife initially sought an accommodation, rather than breaking up the marriage. She asked Lida Baarova to come and see her and astonished her rival with a confession, as the actress recounted later. 'She said: "Well, of course, you know he's a genius, and we must be there for him, both of us. *I* decide what goes on in my home. As to what happens outside, I couldn't care less. You must just promise me not to have a child by him."'

Whether or not the conversation actually went like that – and whether Magda was acting out of conviction, desperation or guile – the parties did in fact attempt for a while to run a *ménage à trois*. As the wronged wife told her ex-sister-in-law, Ello Quandt, in self-justification: 'It is possible that his solid relationship with Baarova, whom he seems to be really in love with, is keeping him away from countless other adventures of the kind which could ruin his reputation and his position. I will try to keep going, try to understand him. Perhaps by being magnanimous I can hold on to Joseph. Sooner or later even this business with Baarova will be in the past. If I leave him now, I'll have lost my husband for ever. But this way I can keep Joseph to myself for later. Then, when we're old, he'll be all mine.'

> When I had to burn his private papers and he was clearing his desk, there was a photo of Lida Baarova. He said: 'Tear that up, please.' And I said: 'I can't do that, Herr Minister; you must do it yourself.' So he took the photo, tore it up and I chucked it on the fire.
>
> *Wilfried von Oven, personal adviser to Joseph Goebbels*

It was easy to see that this enforced threesome could not last long. According to guests of the Goebbels', Lida Baarova would at times assume the role of lady of the house. Goebbels snubbed his own wife in public; once, when visiting a cabaret club with his mistress, he occupied the box next to Magda's. It was no longer a matter of saving face. Magda was on the brink of a nervous breakdown. As often happened with her, the mental turmoil took a toll on her health. But she spent a few weeks at her favourite health-farm, the *Weisser Hirsch* in Dresden, and was soon back on her feet.

While dwelling on ways to get her life back on track, she received an unexpected approach. Of all people, it was Goebbels' permanent secretary and ministerial colleague, Karl Hanke, who took on the role of 'white knight' and made it his job to assemble watertight evidence of his boss's frequent adultery. As proof he furnished Magda with incriminating letters and reports, which his position had given him access to. Hanke, who had been eyeing up the 'Frau Minister' himself, thus strengthened her resolve to put an end to things by demanding a divorce. But under the Third Reich such far-reaching changes in the senior ranks of the regime were a matter for the top man to decide on. Before Magda could present her case to Hitler, Goebbels got wind of her plan and averted the crisis by persuading the Führer that it was all a bit of female hysteria. Meanwhile, the errant husband went back to his spouse with a rueful expression and a bunch of flowers, promising melodramatically that in future he would never stray again. At Magda's behest, he even swore on the life of his children to be faithful. No sooner had he done so than he flung himself once again into the pursuit of pleasure – in blithe disregard of all his assurances. For the propaganda minister, elaborate lies were simply his habitual mode of communication.

> Yesterday: a difficult day. The night before, had a long talk with Magda, which for me was one long humiliation. I'll never forget it. She is so harsh and cruel.
>
> *Joseph Goebbels, diary, 18 August 1938*

Yet thanks to Hanke, her knight in shining armour, the deceived wife swiftly found out about the renewed escapades of her reprobate husband. And this time it was the last straw. She moved out and took refuge in Secretary Hanke's villa in the Grünewald district – not really because she wanted to be near him, but more as a slap in the face for her unfaithful spouse, in the ongoing marital fight. 'Magda is so harsh and cruel', moaned Goebbels in his diary, and then announced self-pityingly that he would rather be sent as consul to Japan than knuckle under.

> Last night she poured her heart out to me. It was all just as I had suspected. Hanke turns out be a first-class rotter. So my mistrust of him was fully justified. I will accept the obvious conclusions from this. Magda is in a frightful dilemma. But I will help her to get out of it.
>
> *Joseph Goebbels, diary 23 July 1939*

Admittedly, he had reckoned without the supreme arbiter in this matter. Hitler would not tolerate any divorce scandal over a Czech mistress, particularly as he was at that moment planning to occupy the woman's homeland. The Third Reich's 'model family' had to keep up the pretence because of its propaganda value. The leader of Germany summoned the distraught couple to the Berghof and demanded their reconciliation, making sure the press were given full details in order to confirm the cosy family image. A strict ban on seeing Lida Baarova was imposed on Goebbels, who for a period was exiled from the charmed circle of the almighty Führer. After a brief period of grace, his mistress was despatched back to Czechoslovakia and the Goebbels marriage triumphantly restored. The façade was firmly back in place.

However, Magda Goebbels was not prepared to return so meekly to the make-believe world of domestic harmony. For a while she seriously flirted with the idea of giving in after all to Hanke's compelling offer of marriage. But in August 1939 she finally decided to return to the family home. The following year another baby, Holde, was born, the 'child of reconciliation'. And Goebbels found an elegant way of getting rid of his faithless colleague. He arranged for Hanke to be promoted and sent as Gauleiter to Breslau, in his eastern homeland of Silesia. This kept him well out of reach of the minister's lady.

> Long palaver with Magda. She tells me all about her dances,
> parties and God knows what else. But I'm not interested in
> any of that.
>
> *Joseph Goebbels, diary, 17 February 1939*

While Magda fought her way out of the marital crisis, the regime
she had committed herself to was driving her stepfather, Richard
Friedländer, ever further into penury. Under the rule of organised
anti-Semitism the man Magda had grown up with lost his
profession and his social position. As head waiter of an open-air
restaurant in Berlin's Tiergarten Park, he had difficulty in making
ends meet for himself and his new wife Charlotte. Nevertheless,
like many Jews, he rejected the idea of emigrating in the mistaken
belief that, since he had served as an officer in the First World War,
his country would be indebted to him. An interview with his
stepson-in-law, Joseph Goebbels, whose support he attempted to
seek, ended with a cool dismissal as soon as the supplicant had
presented his case. Thus we can assume that Goebbels' wife was
well aware of Friedländer's fate, even though she strictly avoided
any direct contact with him.

In 1938 Hitler's authorities abandoned the restraint which for
tactical reasons had been adopted in their policy towards the Jews.
After discrimination, disenfranchisement and being driven from
their occupations, the Jews of Germany were now forced by
deliberately repressive measures to flee the country, leaving their
assets behind. This large-scale blackmail operation began as early
as June 1938 with the first systematic wave of arrests of Jews.
Magda's stepfather was among the earliest victims. Promoted as a
campaign against the 'work-shy' and those with a criminal record,
this led to the rounding up of 2,000 Jews, who were then shipped
off to Buchenwald concentration camp. On 15 June 1938,
Richard Friedländer was arrested at his workplace, taken by train
to Weimar, and from there dispatched by truck to the camp in the
nearby village of Ettersberg.

What faced the new arrivals there, mostly elderly doctors,
lawyers, businessmen or labourers, was later described by one of

the survivors: 'Our introduction to Buchenwald concentration camp took the form of running the most terrible kind of gauntlet. SS men repeatedly set about us with kicks and punches.' As many as 500 of them were crammed into what had once been a shelter for sheep. 'We had no room. There wasn't a table, a chair or a bed for us. At night we had to sleep on the bare earth. We couldn't stretch out; it was much too cramped.' For the first few days the prisoners neither had the chance to wash nor were they given anything to eat. Instead there were hours of parades and physical exercises, beatings, torture and public floggings, merely if a prisoner was caught smoking.

Finally, the inmates had to report for slave-labour in a quarry or on road-building, every day from 6 a.m. to 8 p.m., and on Sundays until 4 p.m. 'As we marched to work, there were men aged sixty-five among us. The SS man, who had a stick in his hand, chased us – or rather flogged us – to our new work-site, the dreaded quarry. Here we were laden with blocks of stone – remember, 80 per cent of us had never done physical work before. They were such a weight that even seasoned labourers had difficulty dragging them along. Many of the blocks were so heavy that it took several people to heave them on to another man's shoulder. Then we had to stagger with these stones for about one-and-a-half kilometres to a roadway, which was also being built by prisoners. The road rose steeply and for the last 500 metres SS men were posted at intervals along it. They kept us on the run with kicks and blows from their rifle-butts. It was the old ones who suffered the worst. They simply couldn't keep up the pace. Then every time, we had to jog back to the quarry. And the chase began all over again.'

In October 1938 alone, more than 100 prisoners died in this torment. Epidemics, which spread quickly among the exhausted and undernourished inmates, raised the death-toll. Richard Friedländer was one of those who succumbed to the inhuman conditions in Buchenwald. 'Deterioration of the heart-muscle, combined with a lung infection', was the laconic wording on the death certificate, dated 18 February 1939. The camp thugs had literally beaten him to death. Years before the industrialised mass murder of the Holocaust, Magda

Goebbels' stepfather fell victim to the racist mania of the Nazis. His widow, who had sent him the maximum permitted allowance of 5 Reichsmarks per week in an attempt to lessen the rigours of imprisonment, received nothing but his coffin. Richard Friedländer was laid to rest in an anonymous grave in the Jewish cemetery of Berlin-Weissensee. His fate has been reconstructed for the first time in this book.

Whether his stepdaughter heard of his lonely death, or even showed any interest at all in it, we shall never know. It seems that like so many supporters of the regime, she unquestioningly accepted the destruction of the Jews, to whom she had been so close in her youth. And this, though she knew better than most of her compatriots what fate the regime had decreed for those it persecuted. Goebbels hid nothing of what he knew from his wife. 'It's ghastly, all the things he tells me about. I simply can't stand it any longer', she confessed to her former sister-in-law, Ello Quandt, at a time when the death factories had long been carrying out their murderous work. 'You simply can't imagine what terrible things he burdens me with, and there's no-one I can pour my heart out to. I'm not supposed to speak to a soul about it . . . He loads it all on to me, because it's too much for him. It's beyond comprehension, beyond thinking about.'

> The woman that I knew . . . I can't believe she was dedicated to any ideology. She was a feminine person. And the whole system was so masculine.
>
> *Anneliese Uhlig, actress*

With the headlong progress of the war of conquest that Hitler unleashed in 1939, Magda and Joseph Goebbels again achieved a mutual understanding. The propagandist was now completely in his element. The war provided him with targets to attack with his armoury of rhetoric. As in the 'fighting days' that he loved harking back to, he could lash out and proclaim real or supposed victories.

Under the banner of a general patriotic offensive, his wife too succeeded in regaining the public-relations function from which she had been banished in peacetime. In the spirit of service to the country now demanded of Germans, she trained as a Red Cross nurse in a military hospital at the very beginning of the war, though she was never required to put her skills into practice. But Magda was constantly to be seen either addressing audiences of women, entertaining the wives of official foreign visitors, organising meals for soldiers returned from the front, or helping out the widows of those who had been killed.

> Frau Goebbels was always very welcome, she was one of the most popular ladies we had up there . . . Well-dressed, attractive, discreet, always reserved, but very friendly.
>
> You could see it . . . Hitler was very at ease. She was one of the few ladies whose advice he asked for, took note of and perhaps even acted on, and in many areas of his work, too.
>
> *Herbert Döhring, Hitler's house-manager*

She put a brave face on things. Very much the 'First Lady', she became the clearing-house for anxious and overburdened wives and mothers from all over the Reich. Hundreds of letters arrived in her office. They attest to the hope of salvation, which they associated with Magda Goebbels. Quite a number of women asked for financial assistance in their desperate straits, and the benefactress had a budget at her disposal to help in these cases. Others sought her support in getting their children back from the *Kinderlandverschickung*, the enforced evacuation of city children to camps and hostels in the countryside. 'Since you yourself are a loving mother', one petitioner wrote in 1941, 'I hope you will fully sympathise with my situation.' The model mother did indeed sympathise and arranged for the woman's son to be brought back to Berlin. Aside from these cries for help, Magda's postbag also included letters from supporters, who expressed deep admiration for the 'First Lady of the Reich' – sometimes in clumsy verse. 'A halo lies upon thy golden hair', wrote a Frankfurt woman adoringly, 'Thine eyes reflect what happiness is yours! Great is the flock of children that surrounds thee, with love they call you "Mother" evermore . . . Thou symbol of German womanhood. Bowed in respect I stand. In thine eyes of blue I descry the richness of thy soul. Thou too must share so many a woman's lot; through trying days thy soul becometh great . . .'

Thus elevated to exemplary status, the 'symbol of German womanhood' also tried, as a 'soldier on the home front', to present a figure true to the party line. For three months, instead of being driven by her chauffeur, she took the tramcar into the city, where she planned to do war-work on the production line in the Telefunken factory. However, frequent illness released her from this obligation. Later, along with her domestic staff, she worked at home winding detonator-reels. Guests at her house were given frugal meals, and then only on presentation of food-coupons.

From the beginning of the war, Harald, Magda's son from her first marriage, served as a front-line soldier. Although his mother followed the young lieutenant's dangerous postings anxiously, she refused to arrange for him to be given preferential treatment – quite the contrary: she and his stepfather, Goebbels, recorded his military decorations with pride, but also demanded his unquestioning readiness for active service. When in early 1944 Harald spent a short time in a Munich hospital with a cold, back home this was disapproved as something close to desertion, as Goebbels noted in his diary: 'I ordered him to get well as quickly as possible and return to his unit. Incidentally, Magda will visit him in Munich on Monday and give him a talking-to.'

The reprimand seems to have had its effect. Harald returned to his unit in Italy and the same year, after heavy fighting, he was wounded and taken prisoner by the British.

*

The change of military fortune on all fronts, following the catastrophe of Stalingrad, brought new activity for the Minister of Propaganda. As 'Reich Director for Total War Deployment', he was given far-reaching powers to stamp out the last remnants of civilian life, and to comb factories and businesses for reserves to serve at the front and in arms manufacture. Announcing this in his notorious speech at the Palace of Sport, Goebbels was treated to frantic applause. His wife, who was in the audience, shared his totalitarian zeal. 'I am very glad', Goebbels wrote proudly in his diary 'that particularly on the question of total war, she adopts a rigid and radical standpoint. If all Nazi women thought as she does, our total war would certainly be in a better state.'

> There were times when Goebbels had a very bad relationship with his wife, and there is no question that he was frequently unfaithful to her. But in the last years of the war they became very close again.
>
> *Wilfried von Oven, personal adviser to Joseph Goebbels*

The reality of this crazy determination to fight on, the nights of bombing, the struggle to survive among the rubble, the forced labour in the armaments factories, were all things from which Magda was largely spared. In August 1943 she and the children moved to the family-owned country property on the Bogensee lake. The peaceful idyll of the Schorfheide, north of Berlin, was broken only by the distant drone of enemy aircraft, like a message from another world. If important business made it necessary to spend some time in Goebbels' official residence next-door to the Ministry of Propaganda, secure air-raid protection was provided. An elevator silently carried the residents down to a bunker apartment, 45 feet below ground. This was fitted out with carpets, armchairs, a fully equipped kitchen, fresh-air ventilation and a well-stocked wine-cellar, so that the Goebbels family should not have to forego any comfort even during nights of bombing.

*

Nevertheless, during the war, Magda found fewer and fewer opportunities to devote herself to the harmony of family life. For weeks, often months on end, she was obliged to stay in clinics and health spas. During her long periods of illness, painful inflammation of the jaw and facial nerves, heart-attacks and severe depression changed the once carefree woman into an exhausted shadow of her former self, someone whose unbalanced behaviour, as well as increasing consumption of alcohol and cigarettes became very noticeable.

> Her illnesses were more of an escape. After all, she had produced seven children – and never stayed in bed for long after each birth.
>
> *Ariane Sheppard, Magda's half-sister*

These symptoms of illness were the external reflection of her inner turmoil. Contrary to all the rhetorical exhortations to stick it out that she produced for public consumption, Magda Goebbels now had little doubt that the Reich, to which she had devoted her existence, was facing destruction. The relentless advance of the Red Army and the failure of the Ardennes offensive at the beginning of 1945 dealt a final blow to any hope of regaining the military initiative. Fireside conversations at the Bogensee country retreat now mainly revolved around a scenario for making their exit. After a long struggle with herself and the shedding of many tears, Magda agreed with her husband that they should remain in Berlin to the end, and keep their children with them. 'I have informed the Führer that my wife is firmly determined to remain in Berlin as well and even refuses to send the children away', Goebbels recorded in his diary for 1 February 1945. 'The Führer does not actually think this is the right decision, but considers it admirable.'

> She had great self-control. In front of strangers, she never let her mask slip, even though underneath she was very emotional.
>
> *Frieda Smyrek, the Goebbels family housekeeper*

The fact that, as parents, they realised their decision amounted to a death-sentence for their children, is confirmed by people who talked to them at that time: 'We will now have to poison ourselves, all of us', Magda announced in a matter-of-fact way, when she arrived with her children on 22 April, on the final trip to the bunker beneath the Reich Chancellery. 'The life you will all have to lead after the collapse of Germany . . . will no longer be worth living.' Such was the justification she gave to her confidante, Ello Quandt. 'Those of us who were in high positions in the Third Reich will, more than anyone, have to take the consequences. We made incredible demands on the people of Germany, we treated other nations with pitiless ferocity. For that the victors will take vengeance . . . We cannot duck this like cowards. The rest have a right to go on living, but not us. We do not have that right . . . We have failed.'

But for her, taking the consequences did not mean standing up and admitting responsibility for that failure. It meant abdicating that responsibility. No amount of false Wagnerian emotionalism about chivalric loyalty to the Führer can disguise that fact. To be close to her idol in the final hours of the Reich was an obsession that suppressed all warnings of common sense.

> Our magnificent idea is in ruins. The world that comes after the Führer and National Socialism is no longer worth living in, and that is why I have taken the children with me. They are too good for the life that will come after us . . .
> *Magda Goebbels, letter to her son Harald Quandt, late April 1945*

Thus it was that Hitler's devotee experienced the apogee of fulfilment when, as the Führer bade her farewell in the bleak corridor of the bunker, he presented her with the 'Gold medal' of the Nazi Party. Magda's usual self-control deserted her and she burst into tears. Never before had a woman received this award. The reality was that she was now worth no more than a piece of tin, but she had long since lost the ability to see this. 'Yesterday evening the Führer took off his gold party medal and pinned it on me,' she wrote in her farewell letter to Harald, who was the only one of her children to survive the war. 'I am proud and happy. God grant me the strength to do the last and hardest thing. We have only one goal now: loyalty to the Führer until death, and the fact that we can end our lives with him is a merciful gift of destiny, one that we never dared hope for.'

Certainly, there was no lack of attempts to rescue at least the children from the bunker. Friends, acquaintances, government officials, even Hitler himself, had offered Magda the opportunity to evacuate them. Finally a woman pilot named Hanna Reitsch tearfully begged the mother to let her take the children in her aircraft away from the besieged city. But Magda Goebbels stuck to her iron resolve.

> She stood by her husband fully and completely; no-one had to persuade or lure her into choosing to die like a Nibelung. It was something the couple decided jointly, for her and for the whole family.
>
> *Wilfred von Oven, personal adviser to Joseph Goebbels*

A day after Hitler's suicide Magda wrapped her children in gleaming white robes as if for a ceremony. 'Don't be frightened, children', she reassured them, as the doctor assisting her stated later. 'You'll be given an injection, just like all the soldiers get.' When the medication took effect and the children were asleep, their mother took over – the doctor had meanwhile chosen to leave the children's room. Magda then administered cyanide capsules to the twelve-year-old Helga, Hilde, eleven, Helmut, nine, Holde, eight, Hedda, six, and Heide who was just four. When another doctor came into the room, so he reported at least, the fatal dose had done its work.

Before Magda herself, with her husband, took her own life, she went down once more to the lowest level of the bunker, to lay the patience cards out on the table. But now she had played the last card.

CHAPTER THREE

THE FILM DIRECTOR –
LENI RIEFENSTAHL

When harmony is achieved, I am happy.

I had always been in the habit of taking up only the things that interested me.

I don't like anything that is run-of-the-mill. I'm attracted by what is out of the ordinary.

I had no intention of falling under Hitler's influence. But I *was* astonished by how he managed to get rid of unemployment, how successful he was in what he did. I could not know that millions of people, millions of Jews, would be killed.

Hitler thought very highly of me. And that's why the party hated me. Because sometimes Adolf Hitler set me up as an example to his men, as someone they could learn from.

I have never had any interest in politics and in the whole of my long life I only worked for Hitler for precisely seven months.

Leni Riefenstahl

As a person, she was completely natural; a fabulous, natural human being. And she was a very pretty woman, too. In those days I thought her the most beautiful woman I had ever met.

Hans Ertl, one of Leni Riefenstahl's cameramen

I admire her as an artist. She is the most revolutionary photographer and film-maker of our time. Even if her Nazi subjects were a load of shit.

Helmut Newton, photographer, 19 October 2000

She lived as 'the Führer's bride without sex', in a sphere that was outside politics and the law.

Rudolf Augstein, Der Spiegel magazine, 10 August 1987

The persecution of this one woman became a witch-hunt, especially in Germany, and it continues to this day.

Alice Schwarzer, Emma magazine, January 1999

Leni Riefenstahl very rapidly became a symbolic figure in the debate over National Socialism – and has remained so for longer than anyone – presumably in part for the very reason that she is a woman.

Rainer Rother in Leni Riefenstahl – the Seduction of Talent, *2000*

Although she shares to a great extent the German characteristics of suppression and denial, she is not a typical representative of them. She is more of a 'super-denier', obsessed with masculinity, and possessing a higher-than-average capacity to remember only those things she wants to remember.

Margarete Mitscherlich, On the Hardships of Emancipation, *1994*

She was a tall, slender woman, and very eloquent; she talked a lot. She was very temperamental and she knew exactly what she wanted.

Ilse Werner, singer and actress

She is playing the greatest role of her life: Leni Riefenstahl presents Leni Riefenstahl.

The cameras have difficulty in staying focused on the old lady; the stage on which she is sitting is besieged by a throng of photographers and TV crews. She appears small and fragile – and unbelievably ancient. She is enjoying the media interest. It is no surprise to her, for Leni Riefenstahl has always been centre stage. 'I know why you're all here. You want to know what the old girl looks like. Is she still alive? Or is that a mummy?' She anticipates the questions in everyone's mind. The laugh is on them, because she is absolutely right. She has come to the Frankfurt Book Fair 2000, to promote an illustrated book about her life. But the media people have gathered to see *her*, the great Riefenstahl, surely the last surviving figure from the front ranks of the Third Reich.

When the parents of the assembled journalists were scarcely born, Leni Riefenstahl was already at the zenith of her career; significant periods of her life were already history. The second generation, and still more the generation after that, are putting questions to her in an attempt to discover the real person behind the Riefenstahl mask. They do so perhaps with less inhibition than their parents, but in almost six decades the burden of their questions has not changed much. Nor have the answers: 'Look, I'm ninety-eight years old, but in my entire life I only did seven months' work for Hitler', Leni Riefenstahl boasts. Her imperious gaze compels her listeners to believe what she says. 'Only 50 per cent of what is written about me is true,' she grumbles. A little later she claims it is as little as '10 per cent'. Then her final summing-up: 'Everything you read about me in the newspapers is lies.' She could 'kill' all journalists. There it is: the Riefenstahl legend that she has donned like a suit of armour – Leni, eternally ostracised, eternally misunderstood. She was a dancer when Germany was still ruled by a kaiser, an actress when the Weimar republic was collapsing in ruins. When the students of 1968 manned the barricades, she was working as a photographer in Africa. Today she is a scuba-diver – surely the oldest woman diver in the world – and is working on an underwater film. Yet the period which defined her whole life was from 1933 to 1945. She was the star director of the Third Reich. Her film *Triumph of the Will*, about the 1934 Nazi Party Rally in Nuremberg, showed the criminal regime in a seductive light. She gave the dictator his audience and she gave the public the 'Führer' they had been waiting for. Her images turned a rabble-rouser into an all-powerful deity and saviour. In the lenses of her cameras the Nazi processions became harbingers of order and strength. It was the force of her imagery that contributed to the seduction of an entire generation.

Is that what people accuse her of today? Probably less than they used to. The films that Leni Riefenstahl directed then are now only familiar to a very few. This is partly because they are seldom allowed to be shown publicly. But it is also true that their visual content appears outmoded to modern eyes. It is over her as a person that people are still bitterly divided. She has never said: 'I am sorry.' In fact she has staunchly resisted making any perceptible form of acknowledgement of having done anything wrong. She claims to have made 'documentary' films. Were they propaganda? No. Never. She merely reproduced reality, she says. That is how Leni Riefenstahl sees it and it is why she has dissociated herself from Germany's efforts to come to terms with its past. But to write her off as an 'unreconstructed Nazi' is an oversimplification. From an artistic standpoint some of her films are masterpieces; they are used as teaching materials at numerous film schools. The question about the responsibility of art and of artists has been posed countless times. Leni Riefenstahl has never given an answer.

> It's impossible to be interested in politics and create works of art as a sideline.
>
> I have always done my job, to the best of my ability.
> *Leni Riefenstahl, 22 August 1997*

When Leni Riefenstahl was born the twentieth century had only just dawned. It was on 22 August 1902 that her father, Alfred, registered the birth of his daughter in Berlin under the names Helene Bertha Amalie. As Leni later recorded in her memoirs, her mother Bertha had prayed during her pregnancy: 'Dear God, give me a beautiful daughter, who will became a famous actress.' But she was disappointed. 'The child seemed the very epitome of ugliness, shrivelled, with tangled hair and squinting eyes.'

Life was strictly regimented in the Riefenstahl household. Father Alfred, owner of a prosperous heating and plumbing business, brooked no contradiction – least of all from his wife and daughter. But little Leni should really have been a son. Noisy and active, she climbed trees with the boys from next door, went swimming, rowing and sailing. Numerous scratches and broken bones did nothing to inhibit the irrepressible child. 'It's a pity you didn't grow up a boy and your brother a girl', Leni remembers her father saying. Her academic achievements at Kollmorgen's High School were thoroughly creditable. It was only with 'conduct' that she had problems. Once Leni was caught clambering on the school roof, where she hoisted the national flag that normally only flew on the Kaiser's birthday. Her reason for doing this was to wangle a day's holiday for the school. By the time Leni left school at sixteen, her father already had firm plans for her. First she was to go to a domestic science college and then to a finishing-school. But his daughter had quite different ideas.

She had spotted a small ad in the *Berliner Zeitung*, saying that the makers of a film called *Opium* were looking for a girl to play one of the roles. As she waited for her audition at the Grimm-Reiter dance academy, she was able watch the girls of the famous school at rehearsal. 'I was overcome by a tremendous urge to join them', as Leni later described the moment. She began taking dance lessons in secret – without her father's knowledge. 'Pansies' was how Alfred Riefenstahl decribed the Berlin dance milieu. When he finally caught his daughter out, he was beside himself with rage. Leni could no longer prevent herself being incarcerated in a girls' finishing-school in the Harz mountains. But after trying for a whole year to wean her away from dancing, Alfred finally gave in: Leni could take dancing lessons.

Now aged nineteen, Leni attempted to catch up on everything her fellow-students had been learning since early childhood. Woken by her alarm-clock in the grey dawn, she took the streetcar from the suburb of Zeuthen into the centre of Berlin. A Russian ballerina named Eugenia Eduardova had taken Leni under her wing. After several hours of ballet instruction Leni would catnap at lunchtime and then complete another training session in what was then called 'expressive dance'. It was now that Leni showed for the first time the quality that would single her out in future: an iron will, which would ultimately lead her to triumph.

*

Coincidence brought a benefactor into her life, a producer named Harry Sokal, who – at least as Leni remembers it – immediately fell eternally in love with her, and knew how to do justice to her talent. He booked Munich's top musical venue, the Tonhalle, on the night of 23 October 1923, for Leni's debut. 'I didn't have first-night nerves', Riefenstahl recalls. 'On the contrary, I could scarcely wait for the moment when I stepped on to the stage. My very first dance, *Study in the style of a gavotte*, was greeted with considerable applause. After my third dance, I had to give an encore. From then on the applause grew louder and louder, until the audience moved towards the stage and demanded more encores. I danced until I dropped from exhaustion.'

A gorgeous child! Full of grace and elegance.
Joseph Goebbels, diary, 1 December 1929

That evening in Munich was the launch of a brief but hectic career. The famous impresario Max Reinhardt presented her at the Deutsches Theater – a great accolade for a dancer who was still practically unknown. Engagements followed all over Germany, as well as in Zürich, Innsbruck, Vienna and Prague. Barefoot, dressed in a clinging silver lamé gown, or else wreathed in diaphanous veils of chiffon, she danced in the ecstatic, expressionistic style popularised by Isadora Duncan in the 1920s. Although at this time Leni was noticeably plumper than in her film-star years, she already possessed a remarkable temperament. Even her slight squint was admired by quite a few men. In a publicity handout she reprinted rave reviews of her performances – an early taste of her skilful public relations.

Thus we find this quote from the *Berliner Zeitung* of 21 December 1923: '. . . this very beautiful young woman . . . is clearly fighting keenly for a place alongside the famous trinity of dancers who are taken seriously: Impekoven, Wigmann and Gert. And when one sees this tall, fully mature creature standing and waiting for her cue, one gets an inkling that there might be some magnificent dancing to come, dancing of a kind that none of the "Trinity" could ever aspire to . . .' Admittedly, what the reviewer went on to say was carefully omitted on the leaflet: 'But then, when the girl begins to unfurl her body, the anticipation evaporates, the lustre is dulled, the resonance decays; what we see moving is an amazing dummy, albeit one filled with the longing for open spaces, the thirst for rhythm, the lust for music. However, the longing for space is never brought alive, rhythm dries up in this thirst, and her lust, like an inflexible cloak, is at odds with the music. It is the longing, the thirst and the desire of a foolish and mesmerised virgin.'

In spite of this, Riefenstahl's early successes were considerable. Yet she would never be able to prove what talent as a dancer she really had in her. While on stage in Prague she sustained a complicated knee-injury, and the doctors could hold out little hope of a cure. At the age of twenty-one, after a getting off to a dazzling start, she found her career in ruins.

*

In Leni Riefenstahl's life there were moments when her career took off in a decisive new direction. There were never any gradual developments. Just such a moment occurred in 1923, when she was waiting for a train at the Nollendorfplatz subway station in Berlin. She was on her way to see a doctor, who might perhaps find a way to restore her damaged knee so that she could continue her career as a dancer. Just as the train was coming in, Leni's eyes lighted on a poster for the film *Mountain of Destiny*, directed by Arnold Fanck. 'Just as I was brooding over the gloomy future ahead of me, I stared at this picture as if hypnotised. It showed a steep precipice and a man swinging from one rock-face to another', Riefenstahl later recalled. Enthralled by the scene, she forgot her medical appointment and hobbled to a nearby cinema to see the film. By her own account she was bewitched by the shots of wild, natural scenery: 'The longer the film went on, the more riveted I became. It excited me so much that even before it had ended I had decided to discover those mountains for myself.' She wanted to become a film-star in movies just like *Mountain of Destiny.*

The question 'Can I actually do it?' seems never to have occurred to Leni. She wanted to star in 'mountain films' – but it was a risky plan, since her injured knee would be just as much of a hindrance as it was in dancing. Undeterred, she drove with her younger brother Heinz south to the Dolomites in the Austrian Tirol. There she would seek out the locations where *Mountain of Destiny* had been filmed. But even more important, she wanted to meet Arnold Fanck's film crew. And sure enough, at a showing of the film in Karersee, she managed to speak to the leading actor. 'Are you Herr Trenker?' she asked him straight out. 'Yup, that's me', Luis Trenker replied. 'In your next film, I'm going to play opposite you', Leni boasted cheekily. Trenker gave an amused laugh, but that is precisely how it turned out.

*

Back in Berlin Leni managed to make contact with Arnold Fanck. 'Doctor' Fanck was in fact a geologist, but he had succeeded in becoming a pioneer of mountaineering films, which he directed himself. His speciality was drama in the ice and snow, short on plot but loaded with action. The real stars of his films were the mountains themselves, which he portrayed with a precision and dramatic impact never seen before. He had gathered around him an enthusiastic group of young cameramen – known as the Freiburg School – who tried out new techniques of shooting and at the same time offered their services as actors and stuntmen. A little later, many of them, such as Sepp Allgeier, Hans Schneeberger and Guzzi Lantschner, were to make up the Riefenstahl film crew.

> Leni was a dancer. And to dance she had to be athletically trained. The control she had over her body – it was unique, incredible. I have never since seen anything like it in a woman. Simply walking, each step she took . . . fantastic.
>
> *Hans Ertl, cameraman with Leni Riefenstahl*

Arnold Fanck was so taken by the young dancer that he engaged her on the spot for the star part in his next film, *The Sacred Mountain*. Fanck's enthusiasm was clearly not limited to Riefenstahl's skills as a dancer. As she remembers it, the film-maker fell hopelessly in love with her. When shooting started, much the same happened to the male lead, Luis Trenker. The real-life situation of a woman caught between two men was reflected in the plot of *The Sacred Mountain*. Leni played the part of a beautiful ballerina, Diotima. Her ethereal movements inflame the hearts of two men, who finally set off on a dangerous mountaineering expedition in which they both lose their lives.

Due to the volatile personal chemistry between members of the cast and crew, the action was sometimes more dramatic behind the camera than in front. Trenker and Fanck were constantly squabbling over the most trivial things – in 'Diotima's' version at least. She even claims to recall a theatrical suicide attempt by Fanck. La Riefenstahl finally fell out with Trenker over the fact that at a press conference the actor publicly referred to his female lead as a 'conceited cow'. The Riefenstahl–Trenker relationship was portrayed in a totally different way in the recollections of each partner. As is so often the case, the truth probably lies somewhere in the middle. But even today it is clear to see that Luis Trenker, never very convincing as a screen lover, delivered his most credible movie kiss – with Leni Riefenstahl.

> She always worshipped everything that was healthy, splendid, wonderful. She had a kind of indomitable narcissism and yet an eternal innocence. She was radiant – but it was the glow of a healthy, tough, unyielding, narcissistic male.
>
> *Margarete Mitscherlich, psychoanalyst and author*

Trenker was not the only man to succumb to the Riefenstahl magic. Her first lover was someone she had quite brazenly pursued. Having been watched like a hawk by her strict father until the age of twenty-one, Leni then decided not only to leave home but to take her love-life into her own hands. The man of her choice was one Otto Froitzheim, a former tennis champion considerably older than herself, to whom she conveyed her unambiguous intentions through a female friend. Froitzheim did not need much persuading and turned up for the rendezvous as arranged. All went according to plan – though without the slightest hint of romance. Afterwards, when Leni emerged from the bathroom, Froitzheim was already fully dressed. He had another date, he told her curtly. Adding insult to injury he left some money on the bedside table, 'in case of an abortion', as Leni remembered with a shudder, decades later.

Despite this scarcely encouraging start Leni stuck by her principle, remarkably sophisticated for those days, always to seek out men for herself. Those she selected were successful, self-confident men, whom she deliberately approached, making no secret of her intentions. In an interview, one of Leni's later cameramen, Hans Ertl, recalled with a gleam in his eye an experience from almost seventy years before. While filming SOS Iceberg in Greenland, Leni had watched him manoeuvring a kayak through the ice-floes. 'Would you teach me how to do that?' she asked the astonished twenty-year-old. 'Why not?' said Ertl. 'Whenever you like.' 'Whenever . . . you . . . like', Leni had repeated, each word pregnant with meaning. A little later she appeared in a sleeveless blouse and very short shorts, ready for the kayak trip. Once aboard, it was not long before Ertl realised the real purpose of the excursion. 'Leni slid forward, close up to me and between my legs, which were meant to be working the foot-rudder. So on that magic arctic night of midnight sun, it wasn't entirely my fault if the paddling lesson was put off until another time.'

Several of Ertl's colleagues behind and in front of the camera had similar stories to tell. 'To Leni, athletic young chaps like us were like candy that you go on nibbling as long as you want', he remembers. Those relationships were usually short-lived and came to an end without much fuss. The only love affair that lasted rather longer was with her cameraman, Hans Schneeberger. When 'snow-flea', as she called him, left her for another woman without first talking it out, Leni was in despair. She later recalled the hours of torment after reading Schneeberger's perfunctory farewell letter. 'The pain seeped into every cell of my body, it paralysed me, until I tried to free myself from it by letting out a terrible scream. Weeping, screaming, biting my hands, I stumbled from one room to another. I grabbed a letter-knife and stabbed myself in the arms, legs and thighs. I felt no physical pain, but the mental agony burned like the fires of Hell. Never again, I swore to myself, never again would I love a man in that way.'

What followed was a series of flings – none of them lasted. Anderl Heckmair, later to become the first man to scale the north face of the Eiger, briefly enjoyed her favours, as did the 1936 Olympic gold medallist in the decathlon, Glenn Morris. 'With a heavy heart, I decided I had to leave him', Leni commented tersely on her Olympic amour. The spurned lover then went off to play the part of Tarzan. It was not until 1944 that Leni finally married. She had got to know her fiancé, Peter Jacob, on the set of her film, *Tiefland* (Lowlands). At their very first meeting Leni was fascinated by the attractive officer from an alpine regiment, but shrank from a more permanent relationship. After jealous scenes, quarrels, reconciliations and letters of flaming passion written from the battle-front, she finally said 'Yes'. The wedding was a typical wartime ceremony, held in Kitzbühel with just a few close friends. Yet Leni and her husband soon drifted apart again and the marriage scarcely outlasted the war. They were divorced in 1947, and Leni wrote without bitterness about it in her memoirs.

The Sacred Mountain was a box-office hit in 1926, and the Fanck–Riefenstahl team was born. Almost overnight Leni Riefenstahl achieved star status. Other films were produced in quick succession: *The Great Leap, The White Hell of Piz Palü, Storm over Mont Blanc* and *White Frenzy* – all directed by Arnold Fanck, and starring Leni Riefenstahl. The plots were usually dramatic adventures in the high Alps, in which the male star's heroism was matched by the beauty of his leading lady.

The director's insistence on absolute realism allowed neither studio shooting nor the use of doubles. Fanck demanded the utmost commitment from everyone involved. Cameraman and actor Guzzi Lantscher can still remember today the breakneck ski-jumps over crevasses and the roofs of mountain huts. 'I usually got away with it all right, being so small and supple. But for the others accidents were an everyday occurrence.' Even Leni suffered the effects of her director's merciless perfectionism. She had to be buried alive by an avalanche or swing on a ladder over the bottomless crevasse of a glacier. When the action of the film required her to perform climbing scenes barefoot, she spent weeks in the Dolomites, tearing her feet on the rocks until they bled. Finally, in *SOS Iceberg*, the last film she made with Arnold Fanck, the cast jumped into the icy arctic waters, to the surprise of some polar bears.

> She was a very good actress – a first-class actress. She played herself. She was kind of unaffected, and that was the great thing about her. She never seemed to be 'acting' like normal actors do when they take on a part.
>
> *Hans Ertl, cameraman*

Working with Arnold Fanck left a great impression on Leni, both personal and filmic. Fanck taught her the basics of movie-making. He would often allow her to direct short sequences and trained her to find the best camera angle. As she was nearly always the only woman on the set she learned at that time to make her presence felt in a man's world. And something perhaps even more important: she learned to reach her own limits, and then go beyond them.

> She had the characteristic of being able to take charge of things exactly like a man. She could handle the crew just like a man would have done.
>
> *Guzzi Lantschner, cameraman with Leni Riefenstahl*

With *Storm over Mont Blanc*, Leni had to handle the transition from silent to sound films. The result was rather laughable at first. In front of dramatic scenery could be heard a thin, reedy voice with an unmistakable Berlin accent. Back in her home city she immediately took elocution lessons and even trained her voice by repeating the recorded announcements of the Berlin Telephone Company. Her voice improved, but for a long time audiences could tell from her exaggerated gestures that she had started out in silent films. To make matters worse, Arnold Fanck's skill in directing his actors was extremely limited. In scenes where Fanck sought assistance from the well-known director, G.W. Pabst, even Leni turned in a thoroughly creditable performance.

As in so many things, Leni rated her own talent as an actress a good deal higher than did most of those who saw her on the screen. As she remembers it, none other than Joseph von Sternberg, the man who discovered and promoted Marlene Dietrich, had long agonised over which of the two women he should take with him to Hollywood. Needless to say, he was 'madly in love' with the mountaineering star, and frequently asked her advice about how to direct Dietrich in *The Blue Angel*. Later, when asked for her thoughts on this, Marlene said that Sternberg would have died laughing at Leni's story, if he weren't already dead.

Though convinced of her own thespian gifts, Leni nevertheless realised that working with Fanck offered limited opportunities for developing them. She recalls with horror how many times she had to exclaim, 'Wow, great!' In the Greenland-based drama, *SOS Iceberg*, filmed in 1933, Leni's role dwindled to that of a decorative accessory. As the only woman in a thin plot, the final scene showed her, draped picturesquely over four kayaks, being paddled across the screen. As if that were not bad enough, the director had chosen to back this with music called 'Dawn on the Mountainside'. We must assume she only made the film in order to restore her overstretched finances and to gain a foothold in the international market, as it was also shown in an English-language version. Personally and professionally she had long since broken free from her mentor.

*

Two years previously Riefenstahl had already conceived a bold plan: she would attempt to make a film of her own, as director and star. With the reckless determination of a beginner she submitted her outline to several leading producers. 'Boring. Not for us!' were words the would-be director got used to hearing. The film was some kind of a fairy-story; and who was going to be interested in that? Despite all her efforts it proved simply impossible to get the money together. Leni decided she would realise her dream with her own resources. *The Blue Light* – the title of the film she planned – was to be her first major independent work, and to this day it remains probably her finest film. Most of her old colleagues from the Freiburg School said they were prepared to work on it for a modest salary; and she was able to persuade a well-known Hungarian screen-writer, Bela Balacz, to write the script. As extras she hired villagers from the remote Sarntal valley in South Tirol, whose characterful faces would set the tone of the film.

The period when she was filming *The Blue Light* seems to have been one of the happiest times in Leni's life. In the Dolomites, under the most primitive conditions, she and her crew made a film which to this day has not lost its timeless magic: a painter named Vigo, played by Matthias Wiemann, comes to a remote mountain village that harbours a secret. Hidden above the village lies a cave containing a rare blue crystal. Only the wild girl, Junta, who lives in the mountains, alone and outcast, knows the way to the cave. Time and again the youths from the village try to follow Junta but always fall to their death. The stranger falls in love with the beautiful savage. In the end, he unsuspectingly shows the villagers the way to the cave – whereupon they plunder it. In a dramatic finale Junta climbs down from the cave and plunges to her death.

The part of Junta, the mountain witch, was taken by Leni herself, attractively costumed in rags. Even today she sees the film as anticipating her own destiny. Junta and Leni – women who were both loved and hated. To this day Riefenstahl sees herself as an outsider, an outcast, though she really wanted no more than to show what was beautiful – and for that the world despised her. To this day she has refused to accept that she was not, like Junta, an alienated creature whose existence was forced on her by others, but had actively shaped her own life with all its aspects of light and darkness.

Leni Riefenstahl's directorial debut was a great success. According to the magazine *Filmkurier*, the first-night audience seemed 'transported', and the review went on: 'Leni Riefenstahl has achieved what she was striving for: a cinematic language that is uniquely poetic.' At her first attempt Riefenstahl had indeed hit the jackpot and created a film of persuasive integrity and rare perfection. Foreign audiences, too, were delighted by the fairy-tale scenario. In London the film ran for fourteen months; in Paris, sixteen. At the Venice Biennale in 1932 it was awarded the Silver Medal. 'The finest thing I have ever seen on film', was the verdict of a man for whom, from then on, Leni would be working.

Riefenstahl was lucky, of course, in getting on terms with Hitler, from a film-making point of view, even before there was any talk of his seizing power. At that early stage she had already won for herself Hitler's approval and involvement.

Dr Fritz Hippler, then Reich Director-General of Film

In those days, enjoying the Führer's esteem, and having access to him, meant everything.

Hans Ertl, cameraman, 1982

Leni Riefenstahl has never made any secret of her – at least initial – enthusiasm for Hitler. She described her first encounter with him, when she heard him speaking at the Palace of Sport, as a moment of awakening. 'To me it was as if the surface of the earth was spreading out before me – like a hemisphere, which suddenly split down the middle and a huge column of water gushed out, so powerful that it touched the heavens and shook the earth. I felt as though I were rooted to the spot. Although there was much that I did not understand in the speech, it had a hypnotic effect on me. A constant barrage of words rained down on the audience and I could tell that this man held them in his power.'

On 18 May 1932, while still under the influence of the Sport Palace speech she wrote Hitler a gushing letter. Addressed to the Brown House, Munich, it read: 'Dear Herr Hitler, A short time ago I attended a political gathering for the first time in my life . . . I must confess I was greatly impressed by you and by the enthusiasm of your audience. I would very much like to get to know you personally.' This early fan-mail proved effective. Shortly before she was due to board a ship for Greenland, to film *SOS Iceberg*, the phone rang in her apartment. 'Bruckner here, Adjutant to the Führer', a brisk voice announced. 'The Führer has read your letter and I am to ask you if it is possible for you to come for the day to Wilhelmshaven tomorrow.' You bet it was possible. Leni hastily cabled the production team to say she would join them in Hamburg; they were not to worry, she would be there on time. 'I wondered whether this was coincidence or fate', she wrote later. It was neither. Riefenstahl had deliberately sought a meeting with Hitler, and she had got what she wanted.

Hitler greeted her on a beach by the North Sea, and they quickly set off for a walk – or so the film queen remembers. The conversation which then apparently took place reads like the contents list of the Riefenstahl book of self-justification. 'Once we're in power, you must make my films', Hitler announced. Taken aback by such an honour, Riefenstahl 'impulsively' demurred: 'I couldn't do that! Please don't misinterpret the meaning of my visit; I am not in the least interested in politics. Nor could I ever become a member of your Party.' And so that there should be no doubt as to her staunchly anti-Nazi credentials, she claims to have immediately gone on to say: 'You are racially prejudiced. If I'd been born an Indian or Jewish woman, you wouldn't even speak to me. How could I work for someone who makes such distinctions between human beings?' And did the dreaded Hitler not react with some displeasure? Far from it. He apparently said: 'I only wish the people around me would speak as frankly as you do.'

While the amount of truth in this account can never be proven, it is significant in that it shows the image Leni had of Hitler. She always strove to separate her picture of the private Hitler, pleasant, charming and chivalrous, from that of the greatest criminal of the century. There was nothing, she claims, that led her to suspect he was a wolf in sheep's clothing. She was born into a generation for whom the saying 'If the Führer only knew about this', was common currency. Yet she has retained her deluded image of the 'private Hitler' to this day. That he was 'schizophrenic', she would probably admit. But the image she paints of the Führer remains that of a normal human being.

> People have attempted to confront this most gifted promoter of the master-race concept with the fact that she probably contributed to the racial hysteria of 'sacred Germany' and thus shares responsibility for the universal misery caused by that unholy regime. But in doing so they only arouse her rage and indignation, and never the process of grieving and remembering, which might lead to self-knowledge and the desire to make good the harm done.
>
> *Margarete Mitscherlich, psychoanalyst and author*

On Christmas Day 1935, as Riefenstahl tells us in her memoirs, she had a second meeting with Hitler. She enquired solicitously where he had spent Christmas Eve. The Führer 'gloomily' replied: 'I drove around aimlessly in a car with my driver, along country roads and through little villages, until I got tired . . . That's what I do every year on Christmas Eve. I have no family, and I'm lonely.' And as if this revelation was not sufficient, she goes on to make further confessions. On that walk beside the North Sea, Hitler had suddenly fallen silent, Leni tells us. 'After quite a long pause, he stopped, looked at me for a long time, then slowly put his arm around me and drew me towards him. He gazed at me excitedly. Then, when he saw how unwilling I was, he immediately let go of me. He turned away from me slightly and I saw him raise his hands and say solemnly: "I may not love any woman until my work is completed."'

*

Adolf Hitler, a thwarted lover? Leni Riefenstahl is quite certain of this. 'Ever since I made the decision to become a politician, I have dispensed with a private life', he apparently told her. Ever the sympathetic listener, Leni asked him if he did not find that hard.

'Very hard, especially when I meet a beautiful woman, who I would like to spend time with. But I'm not the type of man who enjoys brief flings. When my heart is set on fire, my feelings are deep and passionate – how could I respond to that when faced with my duties towards Germany? How sorely I would have to disappoint any woman, however much I loved her.' This romantic scene is brought to a fitting climax, with the author's self-serving conclusion: 'That evening I felt that Hitler desired me as a woman.'

As to her own feelings towards Hitler, Leni Riefenstahl has never vouchsafed much detail.

> Once Hitler was in power I wanted to have no connection with him any longer.
>
> *Leni Riefenstahl in her memoirs*
>
> She was certainly not the typical German woman – submissive, bearing children for the Führer and her husband.
>
> *Margarete Mitscherlich, psychoanalyst and author*

Preserved in the basement of the Federal German Archive is an effusive telegram that was received at the Reich Chancellery: '*Good wishes sent me by my Führer are fulfilment possible* [sic]*; that is why heart gives thanks to him. Today I hold in my two arms the roses as red as the mountains around me, kissed by the last rays of the sun. So I look up at the Rosengarten range, to its gleaming peaks and cliffs, and with my hands I caress the crimson blooms and know only that I am unspeakably happy. Leni Riefenstahl.*'

The signatory has always disputed the genuineness of this document. It is true that the syntax of the text is unusual. On its own, this could be explained by the fact that the telegram was sent from Pera di Vassa, in the far north of Italy, where the language spoken was, and still is, Ladino. The grammatical oddities could thus be explained by mistakes in transmission. The telegram was handed in on 24 August, and arrived in Berlin the following day.

Next to the date is a sequence of numbers: '00.38', which hitherto has been taken to signify the year 1938. Leni has rightly objected that she was nowhere near northern Italy in the summer of that year. However, the figures actually represent the time of receipt (38 minutes past midnight), while there is no indication of the year. The latter can however be deduced from the serial number of the paper on which it was printed, and that only came into use in 1939. A week after 24 August 1939 Leni Riefenstahl was, according to her own memoirs, staying not far away in Bolzano. She wanted to relax before tackling her new project, a film version of Kleist's drama, *Penthesilea*. On 21 June 1939 we find the following entry in the diary of Joseph Goebbels, Minister of Propaganda: 'He [Hitler] wants to finance Leni Riefenstahl's Penthesilea film himself.' From this we can tell that at this time the relationship between Hitler and Riefenstahl was extraordinarily good. On 22 August 1939 Leni had her thirty-seventh birthday. Thus it is perfectly conceivable that she could have received the flowers from Hitler and been moved to this emotional response.

I was interested in Hitler mainly for sociological reasons – like the plight of the unemployed – and not for aesthetic ones. Those Nazi extravaganzas didn't appeal to me at all.

Leni Riefenstahl, 18 August 1997

It is absolutely clear that here is a woman implacably in love with herself, who forces everyone, from her mother onwards, to revere her. Even Hitler revered her, and she him of course, but somehow the two admired each other on an equal footing.

Margarete Mitscherlich, psychoanalyst and author

There can be no doubt that Adolf Hitler admired Leni Riefenstahl – as an artist, certainly, and perhaps also as a woman. But we can be sure that no relationship that went beyond friendship ever existed between the dictator and the film-maker. Nonetheless, even in the 1930s, rumours of this kind were circulating. When

Leni Riefenstahl travelled to New York in November 1938, the American press greeted her with the question, was she Hitler's mistress? The newsreel film containing Riefenstahl's reply was recently discovered. 'Oh, no!' she objects, 'That's just newspaper stories.' And with a coquettish smile she lowers her eyes.

Even in the early postwar years the question of a possible liaison between Hitler and Riefenstahl was hotly debated in the press. The basis for this speculation was the alleged 'Diary of Eva Braun', in which there are descriptions of wild orgies on the Obersalzberg and of a naked Leni dancing for Hitler. Only later was it discovered that the 'diary' was a forgery from beginning to end – the work of Luis Trenker, no less.

Nonetheless, Leni Riefenstahl and Adolf Hitler had much in common. She was the mirror in which Hitler could see himself exactly as he wanted to. And Hitler, who considered himself an artistic genius, ever since the days in Vienna when he had kept body and soul together by painting watercolour postcards, found a kindred spirit in Leni. She was an understanding listener to his interminable monologues about art and what he considered to be 'culture'. Riefenstahl for her part resembled Hitler in her unquestioning narcissism, and basked in the interest this mighty man showed in her. He was her key to fame, her big chance. In 1933 Joseph Goebbels had called her: 'The only one of the stars that understands us.' But Riefenstahl never became a member of the Nazi party; her enthusiasm for 'the Movement' was focused on the personality of Hitler. It was far from coincidental that his choice fell precisely on Leni Riefenstahl, and it was equally no coincidence that the first subject to which she would devote a documentary film was the dictator himself.

> Leni made documentaries, not propaganda. She didn't make propaganda films to order.
>
> *Hans Ertl, Leni Riefenstahl's cameraman*

On 17 May 1933 Goebbels, the propaganda minister, noted in his diary: 'P.m. Leni Riefenstahl: she tells me about her plans. I suggest to her a film about Hitler. She likes the idea very much.' It seems that the 'Hitler film' was quickly taken up. On 14 June we find this entry in Goebbels' diary: 'Riefenstahl has spoken to Hitler. She is now starting on her film.' It is true that a 'Hitler film' as such was never made. But in the autumn the commission was revised; Riefenstahl was now to make a film of the Nazi Party congress in Nuremberg. Eight months after the seizure of power by the National Socialists, this massive rally, under the resounding name of 'Party Congress of Victory', was to demonstrate the absolute supremacy of the Nazis in the German Reich. It was in Nuremberg, the historic city of the medieval German emperors, that the Führer would receive the tribute of his people. And the whole world would see it – through the cameras of Leni Riefenstahl.

Victory of Faith, as the film was sonorously titled, is a work that Leni Riefenstahl has never been happy to talk about. But not because of its political message. No, it is the technical shortcomings of the camerawork that even today can drive her into a rage. 'It's not even a film, it's just exposed material', is how she contemptuously dismisses it. Lost and forgotten for decades, *Victory of Faith* has only recently been rediscovered in its complete form – and it is an eloquent reflection of the beginnings of Nazi dictatorship.

> The backdrop was there already, both in Nuremberg and Berlin. I did not shape my subject. I did not manipulate the material or add any propaganda; I simply got my cameramen to film what I saw, as well as they could.
>
> *Leni Riefenstahl, 18 August 1997*

Riefenstahl was commissioned to make the film at short notice. Hastily she assembled cameramen and equipment. The assignment represented a great challenge; she had never attempted a documentary film before. But her own faith in herself had emerged triumphant long ago. There was no time to work out a definitive shooting-script or even to test different camera positions. Since most of the shots were created spontaneously and more or less at random, failure piled upon failure. Time and again the camera swung round to focus on nothing, or at the crucial moment was not focused at all. But more noticeable even than the technical shortcomings are the flaws in the presentation of Hitler and his paladins. There is Hitler, his expression of concentrated earnestness repeatedly disturbed by unruly strands of hair. There is Reich Marshal Goering marching past Hitler at a brisk pace, just as the Führer tries to shake him by the hand. There is something slightly comic in the sequence where the Reich Youth Leader, Baldur von Schirach, attempts to calm down the cheering youngsters of his Hitler Youth, so that the Führer can get a hearing. If you listen closely you can hear Hitler tittering: 'Now they're startin' all over again!' Time and again a nervous steward distracts the attention of the 'star' just at the critical moment, or – worse still – Hitler's henchmen peer at the camera, thus destroying the effect of the shot.

Victory of Faith provides a snapshot at a moment in the careers of Adolf Hitler and of Leni Riefenstahl. Both were still practising; but a year later they had perfected their image-making.

> As a great artist, what meant most to her was producing a convincing and artistically acceptable film. Nothing else interested her.
>
> *Dr Fritz Hippler, then Reich Director-General of Film*

In the late summer of 1934 Hitler again summoned the faithful to Nuremberg. This time Riefenstahl had mastered film production – and Adolf Hitler was the sole ruler of Germany. Whereas in *Victory of Faith* he had been obliged to share the attention of the public and the cameras with the head of the SA storm-troopers, Ernst Röhm, he now stood alone in the spotlight. In June of that year Hitler had ruthlessly ordered the murder of Röhm and other political rivals. The name of the 1934 party rally and of the film was *Triumph of the Will*. For Riefenstahl this became her greatest success, but it was also the writing on the wall: to this day it is considered the most accomplished propaganda film in the history of cinema.

> She is a very strong-willed woman. In her case you can
> certainly say it was a 'triumph of the will'.
>
> *Hans Ertl, cameraman*

The director had learned from the mistakes of the previous year.
This time she had accepted the commission well ahead of time and
used the run-up to plan the film like a military operation. Having
been given detailed information about how the event would be
staged, she planned her camera positions carefully and had rails
laid down around the speakers' podium so that the cameras could
circle it without interruption. The cameramen practised using
hand-held cameras while moving about on roller-skates. At Leni's
instigation a hoist was installed on the flagpole enabling shots to
be taken from aloft. Probably the most famous scene in *Triumph
of the Will*, showing Hitler, Himmler and the new SA chief, Lutze,
inspecting the ranks on parade, was made up from these high-
angle shots.

Shooting throughout this mammoth event required enormous
logistical organisation on Riefenstahl's part. It involved bringing an
army of cameramen at countless locations under the control of one
mind. The director was in her element and visibly relished her role.
Still photos taken on location show her in a tight-fitting, pale-
coloured uniform of her own design. Her costume befitted her
image and singled her out from the monotonous brown of the party
rally. A book of photos was published to accompany the film. It
contained sixteen photographs of Adolf Hitler – and thirty-seven of
Leni Riefenstahl. However, as Riefenstahl remembers it, the time
spent preparing for the film was torture from beginning to end. In
her memoirs is a photograph, which she has captioned as her 'final
attempt' to persuade Hitler to spare her the task of filming the party
rally. The photo shows Adolf Hitler bent over plans of the ground
where the rally is to be held. Next to him, looking very interested, is
Leni Riefenstahl. Evidence of anti-Nazism? I think not. Leni
Riefenstahl took on an assignment that offered her unprecedented
scope and the certainty of fame. Others chose differently. When a
cameraman named Emil Schünemann refused to work on *Triumph of*

the Will for political reasons, Riefenstahl denounced him for 'boycotting the Führer'.

To this day Riefenstahl insists that she made *Triumph* as a documentary film. She merely reproduced what was there to see. She once said: 'Whether it was about politics or about vegetables, was of no interest to me.' But those were no vegetables. *Triumph of the Will* is a political manifesto. True, it documents the genuine enthusiasm of the people. But it presents a new, heightened form of party rally, an awakening for the *Volk*, for all those who could not be in Nuremberg themselves.

As the film opens the following words appear on the screen: 'On 5 September 1934, twenty years after outbreak of the Great War, sixteen years after the beginning of Germany's suffering, and nineteen months from the start of Germany's rebirth, Adolf Hitler once more flew to Nuremberg to hold a review of his loyal followers.'

The action of the film, a rather unexciting series of parades and speeches, was condensed by Riefenstahl into a two-hour drama. By dint of skilful editing she became the mistress-of-ceremonies of the whole event. Hitler and the *Volk* face each other in a silent dialogue. Riefenstahl describes the history of a relationship – one might say a love-affair – between the Führer and his following. Through careful cutting, Hitler is made to appear as though having a personal conversation with each of his interlocutors, whether they be workers, SA men or members of the Hitler Youth. At the same time the Führer constantly towers above his people. By placing the camera at a low angle, the unprepossessing man is given a heroic aura. 'No-one who has personally seen the face of the Führer in *Triumph of the Will* can ever forget it. It will stay with them day and night, and like a silently glittering flame it will burn itself into their soul.' Those sententious words were spoken by Joseph Goebbels, when he presented Riefenstahl with the National Film Prize for 1935. The propaganda minister of the Third Reich had correctly assessed the 'value' of the work. *Triumph of the Will* was seen by an estimated 20 million people in German cinemas – and it gave them their own very personal experience of the Führer. And this time Leni had also taken care to show Hitler's henchmen in a good light.

> As the only woman with official status in the running of the party rally, she was often in conflict with the party bureaucrats, who at times came close to staging a revolt against her . . . Intrigues were cooked up, and slanderous reports presented to Hess, in order to have her ousted.
>
> *Albert Speer,* Inside the Third Reich, *1969*

Without any hesitation she summoned the top-ranking Nazis to her studio to re-shoot those scenes which she did not think had come out well. After the war, Hitler's architect, Albert Speer, recalled the strange scene: '. . . in the background you saw Streicher, Rosenberg and Frank walking up and down with their scripts, eagerly memorising their lines. Hess arrived and was the first one to be called in front of the cameras. Exactly as he had done before an audience of 30,000, he solemnly raised his hand. With the genuine emotion that only he could muster, he began to turn towards the place where Hitler should have been sitting, but wasn't and, standing strictly to attention, shouted out: "*Mein Führer*, I salute you!"'

The film was never given a voice-over commentary, and today Riefenstahl considers this proof that it could not have been a propaganda film. Yet *Triumph of the Will* needed no words. It was the power of the images that made this film so seductive.

When *Triumph* finally reached the cinemas in March 1935, Leni Riefenstahl was completely exhausted from spending months in the cutting-room. Adolf Hitler, overwhelmed by the way in which the director had portrayed him, presented her with a bunch of lilac. At that moment Leni, to use her own words, 'lost consciousness'.

> A woman who knows what she wants!
>
> *Joseph Goebbels, diary, 5 October 1935*

If she was not already there, *Triumph of the Will* certainly placed Leni Riefenstahl at the pinnacle of society in the Third Reich. Although to the film industry she remained something of an outsider, she gossiped with Hitler's senior colleagues at balls, film premières and parties. There was dancing, entertainment and more than enough to drink. But all that is dismissed by Riefenstahl today. She says that Goebbels hated her, so is that not ultimate proof that she was actually one of those persecuted by the regime?

The beginning of this 'hostility' dates from the year 1932. The 'Babelsberg Buck', as Goebbels was surreptitiously dubbed on account of his numerous amorous adventures, had apparently been pursuing her. Once when Goebbels, then Gauleiter of Berlin, paid a call on Leni, he lost all self-control and cried desperately: 'You must be my mistress, I need you – without you my life is a torment! I've been in love with you for a long time now!' He had collapsed sobbing in front of her, and clasped her round the ankles. Riefenstahl later claimed she pushed him away brusquely and showed him out of the house. 'The man who later became Minister of Propaganda never forgave me for that humiliation.' Such is the version of the story that Leni stuck to all her life. However, Wilfried von Oven, then an adviser to Goebbels, today allows himself a quiet smile over her account. 'I'm not saying he didn't try it on with countless women, but Leni Riefenstahl? No. He knew only too well that she was a woman who could make things difficult for him.' If Riefenstahl's memoirs build Goebbels up to be a sworn enemy, the little minister's diary-entries about Leni are thoroughly benevolent. He describes evenings spent with her as 'very pleasant', and calls her 'a clever girl'. Nonetheless there was certainly a rivalry between Goebbels and Riefenstahl, albeit not for the reason that Leni gave.

'Goebbels was jealous. There was a certain envy about the fact that someone like her could be accepted by Hitler, without Goebbels having somehow had a hand in it,' recalls Fritz Hippler, who at that time was Reich Director-General of Films. Wilfried von Oven has a similar view: 'Purely through her good relationship with Hitler, she kept on interfering with Goebbels' work and messing things up.' It was particularly during the filming of the 1936 Berlin Olympics that the minister and the star director constantly trod on each other's feet. 'I bawled out the Riefenstahl woman. Her behaviour has been indescribable. A hysterical woman. Not like a man, of course', the minister noted in his diary for 6 August 1936.

The squabbles between Goebbels and Riefenstahl were no

secret to the press, and foreign newspapers reported on them. In spring 1937 the *Weltwoche* of Zürich ran the headline: 'The fallen angel of the Third Reich'. And even though the story cobbled together below it was plainly rubbish, Hitler was alarmed. A photo-call with Leni, her family, Goebbels and Hitler was hastily arranged to scotch the rumours circulating around the world. Pictures were taken in the Riefenstahl garden, showing the propaganda minister and the director in perfect harmony, taking tea among the rose-bushes.

Goebbels and Riefenstahl were fighting over the same turf. And both were masters of their trade. Nonetheless, even though Goebbels was often irritated by Leni and her attention-grabbing star quality – the minister knew how important she was to the propaganda of the Third Reich.

Leni Riefenstahl's third film commissioned by the National Socialist Party also had a party rally as its theme – the one held in 1935. She was as unhappy with *Day of Freedom* as she had been with *Victory of Faith*, and she has always played down its importance as being nothing more than a tiresome exercise she was obliged to go through. The content of *Day of Freedom* can be quickly summarised: the troops of the newly rearmed Reich parade past in a gigantic military review, and the Führer casts a satisfied eye over the range of weaponry. In front of the cameras the cavalry shows its paces, and artillery, tanks and aircraft demonstrate their capabilities. Riefenstahl transformed the clanking, rattling procession of armour into a dramatic military manoeuvre, which might almost have been a real battle. Wreathed in clouds of dust, tanks screeched to a halt at the last moment in front of the cameras, or even rolled right over a cameraman positioned in a trench. Thanks to extremely swift cutting the film gave the impression of enormous power and movement. Germany would never again engage in a static war of attrition – that was the message the images suggested to an audience for whom the trauma of the First World War was still a fresh memory. Backed by a soundtrack of stirring martial music and shown shortly after the reintroduction of military conscription, *Day of Freedom* left audiences with an elating sense of strength regained. Germany was 'somebody' once again, after years of servitude under the 'shameful *diktat* of Versailles', which German forces had now emasculated.

Four years later, almost to the day, German tanks would roll over the Polish frontier, but for the time being Hitler the warmonger was posing as a prince of peace.

> Anyway, she put the emphasis on the documentary elements. She expressed no political comments or opinions. The Olympic film was certainly not political; it had after all been commissioned by the IOC.
>
> *Guzzi Lantschner, one of Leni's cameramen*

Back in 1931 the International Olympic Committee had awarded the 1936 Olympics to Germany – a well-meaning gesture towards the prostrate Weimar republic. In Berlin the 'youth of the world' were to meet in sporting competition. True, the new men in power made considerable distinctions between different members of the 'youth'. In 1928 Germany had been invited to attend an Olympiad for the first time since the First World War. But at the time Alfred Rosenberg, chief editor of the Nazi newspaper, *Völkischer Beobachter*, had claimed that even to attend such an event would be a 'crime'. 'Aryans' competing against 'non-Aryans'? Hitler and his henchmen also regarded this as an undignified spectacle – until they recognised the propaganda value of such an event. What could be better at a time when the world was watching developments in Germany with growing alarm? The event was going to cost around 100 million marks – a sum worth paying to convince the world of the international benevolence of the new regime. For the period of the games the anti-Semitic notices vanished from Berlin's shops, parks and public transport. An official order banned the singing of normally popular Nazi songs. The anti-Semitic smear-sheet *Der Stürmer* disappeared under newsagents' counters. This anodyne exterior was enough to distract the world from Germany's preparations for war and genocide. The images of white and coloured athletes engaged in friendly combat went around the world. Jesse Owens, the black American Gold Medal sprinter, was photographed with the

German Luz Long, the two men lying side by side in a meadow chewing grass-stalks.

Although the USA achieved great success in the 1936 Olympiad, the film showing their victorious athletes is not being shown here in Germany, because the American film industry, both production and distribution, is controlled by people who are not acceptable to today's Germany.

Film-Kurier *magazine, 10 January 1939*

For Leni Riefenstahl the Olympics were the subject she had always dreamed of. She now no longer had to portray monotonous mass parades and interminable speeches. Being an enthusiastic sports-woman herself, she could instead create from a wealth of sumptuous images a drama with tension guaranteed.

The facilities provided by the Minister of Propaganda for his star director were extremely generous. Even so, she herself maintains to this day that *Olympia* was carried out as an independent project by her own production company. She herself was guaranteed an exorbitant salary of 250,000 Reichsmarks, and the film had a budget of 1.5 million.

By May 1936 the camera teams, which Riefenstahl had put together from the best in the business, were already rehearsing. Willy Zielke would film the narrative prologue, Hans Ertl, Walter Frentz and Guzzi Lantschner were selected for the action sequences. A new face on the team was Hans von Jaworsky who had made a career in Hollywood after the First World War. Over and over again the cameramen practised tracking the swift movements of the athletes and tried out new camera-angles. It was at this time that the idea arose of filming the athletes from ground-level with the sky in the background. Hans Ertl developed a catapult-mounted camera, which could career along beside the 100-metre track at the same speed as the runners. A small balloon was fitted out with a miniature camera for taking aerial shots. When the sportsmen started their training, Leni's men were there to shoot close-ups, which they would have been prevented from getting in the actual heats.

In the making of the Olympic film she was just a spectator.
She just wanted to be seen. The audience quickly noticed
that and then they shouted: 'Leni . . . Leni, let's see you!' But
when she arrived they shouted down at her: 'Boo, you old
cow, you old cow!' They saw exactly how she was showing
off. The one actually making the film was me. Because I was
there with the camera – I was the guy turning the handle.

Hans Ertl, one of Leni's cameramen

When the Olympic flame was kindled in Berlin, Leni Riefenstahl had
to prove that all the expense had been worth while. She had to co-
ordinate an army of cameras covering countless different events.
What would be visually exciting? Where could a dramatic finish be
expected? Which athletes should be highlighted? When the sun
went down the director sat for hours with her teams, issuing
instructions for the next day. And Riefenstahl's word was law, even
for her self-confident and predominantly male colleagues. Today,
cameraman Guzzi Lantschner still admits with respect: 'She could
manage just as well as a man, and she handled her team just like a
man would do.' Leni knew just how to behave towards her 'boys'.
It was something she had learned from Arnold Fanck. She used the
same knowledge when dealing with the party bigwigs at the Games.
Whenever there was a problem she would dip into her own personal
bag of tricks. Cameraman Walter Frentz recalls how she once 'came
back beaming all over her face and said with a giggle: "We're getting
what we want. I just burst into tears again!"'

Riefenstahl fought like a tigress to get the best positions for her
cameramen. If this meant spoiling the view for the spectators, she
frankly didn't give a damn. One short sequence, whose inclusion
in the film is surely no coincidence, shows Leni at a swimming
event, gesticulating wildly as she harangues the unfortunate
umpire. The expressions on their two faces leave us in no doubt as
to who emerged the victor in this verbal duel. If ever she was
getting nowhere on her own, she would loudly refer to her
eminent Nazi patrons. The Berlin journalist Bella Fromm recalled
that during the Olympics Leni introduced a kind of warning-

system. As soon as she noticed that a newsreel cameraman was trying to muscle in on a position where her own team were still shooting, she would send a messenger-boy over with a note containing a dreaded message: 'Leni Riefenstahl demands that you remain in your place when taking pictures. Do not try to circumvent this. Failure to observe my instruction will lead to the withdrawal of your press pass.' The then Reich Director-General of Film, Fritz Hippler, is still incensed when he remembers Riefenstahl's behaviour: 'She seriously handicapped my newsreel men. But what could we do? Riefenstahl's army was a lot stronger than mine.'

Admittedly there were occasions when even Riefenstahl's steely charm was not enough. Hans Ertl remembers once leaving his camera running when a young woman with a bunch of flowers approached Hitler on the podium. In the act of handing him the flowers she bent over and, with lightning speed, kissed the Führer on the cheek. A clear imprint of lipstick was left on the face of the 'unattainable' Hitler. Hardly had the determined fan been removed than Ertl was also relieved of his reel of film. Two SS men had confiscated the 'compromising' material.

> The Olympics film was certainly the most interesting. Because everything was done so quickly and with such verve. It was exciting, because you could do such a lot without discussion beforehand. That's what the situation demanded. You were left to your own devices.
>
> *Guzzi Lantschner, one of Leni Riefenstahl's cameramen*

With the release of *Olympia* Leni's public profile received a further boost. A lot of advance publicity and 'backstage' reporting celebrated her as the new superstar. Leni was attractive and she knew how to show herself off to advantage. Wearing slacks and a tight-fitting jacket à la Marlene Dietrich, with her hair tousled by the wind, she had herself photographed standing behind Walter Frentz on a camera-truck. Her hand rests reassuringly on the man's shoulder, as though she were controlling his operation of the camera – though it would more probably have made Frentz's work harder rather than easier.

However, the public's reaction to the ubiquitous director became increasingly allergic, particularly as she never went anywhere without a personal photographer in tow. In the end, even her own team became irritated by her diva-like behaviour. Decades later, Hans Ertl was still annoyed by his one-time boss: 'She kept running around – even during the tensest competitions – from one camera-crew to another, acting the big director, supposedly giving important shooting instructions. If she'd been sitting up in the VIP box, it would have been far more helpful to our work than all that endless dashing about.'

> When she stepped into the limelight, it was never in a minor role.
> *Rainer Rother,* Leni Riefenstahl – The Seduction of Talent,
> *2000*

Riefenstahl's real contribution only began after the Olympic flame had been extinguished. No matter that some of her cameramen laid claim to this or that idea for setting up a shot – the editing-desk was Leni's true métier. It took her several months simply to view all the material – no less than 240 *miles* of film had been exposed. Only then could the actual editing process begin. Guzzi Lantschner, who assisted Leni in the cutting-room, remembers: 'We sat at the editing-desk night after night until one or two in the morning, and we would continue the next day without a break.' The work of preparing the film dragged on for month after month. Despite the generous budget, the project soon ran into financial problems. By mid-September 1936 a good 1.2 million Reichsmarks had gone up in smoke. Goebbels, the propaganda minister, was furious: 'Check on the Olympic film; the Riefenstahl woman is making a hash of it. Must intervene!' he noted in his diary for 25 October. Then a few days later, when he discovered the true extent of the financial disaster, he was foaming at the mouth: 'Fräulein Riefenstahl tries to fool me with her hysterics. There's no way I can work with this crazy woman. She now wants another half-million for her film – to make two films out of it. At the same time the mess she's making gets worse than ever. I go very cold on her. She cries. That's always a woman's last weapon. But it won't work with me. She has to get on with the job and keep things in shape.' However, progress at the editing-desk, which he personally went to take a look at, calmed the storm fairly quickly.

> Saw Frl Riefenstahl. Looked at part of the Olympics film. Indescribably good. Grippingly photographed and presented. A very great achievement. In certain parts deeply moving. That Leni really knows a thing or two. I am thrilled and Leni very happy.
>
> *Joseph Goebbels, diary 24 November 1937*

> Dinner with the Führer this evening . . . I tell him about Leni Riefenstahl's Olympic film. He's glad that it's so successful. We intend to do something about honouring Leni in a small way. She has earned it.
>
> *Joseph Goebbels, diary, 26 November 1937*

After two years in the cutting-room, the mammoth work was finally completed. It had become two films: *Festival of Nations* (Fest der Völker) and *Festival of Beauty* (Fest der Schönheit). To this day they are considered milestones in sports reportage. It was not just the new camera techniques, it was chiefly the way Leni had edited the Olympiad into a 'story'. Among the finest sequences in *Olympia* are unquestionably those of the high-diving competition. For the first time ever, Hans Ertl made masterly use of an underwater camera, and from this, together with Guzzi Lanstschner's shots from top of the diving-tower, Riefenstahl composed a sequence in which the divers lift themselves off the high board like birds and twist weightlessly in the air.

In the film's opening sequence she completely abandons the actual events of the Games. A picture of the ancient Greek statue of the

> By any comparison *Olympia* remains one of the best, if not
> the best, sports film ever made.
>
> *Taylor Downing*, Olympia, *1992*

discus-thrower, by Myron, dissolves into the figure of the German
decathlete Erwin Huber. Well-built athletes demonstrate – with
remarkable facility – the classic Olympic contests such as javelin- or
discus-throwing. These sequences were filmed on the Baltic. The
'rushes' that have survived show the effort that Leni's assistant
director, Willy Zielke, put into getting everything right. Between
takes the naked athletes shivered in the Baltic wind. Their bare feet
kept treading on thistles, yet in the finished film they seem like
demi-gods from a far distant age. Filmed from trenches, they
appear to be giants. The camera crews had applied Vaseline and
powder to accentuate the sportsmen's muscles. Every one of them
was a Hercules. After the war, Riefenstahl's fascination with
strength and beauty would be branded as 'fascistic'. Leni has always
staunchly rejected this: 'I'm only interested in what is beautiful.
Misery and illness depress me!'

Olympia is undoubtedly a political film, precisely because it does
not aggressively bang the drum for National Socialism. Naturally
the black Olympic star Jesse Owens was suitably acknowledged,
and of course the German sportsmen were not given undue
prominence. That chimed exactly with the image that the Nazi
leadership wanted to create abroad. The desired effect was
achieved by *Olympia* at a more subtle level.

Hitler, the hero of *Triumph of the Will*, now appeared as a good-
natured sports fan, who sweated and suffered along with the
competitors, for example when the last German runner in the
women's relay dropped the baton just before certain victory. Beside
Hitler, his henchmen in the VIP box bask in the glamour of the
Games. And they all look so *human*: Reich Marshal Hermann Göring
turned up in a different outfit every day, and Hitler's deputy, Rudolf
Hess, seemed unable to shake off his notoriously anxious expression
even during this enjoyable occasion. They all posed as peace-loving
promoters of international understanding. At the close of the Games,

searchlight beams formed Albert Speer's pretentious 'Cathedral of Light'. A few years later they would once again illuminate the night sky over Berlin – this time to pick out enemy bombers.

*

Hitler's forty-ninth birthday, 20 April 1938, was marked by the première of *Olympia*. Leni claims to have held out for this date herself, after the first night had twice been postponed. The Führer had been occupied with the annexation of Austria.

The première, held at Berlin's Ufa-Palast cinema before the assembled Nazi leadership, turned into a triumph for the director, who quickly forgot the stresses of completing the marathon work. 'Everywhere one hears nothing but unstinting praise. I'm making Leni Riefenstahl a gift of 100,000 marks', Goebbels noted patronisingly in his diary.

Vienna, Paris, Brussels, Copenhagen, Stockholm, Helsinki, Oslo, Rome . . . At almost every stage on Leni's foreign tour with *Olympia*, the film was greeted with a frenzy of enthusiasm. Only in Paris and Brussels, where demonstrators sang the communist *Internationale*, did she have to face criticism. But she did not fight back. Failing to recognise the tune of the *Internationale*, she mistakenly took it as a tribute. In general, though, the tour was a complete success. Riefenstahl perfectly fulfilled her role as an advertisement for the Nazi regime. Received by the German ambassador in each capital, she met the heads of government and crowned heads of most European countries, graciously accepted bouquets of flowers, and conversed with a beguiling charm. 'That Riefenstahl is a female with spirit', the propaganda minister allowed.

*

After Europe, the ambassadress of the New Germany intended to conquer the New World. In November 1938 Riefenstahl boarded a ship for New York. But there, spoiled as she was with success, she found a very different wind was blowing. The streets of Hollywood were adorned with posters reading: 'There's no place here for Leni Riefenstahl.' Studios cancelled planned previews of

Olympia, and scarcely a single celebrity wanted to be seen with Leni. Even in 1938 people had long since ceased to accept her pose as an independent artist. The moment she arrived she was bombarded with questions: 'What have you got to say about the fact that Germans have been setting fire to synagogues, and destroying Jewish shops, and that Jews are being killed?' A few days earlier the pogrom in Germany had reached its terrible climax. 'It can't be true!' the director cried.

> Riefenstahl was neither interested in the victims nor in the perpetrators. It was enough for her not be counted among the latter.
> *Rainer Rother*, Leni Riefenstahl – The Seduction of Talent,
> *2000*

Leni Riefenstahl has always denied that she had any idea of the extent of anti-Semitic developments in Germany. Indeed she even claims to have repeatedly and openly criticised Hitler for his racial policies. She says she was unaware that thousands of intellectuals, artists and opponents of the regime were leaving the country, and that she never saw anything of the tens of thousands of deportations. Did she not listen to the radio, read newspapers? No, she says; it was work, work, work, to the exclusion of everything else. Having never come into contact with anti-Semitism, the *Kristallnacht* pogrom came, she says, like a shock to her out of a clear blue sky.

The documentary evidence certainly tells a very different story. We learn that Leni Riefenstahl did not hesitate to exploit the 'opportunities' offered to her by the ostracising of Jewish artists. On a sheet of writing-paper from Berlin's Kaiserhof hotel, we find a note scribbled in a faint hand and dated 11 December 1933: 'I hereby grant Herr Julius Streicher, Gauleiter of Nuremberg, and editor of *Der Stürmer*, full powers to deal with the claim against me made by the Jew Bela Balacz.' That was how Riefenstahl contrived, after the Nazis seized power, to get rid of her co-author on *The Blue Light*. When the film returned to German screens in

1938, Balacz's name was missing from the credits. Suddenly it was 'a Leni Riefenstahl film'. She claims to have met Julius Streicher, an anti-Semitic psychopath, who died on the Nuremberg gallows in 1946, only once in her life, and on that occasion she flung the criticism at him: 'How on earth can you publish such a dreadful newspaper as the *Stürmer*!'

> Essentially Leni Riefenstahl follows the well-known motto of denial: 'I knew nothing.' Whenever the subject turns to the Nazi seizure of power, book-burning or the persecution of the Jews, we soon find in her memoirs the code-words 'mountain-hut', 'Greenland' or 'Dolomites' – actual or alleged places and synonyms for remoteness and absence from the brutal reality of Germany.
>
> *Felix Moeller,* Leni Riefenstahl, *1999*

Yet a letter from Streicher to Leni, dated 27 July 1937, has survived. He writes in very familiar terms: 'The hours we spent at your home were a great experience for all of us.' After adding all kinds of flattery, the fanatical racist lapses into emotion-laden, pseudo-poetic mode: 'Remain inscrutable to those who understand nothing, let them make their jokes, let them mock! Go on your way with a laugh, along the path of your great calling. It is here that you have found your heaven and in it you will be eternal. Yours, Julius Streicher.'

Later, Streicher's extremism became intolerable even to the party authorities and he was removed from office. Yet even then Leni remained in contact with him. Gestapo informers followed her on 29 October 1943, and made the following written report: 'Leni Riefenstahl was in Nuremberg with her fiancé, Major Jacob, staying at the Hotel Deutscher Hof. She immediately got in touch with the former Gauleiter, Julius Streicher, in Pleikerhof and visited him there.'

There were other times, too, when Riefenstahl apparently shared in full Germany's rampant anti-Semitism. Her producer at the time, Harry Sokal, a Jew himself, wrote a letter to *Der Spiegel* magazine after the war, in which he described Riefenstahl's fits of rage on reading bad reviews of *The Blue Light* by Jewish journalists. She was not about to let her work be torn apart by these 'miserable aliens who do not understand our mentality, our soul'. As Sokal remembers, Leni rightly guessed that as soon as the Führer was in power, these 'scribblers' would only be allowed to write for a Jewish readership. Leni Riefenstahl naturally tells a different story.

Yet there are other, more favourable, recollections about the famous director. The actress Evelyn Künneke revealed in an interview that her father, who had been expelled from the Reich Chamber of Film on racial grounds, turned to Leni Riefenstahl for help. Leni did in fact intercede with Hitler who heard her out, and Künneke, a producer of operettas, was allowed to go on working.

*

On 1 September 1939 German troops marched into Poland – and started the Second World War. Leni Riefenstahl decided to place her talents at the service of the cause, and stayed close on the heels of Hitler's armies as they advanced eastward. On 10 September she turned up in the sector commanded by the brilliant general, Erich von Manstein. But even he was at loss as to how to deal with this exalted personage. Manstein later recalled: 'She appeared in our headquarters "following in the steps of the Führer", as she put it. This famous film-actress and director, accompanied by a horde of cameramen . . . I must say, she looked pretty and rather dashing, a bit like a fashion-conscious partisan girl, who might have got her outfit from the Rue de Rivoli in Paris. She was wearing a kind of tunic, with breeches and high, suede boots. A revolver hung from the leather belt around her hips. And this close-combat gear was completed by a knife stuck into the top of her boot, Bavarian-style. I must confess that I and my staff were a little perplexed by this unusual apparition.'

Finding his lady visitor rather *de trop* at the front line, Manstein shifted her on to General von Reichenau, with the instruction that she and her retinue should make their way to the village of Konskie.

> It was only as a prisoner after the war that I heard about those crimes. It has almost driven me insane and I fear that I shall never be able to free myself from the nightmare of that appalling suffering.
>
> *Leni Riefenstahl in a letter to Manfred George, 1949*
>
>
> I knew about Dachau and Theresienstadt, but I didn't learn about the other camps until after the war.
>
> *Leni Riefenstahl, 18 August 1997*

It was on 12 September 1939 that Konskie was the scene of a war-crime, one of the first of its kind. The sequence of events is documented in the recently discovered photo-album of a German infantryman. 'Leni Riefenstahl with the film-crew', is the caption under one of the pictures. The lady director can be seen striding along a street, accompanied by several men. 'Our Führer in Konskie', is a picture of Hitler driving up in an open car. On the next page a photograph of four bodies is captioned: 'Four of our comrades attacked on patrol by Jews and treacherously murdered, on the night of 11 September.' 'The Jews have to dig the graves for our fallen comrades', are the words under the next picture. What had happened? Apparently four German soldiers had died in the battle for Konskie. The Wehrmacht rounded up the resident Jewish population and forced them to dig graves near the centre of the village. When the involuntary grave-diggers were later being pursued along the village street, there was a violent burst of shooting which left at least twenty civilians dead. In the album there is a picture of Riefenstahl surrounded by soldiers, crying out in horror. 'Leni Riefenstahl faints at the sight of the dead Jews', is the infantryman's laconic comment.

What had Leni just seen at that moment? After the war she herself claimed to have protested against the rough treatment of the civilians digging the graves. The soldiers then became aggressive towards her, she said. 'One of them shouted:

"Shoot that woman down!" and pointed his rifle at me.' That at least is how she remembered the incident later. She did not herself see the Jews being shot, she says, but only learned about it later. On this point, Riefenstahl's testimony is scarcely credible – not least because the photo-caption in the infantryman's album is pretty unambiguous – but she was speaking from the perspective of the 1950s, when the events in Konskie were being publicly debated. The criticism was aimed less against the Wehrmacht, members of which had indisputably committed a crime there, and more against a presumed witness of a crime in which she had taken no part. The question being asked was not: 'Who did it?' but 'Who saw it?' In the face of public criticism, Riefenstahl had defended herself and probably opted for the mildest version of the story. However, there is no doubt that she *did* protest about the events in Konskie. It is a proven fact that she went to see General von Reichenau and told him how appalled she was at what she had witnessed. Her objection had absolutely no effect on the hard-line Nazi general – but at least she raised her voice in protest, and that is more than all but a precious few did at that time.

> I regret having lived through that time. If I had known everything then, I would have killed Hitler.
>
> *Leni Riefenstahl, July 1996*

Following the events in Konskie, Leni flew to Danzig and filmed the triumphal entry into the city by Hitler and his troops. She herself described her experience in Konskie as a rude awakening, which persuaded her to give up working as a war-reporter. Indeed, after that she never again visited the front line with her cameras. Yet what she was rejecting were only the horrors of war, not the triumphs of the man who had fomented that war.

Six months later, when Hitler made his entry into a defeated Paris, Leni cabled him: 'It is with indescribable joy, deep emotion and sincere gratitude that we share with you, *mein Führer*, your and Germany's greatest victory, the entry of German troops into Paris. Beyond all powers of man's imagination, you are performing deeds that are without parallel in human history. How can we ever thank you? Expressing my congratulations is not nearly enough to show you the feelings that stir me.'

I have never denied that I was captivated by Hitler's personality. The fact that I recognised too late the demonic in him, is without doubt my fault or my blindness.
    Leni Riefenstahl in a letter to Manfred George, 1948

In the years that followed, Riefenstahl did not turn her back on Hitler, nor did she refuse his patronage. As early as the spring of 1939 discussions had started about building spacious studios for Leni Riefenstahl in Berlin. Not far from her villa in the Dahlem district, a 5.5 acre facility was to be provided for Leni's productions. This was to be done at government expense and was authorised by Hitler himself.

Editing-suites, preview cinemas, a kitchen and canteen for the workers, even a gymnasium was planned. And for her private offices, Leni had requested a picture window that could be lowered into the floor, with a view on to the garden. In his Berghof mountain retreat Hitler boasted an identical window. True, the plans were held up by the outbreak of war, but work continued nonetheless. By 1940, the area had increased to 7 acres and as late as 1942 we find references to the film studios in the correspondence of Albert Speer, Hitler's architect. The studios were envisaged as part of the new capital, 'Germania', which Speer and Hitler wanted to make the centrepiece of the 'Thousand Year Reich'. Yet before the foundation-stone of the 'Riefenstahl Studios' could be laid, the 'Reich' already lay in ruins.

Having decided to abandon her work as a war reporter, Riefenstahl returned to feature films. *Tiefland* (Lowlands), a heavily emotional saga of the victory of good over evil, was to be her second full-length feature and the last she ever made. The idea for it had been in her mind for twenty years. The screenplay tells the story of Pedro, a guileless shepherd from the highlands of Spain, and his love for Martha, who in turn is in thrall to an evil despot from the lowlands. Riefenstahl had started work on it as early as 1934, but from the outset

Tiefland had been dogged by financial and technical problems. For example, a leading part was to be played by a wolf. A certain Dr Bernhard Grzimek was hired to provide a trained animal. The first wolf was too well-behaved, and the second choked to death on its food. Only the third in line 'acted' to Leni's satisfaction. Problems were also caused by the herd of sheep intended to enliven the picturesque mountain backdrop. A lake had been specially created and the sheep tempted there with salt, but so thirsty were they that they very swiftly drank the 'lake' dry, and it had to be laboriously refilled. The war, too, imposed increasing difficulties on the production. Filming in Spain, where the action of the film was set, was no longer possible. The village of Rocabruna in the Pyrenees had to be relocated and rebuilt from scratch in the Karwendel mountains of Austria. Costs escalated uncontrollably, and Joseph Goebbels very soon lost patience. On 8 March 1941 he noted in his diary: 'The new Riefenstahl film is a worry. A ridiculous amount of money is being thrown away on it.' But time and again Riefenstahl managed to shake down more funds. Martin Bormann, Hitler's secretary, had become her new route to the Führer's wallet.

In the history of cinema *Tiefland*, unlike Riefenstahl's other films, has left little impact. A major factor was that Leni did herself no favours by opting to play the principal female role herself. Now in her early forties, no-one could accept that she was the same age as her 23-year-old leading man, even given the most favourable lighting. What is more, when the film finally came to the screen in 1954, its emotionally loaded imagery looked outmoded. The newspaper, *Stuttgarter Zeitung*, poked fun at this 'textbook example of boredom taken to a virtuoso level with cutting that is about as fast as a snail with arthritis'. The *Deutsche Zeitung* accused Riefenstahl of acting with as much animation as a 'wax flower'.

*

Despite the project's lack of success it was the production of *Tiefland*, more than anything, that led to the bitterest charges against Leni after the war. In 1940, when filming began more intensively, the war meant that the large-scale transporting of extras from Spain to Austria was out of the question. But Leni wanted 'local Spanish colour' in the faces of her cast. The solution lay nearer than she had at first dared to hope.

Rosa Winter, a *sinta* gypsy, was seventeen years old when her family were locked up in the Maxglan internment-camp, near Salzburg. Today she can still remember the day she first saw Leni Riefenstahl. 'She came to the camp with some men in uniform and picked out some of us.' The gypsies from Maxglan were taken in buses to the film location at Mittenwald, north of Innsbruck. Rosa Winter can still remember how very glad they all were to have escaped the miserable living-conditions in the gypsy camp. As extras in *Tiefland* they were given adequate board and lodging – but were under constant supervision. Today, Rosa Winter describes Leni as being extremely friendly and kind to the extras. Did the director never stop to wonder where the road would lead for her walk-on actors?

> We were all in the assembly-camp, you see. And then she came along with the police and picked out several of us. And I was one of them. We were just ordinary young people she wanted to use.
>
> *Rosa Winter, extra in* Tiefland

After the war people accused Riefenstahl of having known that when filming was finished the gypsies would be shipped off to Auschwitz and murdered. It is unlikely that as early as 1941 the name of Auschwitz rang any bells. Yet Leni had seen the gypsies interned in Maxglan. It cannot have escaped her that her extras – whom incidentally she never paid or compensated in any way – faced a terrible end.

How much Riefenstahl actually knew about the Holocaust is something that must remain unclear. For decades now, she herself has repeated the same phrases over and over again. In her memoirs she even maintains that the gypsies were her 'special favourites. After the war we saw them all again.' Yet scarcely a single one of her extras survived Auschwitz.

Leni Riefenstahl personally never deported anyone, and she

never killed anyone. Yet she must be open to the accusation of having exploited the opportunities offered her by an inhuman regime. For her own purposes she made use of people who looked 'different'. And they were supplied to her by a regime which marginalised, incarcerated and finally murdered them.

> They are simply history, pure history.
> *Leni Riefenstahl on her films*

The ending of the war on 8 May 1945 cut deeply into Leni Riefenstahl's life. The oft-quoted 'Hour Zero' that was felt by most Germans to be a liberation and a new beginning deprived the film-director of her entire *raison d'être*. She did no filming at all among the ruins of the Reich to which she had owed her triumphs.

In a very short time American troops had arrested her in Kitzbühel and transferred her along with high-ranking Nazis to an assembly-camp for interrogation. One of her interrogating-officers was Irving Rosenbaum. As a Jew who had emigrated to the USA at the age of seventeen, and was now back with the American army in his native land, he was quite familiar with Leni's name. 'As a child I had seen her mountain movies. But the woman we were to question was the creator of notorious Nazi propaganda films', he recalls. 'She seemed like a nervous wreck.' Whereas Leni Riefenstahl herself prefers to remember how shattered she was to see photographs of the concentration camps, the interrogation report, which can be seen today in the American archives, states succinctly: 'Fr. Riefenstahl is chiefly concerned about her film *Tiefland*.' The rest of Leni's statements under Allied interrogation are well known today. Since 1945 she has repeated most of them countless times: she had been forced to make films of the Reich party rallies. She had been persecuted by the Ministry of Propaganda, and she had absolutely no idea about what went on in the concentration camps.

The interrogations in the spring of 1945 were the beginning of the Riefenstahl legend that would be with her for the rest of her life. Three denazification tribunals in the years that followed examined the director's relationship with

National Socialism. On two occasions the verdict was 'not implicated', but a third tribunal classified her as a 'fellow-traveller' – in other words, like all too many Germans, she had happily collaborated with Nazism. With that verdict the 'Riefenstahl case' might well have been put on the shelf and forgotten. But to this day that has not happened.

> The person under investigation is classed in the category of fellow-traveller . . . In formal terms it has been established that Frau Leni Riefenstahl, born 22.8.02, was neither a member of the NSDAP nor of any of its subsidiary organisations, and that thus there is no presumption of guilt under Directive 38. However, it remained to be examined whether and to what extent Frau Riefenstahl furthered the Nazi tyranny in ways other than by working in the Party or its organs, or whether she emerged as a beneficiary of that tyranny . . .
>
> *From the proceedings of the Denazification tribunal against Leni Riefenstahl, 16 December 1949*

For a long time after the war Leni Riefenstahl was unable to get re-established in her profession. She has never again completed a film. This has nothing whatever to do with being blackballed by the industry for, contrary to a widely held belief, that never happened. But to her dying day she saw herself as a scapegoat, symbolically crucified by post-war Germany and representing all those who concealed far more heinous crimes. The resentment that Riefenstahl had to contend with was largely the consequence of her own self-imposed ostracism. Even when her 'recollections' had long since been proved wrong on many points, by eye-witnesses or rediscovered documents, she scented conspiracies and mounted massive counter-attacks against critics who branded her as 'unreconstructed'. Leni Riefenstahl did not discuss, she sued – taking legal action against anyone who even tentatively associated her with Nazi policies or her beloved Führer. Though she won most of her lawsuits, her reputation suffered in the process.

Her comeback in film making was hindered not so much by her

unpopularity as by the fact that she was no longer able to do things the way she wanted to. It was the disappearance overnight of the accustomed framework for her productions that led to the failure of almost all her projects. Her taste in subjects and treatments had been overtaken by the passage of time. She could no longer draw on virtually unlimited budgets, and she lacked her seasoned camera team – the beautiful images of a Hans Schneeberger, the inventiveness of a Hans Ertl or the dedication of a Guzzi Lantschner. The conditions she worked under were no worse than for anyone else – they were simply the same.

Her eventual comeback was achieved not as a director but as a photographer. In November 1962, on an expedition to the Sudan, she came to the village of Tadoro, in order to discover 'her Nubas' there. Living among this tribe, then still largely untouched by western civilisation, was like a return to paradise for Leni. For among the Nuba she was a woman without a history. Her photographic study of different Nuba groups became a success, even though she was censured for once more overemphasising the qualities of strength and heroism. The photographer rejected this criticism by saying: 'They are so beautiful. But I did not make them. It was the good Lord who created them.' She had not understood what her critics were trying to say.

> The most controversial German woman there has been since 1945.
>
> *Alice Schwarzer,* Emma *magazine, 1999*
>
> No other woman in the twentieth century has been at the same time so admired and so vilified.
>
> *Jodie Foster, actress, 2000*

In 2002 Leni Riefenstahl celebrated her hundredth birthday. She did not have much longer to live, and only her past to dwell on. Yet over the previous few years attitudes towards her had changed noticeably. The old lady was admired for her impressive vitality. Throughout the world exhibitions of her photography and even showings of her films began to enjoy great popularity. Top Hollywood director Steven Spielberg expressed interest in getting to know her; and his colleague George Lucas freely admits to having borrowed ideas from *Triumph of the Will* for certain scenes in his *Star Wars* trilogy. The American actress and producer Jodie Foster is going to make a film of her life, and has described Leni Riefenstahl as 'one of the most interesting women of the twentieth century'.

There is now a Riefenstahl renaissance – increasingly the propagandist is taking second place to the unquestionably great artist. The years of fierce criticism are over and critics shy away from referring to transgressions she committed more than half a century ago. She was someone who had always been talked about. Talking *to* her was never really possible since Riefenstahl consistently avoided a truly profound examination of her creative motivation under the Third Reich. Neither in her films nor in her life were there any nuances, only black and white. She would never draw fine distinctions. The armour of her memories had long since become her truth.

> I lived under the Third Reich with all its horrifying crimes. We left a terrible legacy behind. I have a certain debt to pay. There remains something that can be called guilt.
>
> *Leni Riefenstahl, May 2000*

CHAPTER FOUR

THE MUSE – WINIFRED WAGNER

Between 1925 and 1933 Hitler used to stop for a brief rest at Wahnfried on his journeys between Berlin and Munich. In our family circle Hitler could be completely at ease, as a normal person in human surroundings, and he could recover from the gruelling activity of making propaganda speeches for the Party.

After all, I knew him [Hitler] for 22 years and was never once disappointed in him as a human being. I mean, apart from the things that went on elsewhere, but of course those things did not affect me.

I remained more or less loyal to him to the bitter end, because I knew the man as a friendly, high-minded and helpful person. It was the man, not the Party, who held my loyalty.

At the Festspielhaus in Bayreuth, you were not questioned about your party affiliation, only about your performance.

The bond between us was purely human and personal, an intimate bond founded on our reverence and love for Richard Wagner.

USA – *unser seliger Adolf* (our blessed Adolf).

Winifred Wagner

My mother had . . . an idealistic view of the belief in a 'national renewal', which Hitler propagated.

Wolfgang Wagner, autobiography, 1994

She brought Richard Wagner into this diabolical marriage with the German Reich, and into a very personal relationship with its Führer. In so doing she made Richard Wagner a posthumous accomplice and political participant in the destruction of the nation.

Hans Jürgen Syberberg, 1980

After 1945, of course, the Bayreuth Festival could no longer make any public display of anti-Semitism or glorification of National Socialist ideology. So my grandmother went on expressing those attitudes in her rather more intimate circle. People knew how she felt about the 'blessed Adolf'.

Gottfried Wagner, grandson of Winifred Wagner

Hitler was a man from the lower middle class who tried to get into more elevated circles. Through Winifred he was able to do that.

Erica Jansen, chorus-member at the Bayreuth Festival

Winifred had a hot line to the very top and was able to exploit this time and again, to help a Jewish doctor or friend from Bayreuth, and get them out of the concentration camp. There are over thirty letters of thanks from Jewish men and women, to testify to her kindness . . .

Nike Wagner, granddaughter of Winifred Wagner

It was the middle of May 1945. Hitler's suicide and the surrender of the Wehrmacht had finally released Germany from the din of battle and the stench of blood. While most Germans were still wondering numbly whether they felt defeated or liberated, the victors went off in pursuit of those responsible for the catastrophe. In the uniform of a US Army officer, Klaus Mann, son of the emigré German novelist Thomas Mann, was tracking down a woman whose name was near the top of their list. It was in the remote hamlet of Oberwarmensteinach in northern Bavaria that he found her. There, in a little summer cottage, he was received by

Winifred Wagner, the daughter-in-law of that most German of all composers. Her manner was friendly but firm: 'There is one question, Herr Mann, that you do not even have to ask me: I did not sleep with Adolf Hitler.'

Even in her first interrogation she displayed what well-meaning biographers have described as 'candid openness', but which her granddaughter Nike calls culpable 'impenitence'. Klaus Mann was astonished to find that he had to travel 'almost to the Czech frontier' to find at least one German who admitted to having been a supporter of Hitler. 'She was the only person who did not distance herself as far as possible from Hitler, but frankly admitted her friendship with him. We talked about Hitler! "Were we friends? But of course we were! Certainly! And how!" She actually seemed proud of it. With her head held imperiously high, she sat facing me, a valkyrie of imposing stature and impressive lack of inhibition. "He was delightful", she asserted. "I don't understand much about politics but I know a lot about men. Hitler was charming. An Austrian, you know! Warm-hearted and sociable. And he had a simply marvellous sense of humour!"'

That was the story she stuck to. In her two denazification tribunals Winifred Wagner did admittedly try to shed the best light on her conduct during the Nazi period, by saying that she was concerned exclusively with the heritage of Richard Wagner; yet she never let there be any doubt about her close relationship with Hitler as a private individual. When her two sons, Wieland and Wolfgang, revived the Bayreuth Festival in 1951, they had difficulty in keeping Hitler's obdurate lady admirer out of the limelight. However, they managed to do so until 1975. In that year the old lady gave an interview lasting over five hours to the director Hans Jürgen Syberberg, the publication of which created an unwelcome furore. 'If Hitler came through the door today', said Winifred Wagner in a firm voice, 'I would be just as happy and overjoyed as ever to see him and have him with me.' As far as she was concerned, her blood-spattered 'friend' was still a 'unique personality'.

*

Statements like this are off-putting. Winifred Wagner presents us with riddles – even more since the death of her admirer Hitler than during the dark years of his empire. Is it possible for an intelligent person, knowing about Auschwitz, to praise the mass murderer as a 'charmer'? Why does an old woman in full possession of her mental faculties make herself a target for massive public criticism – which naturally was not long in coming? And above all: what was it that cast such a spell over the *grande dame* of Bayreuth that she never broke free from it?

A glance at her life history does something to clear up the mystery. Neither Hitler nor Winifred Wagner were born German, and probably for that reason they both cultivated that fanatical nationalism that is sometimes typical of naturalised citizens of any nation. Hitler's provenance in the backwoods of northern Austria was so murky that the dictator declared his early life a 'matter of state secrecy'. Yet to the end he seemed to be searching for a substitute for the warmth of family life that he lacked. For a time he found this with Winifred.

*

She herself made no secret of her origins: she was born Winifred Williams in Hastings, England, in 1897. Her father, John Williams, was a writer of no more than adequate talent, and her mother Emily had been an actress on the provincial stage. Orphaned at the age of three, Winifred was shunted back and forth between relatives, ending up in the care of strict nuns in a gloomy Victorian orphanage in south London. These were apparently 'very unhappy years', as she admitted in old age, and one may assume that this scarcely conveys the true extent of her misery.

> Because of her whole Victorian upbringing, she was unable to admit openly to her feelings.
>
> *Gottfried Wagner*

The time in the orphanage left her with two indelible traits in her nature: on the one hand she had a rather taciturn, introverted personality that seldom permitted her to show her feelings. Her grandson, Gottfried Wagner, has reproached both his grandmother and his father, Wolfgang, with the same coldness and hardness. On the other hand, though, she had a strong, not to say selfless sense of family, which made her a caring, and in the eyes of many, a model mother and grandmother. Until well into old age she tirelessly helped her offspring change their babies' nappies or laboured over the kitchen stove. She was even prepared to forgive her rebellious daughter Friedelind for writing her mercilessly revealing book *Night over Bayreuth*, even though it provided the prosecution with evidence for her arraignment before a denazification tribunal. After the war Winifred unhesitatingly assumed responsibility for Bayreuth's Nazi legacy, so that her sons, untainted by her past as a protégée of Hitler, could continue to stage the festivals.

> At Wahnfried there are no skeletons in the cupboard.
>
> My mother's political attitude was and is like a fateful intellectual mortgage that I have been paying off all my life, since with her typical Welsh stubbornness she never deviated from it.
>
> *Wolfgang Wagner in his autobiography*

After her first years of schooling, Winifred Williams fell ill. A doctor recommended a 'continental climate', and that is what took her to Berlin, to live with distant relatives, the Klindworths. It was certainly the turning-point of her life. The very elderly, white-bearded Karl Klindworth was a musician who had once been a friend of Richard Wagner, and still kept closely in touch with Bayreuth. He became Winifred's adoptive father, introducing her to Wagner's operas and to the realm of *völkisch* ideas which, particularly among German Wagnerians, had grown up around the tales of *Parsifal*, *The Meistersinger* and the *Ring of the Nibelungs*. As the consumptive English girl turned into a handsome young woman, Klindworth and Wagner's widow, Cosima, acted as matchmakers, and his ward was introduced to the family of the *Meister*. The success of her instruction in matters Wagnerian is shown by the fact that she took on the additional Christian name of 'Senta' – after the mythical woman in *The Flying Dutchman*, who was to redeem the accursed seaman through 'faithfulness unto death'.

> She felt herself to be a German woman.
> *Walter Schertz-Parey, Winifred Wagner's biographer*

At the same time as illness and coincidence brought the young Winifred into the home of a passionate Wagnerian, a certain young Austrian was experiencing his 'awakening' in a cheap seat at the opera-house in Linz. Wagner's early work *Rienzi* was being performed. August Kubizek, a boyhood friend of Hitler and like him an ardent Wagner fan, tells us of the first time they went to a Wagner opera together. 'We were shattered by the death of Rienzi', he wrote of that November evening in 1906, 'and although Hitler would usually begin to talk immediately after being moved by an artistic experience, and to voice sharp criticism of the performance, on this occasion Adolf remained silent for a long time.' Rienzi was a Roman tribune, who wanted to liberate his people but in the end was betrayed, and died amid the ruins of the Capitol. In this story Hitler saw a vision of his own future. 'Gustl' Kubizek described how his pal suddenly announced to him, with 'grand and thrilling images', his 'mission', which was to lead the German people to the 'heights of liberty'. 'It was as if another person inside him were speaking', Kubizek went on, 'someone by whom he was as deeply moved as I was.' In 1939 Hitler, who had long since turned Wagner's Rienzi theme into an anthem for his party rallies, described to Winifred that fateful night in Linz; in a voice trembling with emotion he said: 'In that hour it began!'

Wagner's dramatic and mythical world, which seemed full of bottomless abysses and messages of salvation, was the one which Hitler, even in his youth, had chosen as his spiritual home. 'At a stroke I was transfixed'; those words in his massive manifesto, *Mein Kampf* (My Struggle), sum up Hitler's first encounter with Wagner's music. Even the book's title was modelled on

Richard Wagner's autobiography, *Mein Leben* (My Life). From that moment on, as Hitler revealed to an American journalist, he had been going to Wagner operas 'as other people go to church'. Burning pyres, crumbling Valhallas, ecstatic redemption – in the opera-house Hitler the Catholic found his communion. How much Wagner there was in Hitler would only emerge in the years of his dictatorship.

> Adolf Hitler's passion for Wagner served as a means of legitimising his own political mission. He exploited Wagner's concept of a German national art in his own ideology.
>
> *Wolfgang Wagner in his autobiography*

Winifred Williams saw her first Wagner opera in the summer of 1914, in those fateful weeks before the outbreak of the First World War brought a gilded era to an end. A Serbian fanatic had just shot Franz Ferdinand, the Crown Prince of Austria. But as a dizzy seventeen-year-old, Winifred's head was full of other things. She too, as she wrote later, was 'deeply stirred' by the cascades of sound that swept over her from the orchestra-pit during a dress rehearsal of *The Flying Dutchman*. She was bewitched by the action on stage, in those days still strictly 'naturalistic', with artificial trees, rustling beards and ox-horned Germanic helmets. 'From that moment on', she wrote enthusiastically, decades later, 'all that existed for me were Wagner and the world of Bayreuth.' Perhaps it was the intoxicating harmonies, or perhaps Klindworth's encouraging words, that also sent her into raptures over Richard Wagner's son Siegfried. Only a year later, on 22 September 1915, the unlikely couple were married.

*

World war or no world war, Bayreuth was happy. The most important thing was that the *Meister*'s widow, Cosima, was finally freed from her worry about perpetuating the family line. Her only son Siegfried, known as 'Fidi', was already forty-six years old when he finally reached the altar. True, he had an illegitimate child by a pastor's daughter, but this unlawful issue could not be considered a guarantee of continued control over the 'green hill', the grounds of the Festspielhaus. In his day, Siegfried was thought of as a pretty successful composer himself, and a worthy Wagner heir. It was just that his reputation was tainted by his many dalliances with both the female and male sex – not that a certain promiscuousness did not play a part in the Wagner tradition. After all, even Cosima could not name the father of her daughter Isolde with absolute confidence. Yet in her dignified old age the composer's sensuous wife had become the puritanical keeper of the flame, who knew enough about Fidi's escapades not to enquire further. Whether the Cinderella-like Winifred even knew of Cosima's seal of approval is extremely doubtful. 'Little Winnie' was needed – to uphold the dynasty. Shortly before the wedding she wrote to her Siegfried, as though speaking Senta's lines from *The Flying Dutchman*: 'With body and soul I dedicate myself to you; guide me through life – shape me as you would wish me to be. I have longed so much for love.'

Richard Wagner had christened his stately home in Bayreuth Wahnfried (meaning something like 'peace to the frenzied'), because here his *Wähnen* or frenzied imaginings were to 'find peace'. But when Winifred arrived there as a young bride, what awaited her was anything but peace and tranquillity. Two jealous sisters of Siegfried, both married but childless, made life difficult for her with their hostility and bossiness. The aged Cosima laid down a strictly regulated daily programme for her daughter-in-law and liked her to address Siegfried, her new husband, as *hoch verehrter Meister* (highly esteemed master). Because there was a war on, no festivals were held, a fact that soon brought the family into dire financial straits. In winter they moved into the little annexe beside Wahnfried, because it was cheaper to heat.

Despite all these adversities Winifred lived up to the expectations placed on her. At the rate of one a year she gave birth to young Wagners: first, in 1917 the son and heir, Wieland, then Friedelind, Wolfgang and finally Verena in 1920.

This regular maternity strengthened her position in the clan. When she brought baby Wieland to Wahnfried for the first time, she pointedly laid the son and heir in the arms of Cosima.

Altogether, Winifred seems from the very outset to have joined in the power-struggle in and for Wahnfried with what her son Wolfgang called 'Welsh pig-headedness'. When one of her unpopular sisters-in-law, Daniela Thode, with perfectly good intentions, gave her a trousseau and clothes for the next few years, Winifred wasted no time in donating them to the Bayreuth church 'for charitable purposes'. She, and no-one else, would decide what she wore. Soon 'Little Winnie', the object of an arranged marriage, became a respected figure. One visitor, Count Gravina Gilberto, described the transformation – which was actually visible in her physique – in no uncertain terms: 'After four children she was no longer recognisable. She had almost doubled in size. She was seen as an exemplary mother, a prolific milch-cow, who had brought a thoroughly healthy and vital heredity to the marriage. It was all Siegfried could do to cope with her in a fitting manner.'

> The Wagners were a very nationalistic German family. And Winifred felt very much at home with them, since she had of course been brought up in the same spirit by her adoptive father.
>
> *Walter Schertz-Parey, biographer of Winifred Wagner*

Relations with Fidi, twenty-eight years her senior, gradually declined into a marriage of convenience. Once the family bloodline had been secured, the spouses went their separate ways. The husband returned to his bachelor existence and cultivated his homosexual friendships. One of his lovers was an Englishman, Clement Harris, who boasted that he had shared a bed with Oscar Wilde. Siegfried turned his mixed feelings about the sham marriage into an opera *à clef* with the revealing title *Das Liebesglück* (The Bliss of Love). There was nothing Winifred could do but draw a veil of silence over Fidi's predilections, even though she was deeply hurt by them. Public discussion of the homosexuality of Richard Wagner's son would have incurred the severe disapproval of the festival's conservative audiences. For this reason, attempts at blackmail over Fidi's little games not infrequently proved successful.

For Winifred Wagner her own husband's homosexuality was a very problematic subject. In the 1920s it was something no-one talked about. Then the topic was broached with Hitler and Goebbels: Ugh, how decadent!

Gottfried Wagner

It is proof of her pragmatic temperament that Winifred Wagner nonetheless pursued her family life at Wahnfried with energy and determination. Four lively children, complaining sisters-in-law and the steadily declining Cosima all needed looking after. Now and again Siegfried would appear, choosing to ignore it all and preferring to go on family jaunts through the countryside. What mattered, as their son Wolfgang put it, was to give the 'outward appearance' of being an intact family unit. Winifred, the first woman in Bayreuth to possess a driving licence, was at the wheel. She adored driving, usually with a cigarette drooping from the corner of her mouth, and was not above carrying out her own repairs and maintenance. Wolfgang remembers that she even had a pit dug to make it easier to change the oil when necessary.

Winifred's foster-father, Klindworth, who had died in 1916, had given her a grounding in politics, so that she eagerly soaked up the *völkisch*, or ethnic German, mentality in which Wahnfried was steeped. Eva, the other of her two sisters-in-law, had married Houston Stewart Chamberlain, an English-born Germanic theorist who, like Winifred, had been brought up in Germany. Chamberlain's mentor had been a fanatical Prussian nationalist and he himself felt called upon to uphold and pass on Richard Wagner's message. In 1905, long before Hitler had began to interest himself in these ideas, Chamberlain was writing about an 'Aryan view of the world' and advised Germany's leaders to 'release the empire from the crushing embrace of the Jews'. For this he was commended by no less a personage than Kaiser Wilhelm II: 'It is God who has sent your book to the German people, and you personally to me.' Such was the monarch's endorsement of the Englishman who was so concerned about the continued survival of the Germans.

From the all-embracing and ideologically confused jumble of Wagner's ideas, Chamberlain had picked out the passages that fitted the *völkisch* image. It is chiefly the composer's anti-Semitic utterances that leap out at one: 'Communism and the stock-market' were the 'creeping demons of Jewry', or 'the Jewish race' was the 'sworn enemy of humanity'.

> As an orphan and the wife of a homosexual, she grew up in the whole ideological environment and became a hundred-and-fifty-percent 'Wagnerian'.
>
> *Gottfried Wagner*

There has been much dispute over Richard Wagner's anti-Semitism, which in fact later reached the minds of Nazis through Houston Stewart Chamberlain. Do Wagner's works carry a burden of anti-Jewish thinking? Are the sinister characters in his operas, such as 'Mime' in the Ring cycle, or 'Beckmesser' in the *Meistersinger*, projections of the hated Jew? Was his essay, *The Jewish Character in Music*, the theoretical foundation of a programme of extermination? Is the composer in fact that 'prophet' who was followed by Hitler the 'executor', as has recently been provocatively suggested by the writer Joachim Köhler?* Wagner enthusiasts maintain, on the contrary, that their idol sometimes gave preference to Jewish conductors, and that the characters of 'Mime' or 'Beckmesser' were merely interpreted by later directors in a way that evoked associations with Jewishness.

It is nonetheless the case that Wagner was by no means free from the widespread anti-Semitism of his age. That clearly does not mean that he envisaged the mass murder of millions – indeed no-one in the nineteenth century had any inkling of the Holocaust. His idea was rather that Germany should 'assimilate' the Jews to such an

---

* *Wagner's Hitler*, by J. Köhler, Polity Press, Cambridge, 1998.

extent that they would by 'redeemed' from their Judaism by baptism. Thus Wagner's anti-Semitism was rooted in religious and cultural antipathy, not in racial hatred. Not until the end of the nineteenth century, after Wagner's death in 1883, did more extreme notions become mixed with this mentality. Bayreuth, with Cosima as the keeper of the flame, and Chamberlain as the source of ideas, became one of those breeding-grounds in which *völkisch* German jingoism grew into an aggressive political programme. This increasingly poisonous intellectual brew also shaped the political attitudes of the young Winifred. Her fundamental position was backward-looking, strongly nationalist and hostile to the new Weimar republic. On the occasion of every festival and holiday, messages of devotion were sent from Wahnfried to the Kaiser, languishing in exile in Holland.

*

As early as 1919 word of a new harbinger of hope reached Bayreuth. Political friends from Munich reported that an ex-soldier named Hitler was attracting attention with his inflammatory speeches. At that time the Wagner-obsessed veteran of the First World War was still seeking a political home and a future profession. His success as a political agitator, working for right-wing nationalist officers, seemed like a promising start. Yet without patronage from influential Munich circles, Hitler would probably never have achieved more than limited fame in smoke-filled Bavarian beer-cellars. In particular it was the Bechstein and Bruckmann families, respectively piano-makers and publishers, who assisted at the birth of Hitler the politician. It was in their drawing-rooms that the former inmate of men's hostels was cured of his awkward manners and learned to kiss a lady's hand, eat lobster and dress *comme il faut*. There was only one thing his mentors did not have to teach him: the young man was astonishingly omniscient about the music favoured by those circles. Hitler's knowledge of Wagner went a long way to raise his entertainment-value in Munich's 'select' society.

In the official history of the festival and also in Winifred's retrospective account, the first meeting between her and Hitler took place in Wahnfried on 1 October 1923. An encounter of that

> Hitler had expressed the wish to see the house where the
> Master had worked, and to stand by his graveside. In her
> spontaneous way, Winifred said to him: Why don't you come
> to us for breakfast tomorrow. And so he did.
>
> *Walter Schertz-Parey, Winifred Wagner's biographer*

kind on the 'sanctified ground' of Wagner's home may well have a
certain dramatic value – but there had probably been earlier
contacts. As a schoolgirl in Berlin, Winifred had been a frequent
guest of the Bechsteins. For a time, Edwin Bechstein even took
charge of her education. To Hitler, Winifred spoke of the
Bechsteins as 'our mutual friends', and her daughter Friedelind
wrote this about Winifred's enthusiasm for Nazism: 'It was on a
visit to the Bechsteins' house in Munich that Mother became
infected with this fever.' There is another clue that suggests
Winifred Wagner must have had a more than passing acquaintance
with Hitler, even before 1 October 1923. A surveillance report by
the Bavarian police, dated December 1923, states that 'the female
members of the Wahnfried household, in particular, are practising
a veritable Hitler-cult'. A veritable 'cult', after only one meeting?
The almost intimate familiarity which their early correspondence
exudes, and the parcels full of loving gifts sent by Winifred during
Hitler's imprisonment in Landsberg, leave us with only one
possible conclusion: that Adolf and his muse had been close for
quite a long time.

*

Thus we can well understand the friendly reception enjoyed by
Hitler on his first visit to Wahnfried. On the previous evening he
had given a speech at the 'German Day' in Bayreuth, a *völkisch*
event staged by various parties of the extreme right, at which he
was cheered to the echo. Next morning he finally arrived at the
home of the composer, whom he would soon describe as the
'greatest of Germans'. Friedelind Wagner described the moment
with rich irony: 'He walked around on tiptoe and stood entranced

before individual mementoes, as though he were looking at holy relics in a cathedral.' Hitler then walked expectantly through the garden to Richard Wagner's grave, a massive, unadorned stone slab. In 'devout silence', as Winifred wrote, he stood there for several minutes. Then, with a sombre expression, he turned to the descendants of his idol and promised to return the exclusive performing rights in *Parsifal* to the Bayreuth Festival, if at some future time he was ever to exert 'any influence on the destiny of Germany' – a promise which he was not to keep.

Hitler's first entrance into the Wagner family circle left mixed feelings: whereas Siegfried's two sisters were quite appalled that the visitor had appeared in the Holy of Holies wearing 'short pants', that is to say *Lederhosen*, Siegfried himself, and Winifred, seemed extremely affected. This man was obviously bursting with vitality. And then 'those eyes', 'that passion' – as Winifred would repeatedly rhapsodise. Later, Wagner's son Siegfried wrote enthusiastically to a friend: 'Thank God there are still some real men left in Germany! Hitler is a magnificent chap, a true representative of the German soul. He is bound to succeed.'

I must confess that I immediately gained a very great and deep impression of the man as a personality. It was his eyes, most of all, that were enormously attractive.
Winifred Wagner, interview with Hans-Jürgen Syberberg, 1975

He worshipped her, simply because she was Wagner's successor. You see, Wagner was everything to him. And she always welcomed him and looked after him in Bayreuth . . .
Herbert Döhring, Hitler's house-manager at the Berghof

Late in the evening before his visit to Wahnfried, which had thrown the Wagners into such ecstasies, Hitler had paid a remarkable visit to Houston Stewart Chamberlain, the guardian of the Wagnerian intellectual tradition. The Nazi Party's propaganda transformed this meeting with the bedridden old man into an ideological 'handing on of the torch', in which the 'flame' preserved in Bayreuth had set alight the 'fire of national revolution': 'They stretched out their hands to each other. Chamberlain, the prophet of genius and harbinger of the Third Reich, felt that in this simple man of the people the destiny of Germany would be gratifyingly fulfilled.' Precisely what the old philosopher and the young hothead talked about during this nocturnal encounter, history does not relate. Years later, Hitler merely stated that on that day, 30 September 1923, he made his way to the place where first Wagner and then Chamberlain had forged the 'intellectual sword with which we are fighting today'. Chamberlain, for his part, wrote in an open letter that, after his meeting with Hitler, he no longer needed to fear for Germany's future. For the first time in many years he had found 'long and refreshing sleep' and that he really 'did not need to awaken again'.

In recent years historians have put forward the theory that the Nazi Party's representation of Hitler's meeting with H.S. Chamberlain does in fact contain a kernel of truth, to the extent that on that evening Wagner's anti-Semitism had indeed been passed on to Hitler as a programme of annihilation. This audacious theory has given rise to a great deal of argument and will be difficult to substantiate – especially as there is no written record of the encounter. However, there is no disputing how closely the writings of Chamberlain corresponded with Hitler's ideology. Their common denominator became the foundation of the later Nazi regime. The key words are very similar: 'national revolution', 'solution of the Jewish question', 'ethnic community'. Yet what seems more questionable is whether Chamberlain, in his only conversation with the future dictator, imagined that he was setting him on a new course. Hitler had already been harbouring his hatred for the Jews for a long time; and ever since November 1918, dozens of *völkisch* orators had ranted on about a 'national revolution' as a reaction to the 'red' revolution. It is probable that the importance of the meeting between these two anti-Semites lies rather in the fact that the aged thinker made a gift to the still largely insignificant Nazi movement: the accolade of the sacred mount of Bayreuth, thus appointing it the successor to Richard Wagner. Thenceforth

Hitler was cloaked in an aura of intellectual nobility, which he would emphasise for propaganda purposes, whenever the situation demanded.

*

On 9 November 1923 Siegfried and Winifred were staying in Munich. Siegfried was to conduct a concert that evening. But nothing came of it, because that was the day on which the reverential visitor to Wagner's grave intended to make history. Thus it was that the Wagners witnessed the 'March on the Feldherrnhalle' – and its wretched failure – at close quarters. (It would nevertheless be celebrated year by year throughout the Nazi era to the accompaniment of Wagner's 'Death of Siegfried'.) From their hotel room Siegfried and Winifred could follow the bloody action, as the insurgents scattered under the rifle-fire of the Bavarian police. We may suppose that the Wagners had watched this first attempt at a 'national revolution' with considerable hope, and were correspondingly downcast by its outcome. Now their 'bright hope' needed more help than ever. At Winifred's insistence Siegfried drove straight from Munich to Innsbruck, where the injured Goering was being treated in hospital. Richard Wagner's son paid the medical bill and arranged a discreet hideaway for the war-hero and his Swedish wife in Venice.

Winifred returned home and gave Bayreuth's local Nazi group an instantaneous account of the putsch. An eye-witness reported how the 26-year-old woman jumped excitedly on to a table in a hostelry and gave a vivid description of the deeds of Hitler and his men. A few days later, on 12 November, she drafted an open letter, which was printed in a regional newspaper, the *Oberfränkische Zeitung*. 'For years we have been observing with great sympathy and approval the constructive work of Adolf Hitler', she wrote in her 'confession of faith', which ended with the promise: 'I frankly admit that we too are under the spell of his personality, that we too stood by him in happier days and now in his hour of need we will stay true to him.' This public statement by Winifred, with Siegfried's support, casts a revealing light on the political atmosphere in Bavaria at that time.

Insurgents, threatened with conviction and imprisonment, were looked on as the true heroes of a battered nation by those conservatives whose milieu Thomas Dehler tellingly described as a 'Bavarian swamp'. It seemed that the future was in the hands of the nascent Nazi party, and certainly the Wagners intended, with their public intervention, to make it so. At Christmas 1923 Siegfried wrote: 'The Jew and the Jesuit go arm in arm, in order to wipe out the German character. But perhaps this time Satan has miscalculated . . . my wife is fighting like a lioness for Hitler; splendid!'

> It is a strange paradox that my mother, who as an English-woman thought in democratic terms and certainly did not worship authority, took up with a dictator.
> *Wolfgang Wagner in his autobiography*

Winifred Wagner was indeed 'fighting', but not only that, for she was touchingly concerned that Hitler's far from uncomfortable imprisonment in Landsberg should pass as pleasantly as possible. She sent food-parcels, accompanied by affectionate letters ('. . . you know you are with us in spirit'), and even delivered paper and pencils for Hitler's projected book, which a decade later would be published as the barely readable best-seller of the Nazi era, *Mein Kampf*. It was not just the title, but also one of the key sentences, that Hitler copied from Richard Wagner. Just as the composer had written in *Mein Leben*: 'I decided to become a composer', so did the prisoner now write: 'I decided to become a politician.' Hitler never forgot the letters and parcels posted from Bayreuth. Some twenty years later, in his nocturnal monologues at his East Prussian headquarters, the 'Wolf's Lair', the Führer wistfully recalled the loving gifts 'at a time when things were at their worst for me',

*

In the summer of 1924 permission was finally given for the festival to be held again at Bayreuth – the first since the end of the First World

War. By conducting concerts in half the countries of Europe, Siegfried had laid the financial foundations. A trip with Winifred to the United States was intended to attract further wealthy donors. But reports in America's liberal press about the Wagners' political 'leanings' created unexpected obstacles. When they returned home the collection box only contained $8,000, and that had mostly been the result of Winifred's lectures and Siegfried's concerts. Even a meeting with the billionaire motor manufacturer Henry Ford failed to yield the desired result – at least according to official sources. The industrialist could not afford to have his sympathies with German fascism exposed in the press. Nevertheless, the suspicion arose that he had secretly contributed to the 'cause', which the Wagners, too, apparently supported. When, in 1938, Hitler awarded Ford the 'Grand Cross of the Order of the German Eagle', and conveyed 'words of thanks' to him, this theory seemed to be borne out. For that was the highest decoration that could be given to a foreigner.

In March 1924, on their return journey to Germany, the Wagners once more acted as the political envoys of their imprisoned standard-bearer, going to Rome to visit Mussolini, who had already been successful in his 'grab for power'. Yet the leader of the Italian 'blackshirts' did not make a favourable impression on them. 'Nothing but will-power, nothing but force, almost brutality', his Bayreuth visitors maintained. 'Unlike Hitler and Ludendorff, he has not the strength of love.'

The 1924 Bayreuth Festival was a politically inspired event. It was not the flag of republican Germany that flew over the Festspielhaus, but the banner of the imperial eagle. General Ludendorff, who had marched side by side with Hitler up to the Feldherrnhalle, was guest of honour at a performance of *Parsifal*. The democratic press was sharply critical of Siegfried for putting out a slogan about the 'festival of redemption for the German spirit'. Wagner in Bayreuth seemed to be nothing less than a political demonstration, with musical accompaniment, against the 'November criminals' and their republic. Under the laws of today's Federal Republic, this would have been a clear case for the Constitutional Court, yet the Weimar constitution of 1919 offered no effective defence against the internal enemies of democracy. It was only when the audience stood up and sang the German national anthem after a performance of *Die Meistersinger* that the director of the festival felt things were getting out of hand, and had notices reading 'Art for art's sake' posted on the doors of the auditorium.

> I will always remember him with gratitude, because here in Bayreuth he literally sliced the beetroot for me and helped me in every way.
>
> *Winifred Wagner*

It was a year later that Hitler came to the festival – for the first time in his life. Although sentenced to five years in prison, he had served precisely nine months before being released. His introduction to the hallowed atmosphere of the theatre and his reunion with the Wagners aroused feelings of happiness in him: 'I arrived in Bayreuth at eleven o'clock at night', Hitler remembered exactly during the war, 'and early next morning Frau Wagner came and brought me a few flowers. I was thirty-six years old, still had not a care in the world, and the heavens were filled with the sound of violins.' After his release, his relationship with the Wagner heirs became ever closer. Even Siegfried, whom the 'official' historians of Bayreuth like to credit with arm's-length neutrality, in truth got on extremely well with Wahnfried's frequent guest. On one occasion, as another visitor remembered, Siegfried placed his hands on Hitler's shoulders and said: 'Y'know, I *like* you.'

Winifred displayed even greater commitment. In 1926, on Hitler's insistence, she joined the party – as member number 29349, which made her an 'old campaigner'. Under the Nazi regime she would receive the party's 'Gold Award' for this. On the piano that had once belonged to Franz Liszt she played the popular songs of the 'Movement' to her children. They were easier to sing along to than the parts written by her father-in-law. The Wahnfried children were soon calling Hitler by his *nom de guerre*, 'Wolf', and were always glad to see him. He would play with them for hours and told them bedtime stories. Wolfgang Wagner's memories of his nice uncle are still as vivid as ever: '"Wolf" always behaved in a friendly and courteous way and – contrary to popular belief – never chewed the carpets.'

Hitler gradually took on the role of 'substitute father' to the two Wagner boys, as Wieland's wife Gertrud later confirmed. Only his sister Friedelind, the 'whinger of Wahnfried', told of a rather different Hitler. Later, when in exile in America, she complained that 'his finger-nails always had too much skin growing over them,' and that he 'continually chewed his food while talking, occasionally breaking off to stare critically at one or other of us'.

Winifred fed him, dressed him and gave him lessons in elementary manners, took him to the opera-house, provided him with money and gave parties in order to introduce him to influential people.

Friedelind Wagner

He visited the family but was never drawn into it, in the sense that my mother never said to him: Listen, Wolf, what do you think? Is Wieland right to do such and such? She never asked his advice.

Wolfgang Wagner on Winifred's relationship with Hitler

Winifred, on the other hand, had more important priorities than 'Wolf's' inadequate manicure. In many respects her friend from Munich was a replacement for Siegfried, who was so often otherwise engaged. She would follow Hitler on his election tours, and when they met at night in some remote hostelry she no doubt found a little compensation for the privations of her marriage. It was a close friendship, both personal and political, and one that naturally had the Bayreuth rumour-machine working overtime. Did 'Wolf' and Winifred have a physical relationship? Lacking any proof, we are thrown back on speculation.

After the war Winifred steadfastly denied any intimacy. Nevertheless, we know from reliable witnesses that after 1930 she was more generous with her favours, and shared a bed with Heinz Tietjen, the artistic director of the Bayreuth Festival. Did she give in to Hitler as well? Or should we rather ask whether Hitler had any physical intentions at all towards her? After all, did not Wagner

– particularly in *Parsifal* – praise abstinence as a source of strength? Could Hitler possibly have reconciled his quasi-religious veneration of the composer with a carnal liaison with his daughter-in-law? From the sources currently available to us, no final answer can be given. Thus it remains more than questionable whether there was any justification for the strange jealousy of Hitler, that Siegfried displayed to his wife in his last years. In Wieland's Opus 17, entitled *Walamund*, a tame wolf comes on to the stage, then at the end of the work, reveals his true nature and savages a sheep. The master of the Bayreuth household certainly gave occasional vent to his annoyance by criticising Winifred's now extremely corpulent appearance. 'Wini, don't eat so much', he once hissed at her when they were dining with guests.

> She always wore the trousers, and was always the one who decided things.
> *Erika Jansen, chorus member at the Bayreuth Festival*

> She did everything; there was no job that she wouldn't tackle.
> *Wolfgang Wagner*

The couple's little jealousies actually reflected a relative shift in authority on the 'green hill'. Increasingly Winifred was taking the helm. Her tireless involvement in politics, the firm hand regulating the Wahnfried household, and organising the business side of the festival, all demanded the kind of energy that the happy-go-lucky 'Fidi' could not offer. The age-difference between husband and wife was becoming ever more noticeable. Siegfried Wagner was approaching sixty, whereas Winifred did not celebrate her thirtieth birthday until 1927. Her portrait rightfully appeared alongside Siegried's in the festival programme. We have the assiduous diarist Joseph Goebbels to thank for this snapshot from those days: 'Frau Wagner accompanied me into dinner', Goebbels noted on 9 May 1926, on a visit to Wahnfried, 'and she poured out her troubles to me. Siegfried is so worn-out and flabby. Ugh! His father, the

1 'Me, mistress of the greatest man in Germany and on earth . . .' An entry from Eva Braun's diary, 1935.

2 'She wanted to be centre stage . . .' Eva's respectable middle-class family set clear standards, but the teenage flapper had her own ideas.

3 'The Führer has a right to a private life . . .' To the servants at the Berghof, Eva Braun was Hitler's companion.

4 'A nice German girl . . .' Despite the 'Hausfrau' pose, Eva Braun did not really fit the Nazis' female stereotype.

5 'Eva Braun is not a factor in history . . .' The criminal of the century, and at his side the mistress who remained without influence on his political decisions.

6 'She loved Hitler, she worshipped him . . .' Hitler and Magda Goebbels on an election tour in 1932.

7 'She is very clever and understands things better than many a top politico . . .' Magda and the newly appointed Reich Minister for Popular Enlightenment.

8 'She is a valuable support for me in these difficult times . . .' The Goebbels family (top right: Magda's son, Harald Quandt).

9 '. . . I bore them for Hitler and the Third Reich . . .' The bodies of the six Goebbels children, 1945.

10 'She couldn't tell the difference between the SA and the SS . . .' Leni Riefenstahl and Heinrich Himmler at the 1934 Nazi Party rally.

11 'She's a clever girl . . .' Leni Riefenstahl talking to Goebbels about her film *Festival of Nations*.

12 'He praised Riefenstahl for her great individuality . . .' Leni Riefenstahl holds hands with her idol.

13 'Highly esteemed master . . .' 'Little Winnie' with her husband Siegfried at Wahnfried, the house built by Richard Wagner.

14 'Vigorous heredity . . .' Winifred and Siegfried with their children (from left) Verena, Friedelind, Wieland and Wolfgang.

15 'A friendship based on mutual respect . . .' Winifred Wagner after a motor-trip with Hitler.

16 'I don't know much about politics . . .' Hermann Goering and Winifred Wagner leaving Bayreuth's Festspielhaus.

17 'The commercial success she's had is huge . . .' Zarah Leander with (left) Joseph Goebbels, the Minister of Propaganda.

18 'Absolutely no interest in politics . . .' Zarah Leander collecting money for the Winter Welfare fund.

19 'It's all in that voice . . .' Zarah Leander as a singer, with Paul Hörbiger as her pianist, in the film *Die Grosse Liebe*.

20 'I've only ever played one role . . .' Zarah Leander with director Alfred Braun in 1953.

21 'I wanted a happy, golden childhood . . .' Marlene (right) with her sister Elisabeth, her mother and her father Erich Otto Dietrich, a police officer.

22 'Her beauty was captivating but cold . . .' Two men who were unhappily in love with Marlene Dietrich: Joseph von Sternberg (left) and novelist Erich Maria Remarque.

23 'I'm not going to sit here and let the war pass me by . . .' Marlene Dietrich in North Africa with the great love of her life, French actor Jean Gabin.

24 'I wanted to help bring the war to an end . . .' The star was happy to accept the rigours of service life.

25 'I am, thank God, a Berliner . . .' West Berlin's mayor, Willi Brandt, welcomes
Marlene Dietrich in 1960.

Master, would be ashamed of him. I like his wife. I'd like to have her as a girl-friend. A young woman weeps because the son is not as the Master was.'

> A woman with class. I wish they were all like that. And fanatically on our side.
>
> *Joseph Goebbels, diary, 8 May 1926*

In 1929 the Wagners made a joint will. True, Siegfried was still apparently in the best of health, yet his sixtieth birthday seemed occasion enough to take steps to safeguard the future. Winifred was named as the heiress of 'the entire estate', and the children they had between them were to inherit after her death – a great demonstration of trust in the young woman, which ignored the fact that she had hardly a clue about the artistic side of running the festival. Furthermore, Siegfried added another – decisive – clause, which was quite openly directed at nice Uncle 'Wolf': in the event of Winifred's 'remarriage' the will made sure that all rights and duties under it would pass immediately to their children. This was apparently intended to prevent Hitler, the Wagner fan, from gaining dominance over the 'green hill' by taking Winifred to the altar. From Siegfried's point of view this was no doubt a justifiable suspicion, for as well as the talk of Hitler's secret meetings with Winifred, it had also come to his ear that Hitler had, with his own hand, produced sketches for stage-sets and made suggestions about productions at Bayreuth.

Then something happened that no-one had reckoned with: only a year later the will took effect and thus had a decisive effect on the rest of Winifred's life. In the spring of 1930, her 92-year-old mother-in-law, Cosima Wagner, the master's widow, died. The one-time 'high-priestess' had been bedridden for the final years of her life. Wolfgang Wagner can still remember how the hordes of grand-children made an affectionate if disrespectful rumpus around the old lady. Apparently Wieland, Friedelind, Verena and he would burst into her room and 'tickle her feet to see if she still reacted'. And they took an exuberant delight in 'playing with her false teeth'.

Cosima's funeral was akin to a state occasion. It seems that Siegfried could scarcely cope with the loss. He had only been fourteen when his father died and since then his relationship with his mother had been very ambivalent. He had certainly suffered from her high expectations of him, yet his veneration for her and for the strength she devoted to making Bayreuth the Grail of the Wagner legacy was genuine enough.

Only three months after Cosima was buried, Siegfried suffered a heart-attack during rehearsals for the 1930 Bayreuth Festival. Winifred led him from the stage, supporting him on a strong arm. Three weeks later, on 4 August, the son of Richard Wagner was dead too. The festival, which was now in progress, continued without interruption. At the funeral a column of SA storm-troopers from Bayreuth joined the procession. Hitler sent a wreath, which the mourners felt was 'larger than necessary'.

> . . . I must rely on the future alone . . . Then the time will come in which pride in your friend shall be my thanks for much, which today I cannot begin to repay you for . . .
> *Adolf Hitler to Winifred Wagner, 30 December 1927*

True to her pragmatic nature, Winifred did not spend too much time in mourning. Only a day after Siegfried's death she circulated a note to the staff of the festival, in which she announced her testamentary claim to be director of the Festspielhaus and called for the 'co-operation of everyone' in carrying out her 'weighty task'. From the outset, her sovereignty over the 'green hill' had a dictatorial character. 'The only thing that matters to me', she remarked on her ruling principle, 'is that the operas are staged as I mean them to be.'

This 'seizure of power' by a woman considered a musical innocent led the great conductor, Arturo Toscanini, to boycott the 1931 festival – for reasons of 'artistic disillusionment', as he publicly announced. Yet Winifred had the insight to employ the right kind of people. Toscanini was replaced by the equally renowned Wilhelm Furtwängler; for Bayreuth's stage design she recruited the pioneering Emil Preetorius, and as director, the general manager of the Prussian State Theatre, Heinz Tietjen. She had gleaned these recommended names from her husband before he died. For Bayreuth the most important appointment was probably that of the short, bespectacled Tietjen, whom the Wagner children soon christened 'the owl'. This ambivalent figure, who later became a protégé of Hermann Göring, to all appearances toed the Nazi line, but in truth was as politically volatile – swerving between compromise and resistance – as he was artistically brilliant; in many ways he was comparable with that other man of the theatre, Gustaf Gründgens.

*

With the verve of the new directorial team and Winifred's purposeful style, Wagner productions at Bayreuth in the early 1930s under-went revolutionary changes. The rickety stage-sets, some of which dated from the original era of the Festspielhaus, were replaced by modern and striking décor. Outmoded staging techniques were junked with a positively blasphemous enthusiasm, a move that naturally provoked vehement resistance from traditional Wagnerians. The conflict, in which the 'conservatives' tried to keep unchanged all the elements 'upon which the eye of the Master had rested', lasted for years and even touched on questions of 'ideology'. By appointing Tietjen and Preetorius, Winifred opened herself to reproach for admitting 'racially suspect' or at least politically unreliable staff into the Holy of Holies. However, thanks to her toughness – and to Hitler's protection after 1933 – she emerged as the victor in the 'battle with the nineteenth century'. Her two sisters-in-law, who were among those stirring up the opposition, were pushed out into the cold – 'in the most despicable way', as Eva Chamberlain complained in 1932. In this fight no holds were barred, something that an 'old Wagnerian' named Zinstag, who lived in Switzerland, found out to his cost. He was curtly informed that for the good of his health he should 'never contemplate setting foot again on German soil'.

Winifred Wagner also made a clean break with her own personal past. She seems to have wanted to erase her late husband from her memory. She distanced herself from his works, which bore such unusual titles as *Bearskins, Commandment of the Stars* and *Banadietrich*, and were among the most frequently performed German operas at the beginning of the twentieth century. She tried, with some success, to prevent them being staged. The name of Richard Wagner's son was largely removed from the official history of the Bayreuth Festival. Winifred turned his study into a shrine to Richard Wagner. This 'control of the past' even extended to a certain Walter Aign, Siegfried's illegitimate son by a pastor's daughter, who was employed as a *repetiteur* at the Festspielhaus. He was fired without notice.

Was all this no more than a young widow's effort to establish her own identity, as well-intentioned biographers of Winifred maintain? Or was it rather the belated revenge of a woman who had patiently endured the humiliation of 'Fidi's' escapades? The eagerness with which Winifred went to work after her husband's death suggests, at least, that her grief was accompanied by a sense of liberation.

My grandmother did tell me more than once, that from the autumn of 1930 – my grandfather having died during the 1930 festival – the idea was certainly in Hitler's mind to marry Winifred.

Gottfried Wagner

As the Führer's 'bride', she had no need to flatter the party bigwigs. Uncle Wolf would understand her, she knew that.
Rudolf Augstein, editor of Der Spiegel magazine, 1994

Now at last she was free to meet 'Uncle Wolf' whenever she liked. Hitler's NSDAP was no longer just a right-wing splinter group but a serious force in politics, and almost every time the ambitious agitator travelled north from Munich to Berlin, he would stop over at Wahnfried. However, the atmosphere in the collapsing Weimar republic, now close to civil war, was such that Hitler was obliged to 'maintain the highest secrecy', or so he claimed. It is certainly true that he usually arrived after dark, and the bedtime stories he told the children were descriptions of his 'dangerous political adventures', as Friedelind Wagner recalls with disdain. As before, he rendezvous'd with Winifred in secluded inns and restaurants. Details have survived of various meetings at the Behringersmühle, in the hilly district of northern Bavaria known as 'Franconian Switzerland'.

On one occasion the *galant* even allowed himself to be driven by the enthusiastic Winifred, as she later related with pride: 'There was I, sitting at the wheel with him beside me – something which must have seemed very odd to him, because whenever he was being driven by his usual chauffeur, and they passed a woman driver, he would always shout: "Look out, a woman! Woman at the wheel!" But in order to come here unrecognised, and to avoid attracting attention, he did in fact sit beside me in the car and even complimented me on my driving skill.' Winifred could now indulge her lifelong lust for travel, without having to take into account the plans of a spouse. Outside the festival period she would often turn up in Berlin and visit Tietjen, or go to the cinema with Hitler. On one occasion she even went to the opera with the Papal Nunzio, Cardinal Pacelli, who later became Pope Pius XII.

> As a powerful woman in her own right, my grandmother would never have been satisfied with being Frau Hitler-Wagner. That must be said very clearly. Running the festival was much more important for her, because there she had very different opportunities to make her mark.
>
> *Gottfried Wagner*

Nonetheless, on 30 January 1933 Winifred Wagner was at home in Bayreuth. Wolfgang Wagner tells us that on that day his mother had excitedly called him over to listen to the radio. The speaker announced that Hitler had just been appointed Reich Chancellor by President Hindenburg. Her friend, who had once come to Bayreuth wearing shorts and had made a pilgrimage to the grave of the 'Master', was now Chancellor of the German Reich! Winifred was dismayed rather than delighted. 'Poor Wolf',

Wolfgang remembers her saying, 'I can't imagine he'll be there very long.' Indeed, her fear was shared by many who wrongly predicted that Hitler's cabinet, like its predecessors, would only be granted a brief existence. But 'Uncle Wolf' had no intention of following the 'legal' route to power as a constitutional government. With breathtaking speed the wolf shed his sheep's clothing and replaced the Weimar republic by his 'Third Reich', which was nothing other than an inhuman dictatorship that enslaved the majority of the German people with its dire blend of terror and potent stagecraft.

Needless to say, the new Nazi state's often melodramatic self-presentation reached a climax with the Bayreuth Festival of 1933. Rudolf Bockel, who sang the role of Hans Sachs in *Die Meistersinger*, remembered how the crowds appeared 'intoxicated'. The whole historic town was bedecked with swastika banners. The approach to the Festspielhaus was lined with SA stormtroopers, and the streets echoed to shouts of *Heil Hitler*. Bayreuth's bookshops no longer displayed Wagner's *Mein Leben*, but Hitler's *Mein Kampf*, in pride of place. When the Führer's motorcade finally drove up the 'green hill', the atmosphere was as euphoric as a crowd scene in *Die Meistersinger*. Newsreels from that time show moments of exultation that were not equalled again until the victory parade following the defeat of France in 1940: young girls weeping tears of joy, a collective frenzy, national hysteria. The matronly châtelaine, Winifred Wagner, was waiting at the entrance to the Festspielhaus and greeted Hitler with a devoted smile. He in turn addressed her as 'dear lady' and avoided using the intimate pronoun *Du* that had characterised their many friendly meetings before. She replied with *Mein Führer*. It was as if the high priestess and keeper of the Grail were laying her treasure at the feet of the new arrival. At that moment Bayreuth seemed to be the sacred heart of the new Nazi Germany.

> She permitted and tolerated the way Nazi propaganda exploited the prestige of the festival and in effect used the Bayreuth stage to present itself.
>
> *Wolfgang Wagner in his autobiography*

Once inside the Festspielhaus, however, the man who wished to fulfil the mission of 'Rienzi' in modern times, forbade all tributes to himself. Here in the Holy of Holies attention should be given to the 'Master' alone. Hitler had a leaflet distributed to everyone attending the festival, which read: 'The Führer requests that at the end of the performance there should be no singing of the national anthem or the Horst Wessel Song. There is no finer expression of the German spirit than the immortal works of the Master himself.' Not until the lights went down did Hitler step into the box in which King Ludwig II had once listened to Wagner's operas. And as in the days of the Bavarian monarchy, the audience stood up in silence and did not sit down again until Hitler had taken his seat. The appearances of 'Uncle Wolf' were full of symbolism. They gave the impression that, in his own emotional way, he was taking possession of the temple mount which guarded the legacy of Richard Wagner.

> Hitler is rescuing Germany and Bayreuth from the powers of darkness, from the Bolshevists and the Old Wagnerians.
>
> *Winifred Wagner*

Earlier Hitler had been obliged to take clandestine steps to ensure that the festival could take place at all. In the spring and summer of 1933 Winifred was appalled to discover that hundreds of foreign ticket reservations had been cancelled. Even in Germany demand had been flagging. The financial forecasts showed a deficit and all attempts to obtain state funding appeared to have failed. Hitler himself was so preoccupied with securing his own position that for months he had been deaf to his lady-friend in Bayreuth. 'We have been frozen into isolation', noted Lieselotte Schmidt, a close friend of Winifred, in a tone of voice typical of that time. 'The hate campaign against Bayreuth, which at root is of purely Jewish origin, stops at nothing in its lies and unpleasantness.' But then Winifred did finally manage to get Hitler to answer the telephone. 'Wolf has taken our troubles on himself', Lieselotte rejoiced in another letter to her parents.

'He summoned Frau Wagner to Berlin. She flew there, and within a quarter of an hour we had the necessary help – and how! It is just as we always thought. He has no idea what is going on, but among those around him there are voices which, for all-too-obvious reasons, are far from well-disposed towards us.' Hitler had instructed the SA, the Women's Nazi Movement, and the Nazi Federation of Schoolteachers to make large block purchases of tickets and pass them on to 'deserving' party loyalists. Then, a year later, the Reich Ministry of Propaganda became responsible for the block purchasing of tickets and paid Winifred the sum of 364,000 Reichsmarks – more than a third of her total budget.

In a trice, Hitler's seizure of power had transformed the financially rickety family business into a semi-nationalised undertaking, enjoying generous subsidies. Its task, though never made explicit, was to serve the presentational purposes of the regime. It goes without saying that the festival was exempt from all taxes during the Nazi period. If one also takes into account the 50,000 Reichsmarks that Hitler donated from his 'private money-box' for every new production, the fatal interdependence of the Wagners and Nazism is only too clear. The border between art and politics had virtually disappeared. The great novelist Thomas Mann, himself an ardent Wagnerian, was right when he referred to Bayreuth as 'Hitler's court theatre'. Meanwhile Winifred was particularly pleased about the improvement in the festival's finances: 'At last I have firm ground under my feet', she declared after the 1934 season.

Even outside the festival season it was Wagner who set the tone in Hitler's Germany. The word 'Awake!' from the chorus of *Die Meistersinger*, became the slogan 'Germany awake' on the banners of the Nazi Party, rallies and celebrations resounded to music from Wagner's operas, and the Reich Party Congress opened with the theme from *Rienzi*. Newspapers and magazines in the Nazi-controlled press were filled with articles drawing attention to 'Bayreuth's mission for the Third Reich'. While Jewish and avant-garde artists were branded 'degenerate', Richard Wagner's music was held up by contrast as a shining example of 'healthy national art'.

The first festival held under the swastika was opened by the propaganda minister, Joseph Goebbels, with the words: 'There is probably no work so close in spirit to our age and its intellectual and psychological tensions as Richard Wagner's *Die Meistersinger*. How often in recent years has its rousing chorus, *"Wacht auf, es nahet gen dem Tag"* (Awake, for morn approaches), echoed the faith and longing of Germans, as a tangible symbol of the reawakening of the German people from the deep political and spiritual coma of November 1918.'

In the climate of Bayreuth's elevation to a 'national' institution, rumours of wedding-bells were soon circulating. How fitting it would be if the 'Führer and Reich Chancellor' were to seal his alliance with the 'great lady' of Bayreuth by matrimony, and thus visibly demonstrate the fusion of Wagner's 'mission' with that of the new state. Houston Stewart Chamberlain's companion, Hans von Wolzogen, was already rhapsodising about the dream couple. It was, proclaimed the elderly windbag, as though 'Baldur was consorting with Fricka'. In Berlin jokes were soon going the rounds – how should the fecund Winifred be formally addressed after marrying Wolf: as 'Venerable Reich Mother', perhaps? Hitler's half-sister, Angela Raubal, later told how she had heard of proposals by Winifred that the Bayreuth-Berlin axis should be strengthened by dynastic bonds.

> Then there was another attempt to promote a marriage between Hitler and the Wahnfried household: Hitler was to marry Friedelind Wagner.
> *From the newspaper* Frankenpost, *1 August 1950*

Yet it was probably due to Hitler that the wedding-bells remained silent. True, he is known to have declared that if he 'were ever to marry, Frau Wagner would be a suitable candidate' – but marriage was simply not on his agenda. Winifred's daughter Friedelind remembered how, as a schoolgirl, she would inform anyone willing to listen, in a strong local accent: 'Me Mum'd like ter, but Uncle Wolf ain't 'avin it.' Doubtless only a small consideration in this was Hitler's knowledge of Siegfried's last wish – that Winifred could only marry again at the cost of losing her power over Bayreuth. A man who could drive a coach and horses through the nation's constitution would not allow

mere testamentary stipulations to get in his way. Indeed the true
obstacle was probably Hitler's self-characterisation as the
'solitary' chosen one, who needed all his strength in order to
lead his people. This was a familiar theme that also echoes
through Wagner's operas. Compared with the mythical heights,
which the opera buff from Linz now imagined he inhabited, the
joys of family life seemed to him like an undignified come-down.
Characteristically, he impressed upon Winifred several times that
only by remaining unmarried could she continue to occupy the
position of 'queen' – yes, he really did use the word 'queen'.

*

Since Richard Wagner's day the 'green hill' had been transformed
from an opera centre to a place with sinister political emanations.
The people most responsible for this were Cosima, Siegfried and
Winifred Wagner, who as directors of the festival had welcomed
and furthered this development – but so also were those
conservative and nationalist Wagnerians such as H.S. Chamberlain,
who seemed to follow the supposed message of the 'Master' like
the tail of a comet. After 1933 this 'cauldron of German
nationalism' became an integral element in Hitler's Reich; and
Wagner's 'mission' was now an ingredient in the confused and evil
brew of Nazi ideology. Anyone who dared to voice any criticism
was heading for trouble.

In February 1933 the writer Thomas Mann, an avowed lover of
Wagner's music, gave a lecture on the 'Sufferings and Greatness of
Richard Wagner', in which he bemoaned the exploitation of the
composer by the Nazis and pointed out the diversity of Wagner's
world of ideas. In doing so he provoked a storm of outrage.
Leading figures in the world of arts, among them Richard Strauss,
penned a 'Letter of protest from Wagner's city, Munich', and the
official Nazi newspaper, the *Völkischer Beobachter*, scourged
the 'semi-Bolshevist' Mann for having brought 'shame' on the
Germans with his lecture. The novelist rightly took this smear-
campaign to be an incitement to violence and soon fled into exile.

The Nazis' new 'ethnic community' seemed in many ways to
recall the atmosphere of productions of the *Meistersinger*. It was

no coincidence that Goebbels praised that particular work as 'the incarnation of all that is German'; it contained everything, he said, 'that defines and fulfils the cultural soul of Germany'. Goebbels also reserved special praise for Hitler's favourite opera, *Rienzi* – even though this early work of Wagner's has an un-Germanic, Roman theme and is so weak in its musical structure that to date it has never been produced at Bayreuth.

Yet by this time art had long since ceased to be the 'question'. Nazi writings that have survived are full of examinations of Wagner from an 'ideological' standpoint. For instance, the author of a pamphlet entitled 'Richard Wagner and the New Germany', a certain Alfred Grunsky, described the *Ring of the Nibelungs* as a 'powerful artistic interpretation of racial ideas'. The *Völkischer Beobachter*, needless to say, added fuel to the flames. In a leading article by Goebbels we read: 'Richard Wagner has taught us what a Jew is. Let us listen to him, we who have finally freed ourselves from enslavement by these *Untermenschen* through the words and deeds of Adolf Hitler. Wagner tells us everything: through his writings and through his music, whose every note breathes the pure essence of Germany.' A catalogue of all the Nazi quotations that refer to Wagner would fill a thick book. This does not mean, however, that the composer was the intellectual progenitor of the Holocaust; but its true progenitor, Hitler, saw himself clearly as the self-appointed successor to Richard Wagner.

Incidentally, over the years, Hitler's preferences changed where Wagner was concerned. After the 'seizure of power' he was no longer so keen on hearing the 'ethnic messages' of the *Meistersinger*. He preferred to fill his ears with the particularly dark and emotionally charged passages from the closing act of *Tristan* or the funeral music from *Götterdämmerung*. The latter became his favourite opera of all. On several occasions he travelled to Bayreuth specially to see it performed. One can only begin to understand the perverted personality of this mass murderer if one takes account of his weakness for oppressive and heady musical moods. As a politician he was anything but rational, was incapable of reaching decisions after logical consideration. The dictator acted pretty much as the mood took him, following an 'inner voice', as he often claimed, and believing in a guiding 'Providence'. In the early years of his tyranny, this approach was still bringing him success. In the end his irrational actions led to the pointless death of millions.

*

It is probable that Wagner's late work, *Parsifal*, exerted a special influence on Hitler's view of the world. The solemn religiosity of this opera seems to have been the model for a number of Hitler's speeches in which, with a voice filled with emotion, he regularly succeeded in creating a kind of collective stupor among his faithful. If we look at the films made of the regime's memorial ceremonies, such as the annual charade accompanying the 9 November anniversary of Hitler's (failed) putsch in Munich, it is easy to see their crude affinity with the liturgical elements of Christian worship. The cult of the 'bloodstained banners', the 'eternal flame' on the tombs of the fallen, the monotonous chanting of the names of the 'martyrs of the Movement', and the solitary choreography of the celebrant – on 9 November it was usually the Führer's deputy, Rudolf Hess. All this was intended to underline the fact that National Socialism wanted to be more than just a political programme. Even the many instructions, couched in bureaucratic language, for the 'Order of Political Celebration', reflect the direly pseudo-religious character of the 'Movement'.

However, yet another idea seems to have been filched from *Parsifal*: the summoning of the 'chosen' to a 'Holy Grail' of pure blood. The SS *Ordensburgen* (elite training colleges) were strikingly reminiscent of Richard Wagner's Grail Mount. Was not the Nazi racial obsession, with its 'Certificates of Aryan Heredity' and its notions of selective breeding, just another slant on the Wagnerian principle of the 'chosen'? Can we not derive the call for 'purification of the blood' directly from *Parsifal*? And an even worse suspicion: does the opera not contain hidden instructions for the way Himmler and Eichmann acted under Nazism? Put in such an extreme form, these recently proposed theories do not stand comparison with the actual evidence. There is nothing to indicate a direct link between the opera and Hitler's extermination programme – nor with the 'elite' SS personnel who carried it out.

The president of the Danzig senate, Hermann Rauschning, reported that the dictator had revealed *Parsifal* to him as a call for 'blood purification' by a 'select group of those possessing true knowledge'. However, historians have cast considerable doubt on the reliability of this source. Rauschning probably made the whole thing up. It is true that, in the notorious painting from 1935, Hitler had himself portrayed in the gleaming armour of a knight of the Grail – but then why were performances of *Parsifal* banned throughout the Reich as soon as war broke out? The fact is that Wagner's last opera must be excluded as a direct model, because in Nazi eyes it was too readily misunderstood and was not extreme enough. For in *Parsifal* the future leader of the 'sacred community' was to be no more than an unwitting 'gateway of purity' and Kundry, the character representing 'impure blood', is not in the end 'annihilated' – but 'redeemed' through baptism.

*

'Parsifal is daft' was the refreshingly straightforward verdict of Winifred Wagner's children on their grandfather's complex and significant work. For them, the beginning of the Third Reich brought a youth as untroubled as it was privileged. The fact that all four came home from school with no more than mediocre grades, was amply made up for by the quasi-ennoblement that Hitler conferred on them. When the young Wagners were bored with the Hitler Youth, they simply quit. Mother's good connections with the Reich Chancellery made that possible. Wolfgang Wagner recalls that for him – unlike just about any other young German – there were no consequences to fear. 'I told "Wolf" and he said he would have done exactly the same.'

> She actually approved of her two sons leaving the Hitler Youth.
>
> *Walter Schertz-Parey, Winifred Wagner's biographer*

At school the Wagner heirs were, needless to say, a huge success at coffee-time with their stories about 'Uncle Wolf'.

For a time Hitler even granted the two Wagner boys a special honour – exclusive to them and no-one else except his 'court photographer' Hoffmann – the right to take pictures of him in person. When he posed for Wolfgang and Wieland, an eye-witness tells us, he seemed to have 'all the time in the world'. In this way the boys were able to earn themselves 'a nice wad of cash'. Since Wolfgang also owned a small movie-camera, a number of home movies of the Führer in the Wagner family circle have survived. They show a relaxed Hitler in a pale grey suit, chatting to Winifred as they walk across the lawn, and later lifting a cup, presumably of tea, to his lips. Watching this garden idyll, one cannot help recalling Hannah Arendt's phrase about the 'banality of evil'.

*

Neither in Wolfgang's amateur films, nor in photos, do we ever see Heinz Tietjen with Hitler. The wily genius behind Bayreuth, without whom the festivals would have been almost inconceivable, deliberately avoided Hitler's company. Whenever Hitler stopped over in Bayreuth, Tietjen became 'invisible'. Nonetheless, we are told that Winifred would have been only too happy to see 'Wolf' and 'Heinz' photographed together. For Tietjen had become a permanent fixture in her life. He had rather quickly taken over the position that she would have preferred to give to Hitler – if the latter had not been so abstemious.

Pragmatist that she was, Winifred had also made an unambiguous offer to her 'Heinz', by declaring him to be her 'appointed one', and at the same time naming him 'artistic director'. After the war, Tietjen described it in this way: 'She begged me, she implored me. She all but fell on her knees in front of me. I was unable to resist.'

At that time Winifred Wagner was in her mid-thirties and had always had a weakness for men who had something special. Tietjen – like her late husband Siegfried, and even her 'Wolf' – did not cut much of a figure as a male. The 'Owl' looked weak and weedy, particularly when standing beside the statuesque Winifred. Nonetheless he could,

My mother was then called all sorts of names by senior Nazis like Rosenberg: how could she, as a long-standing Party member, give the artistic directorship to a Social Democrat like Tietjen? I can still remember my mother's retort – two years after the advent of the Third Reich: I hire people for their ability not for their party card.

Wofgang Wagner

Politics meant nothing to Winifred. She was interested in people.

Walter Schertz-Parey, Winifred Wagner's biographer

as Wolfgang Wagner tells us, be quite a charmer, witty, intelligent and somehow mysterious. Whenever he came to Bayreuth for rehearsals, Winifred was alive with anticipation. 'Frau Wagner was in raptures, a totally different person', the children's nanny, Liselotte Schmidt, recalls. She had acquired an apartment next to Tietjen's in Berlin, and we know from the opera-singer Bockelmann that this relationship, if not others, went beyond the purely platonic. On one occasion, Bockelmann tells us, he called unannounced on the two guardians of Bayreuth in Tietjen's Berlin office and caught them in a 'richly comic posture'.

As opera-lovers saw it, the part played by Tietjen was highly beneficial to Bayreuth. Since he also controlled the Berlin Opera House, he was able to engage 'the best voices in the Reich' for the festival. Thanks to him, Preetorius and Furtwängler achieved the highest artistic standards in such productions as the 1936 *Lohengrin*. Recordings made at the time can fully stand comparison, the experts assure us, with the best of today's offerings. Yet the moral judgement that should be passed on these artistic treasures remains a matter of controversy.

Many of those artists, who in the Third Reich enjoyed state support and generous salaries, insisted after the war that they had only been trying to ensure the survival of art through those dark days. Quite a number, including Winifred Wagner and Heinz

Tietjen, were occasionally able to use their good connections to save people from persecution. As Tietjen wrote in a 1945 statement justifying his actions, they had never served the purposes of propaganda. In fact, they had maintained a constant attitude of 'inward rejection'. It is certainly difficult to judge them according to the prevailing conditions of the time. It is a fact that even the Bayreuth productions during the Nazi era hardly display any evidence of distortion for propaganda reasons. There were no swastikas decorating the auditorium – as there were in many other German theatres. After the war, Tietjen was able to claim links – albeit loose ones – with the resistance movement headed by Field-Marshal von Witzleben and the ex-mayor of Leipzig, Carl Goerdeler. Yet against Tietjen and all the others the accusation stands, that their supreme artistry provided Hitler with just the platform he needed for his propaganda and self-promotion. Even if the orchestra-pit did offer a refuge for a few persecuted for their homosexuality or political convictions, what was the value of artistry, when in the stalls sat the tormentors and exterminators of millions, listening reverently to the performance. The fact that Hitler, by way of a thank-you, elevated both Tietjen and Furtwängler to the rank of Councillor of State makes a fair judgement even more difficult.

> It was typical of Winifred Wagner that she constantly repeated the opinions of others. Those instances of derogatory comments on the Nazi elite or about other women . . . if one examines them critically they were basically an accumulation of other people's views. So it was never her own critical analysis.
>
> *Gottfried Wagner*

It was Winifred who played a particularly important part in rescuing victims of persecution, by virtue of her good connections with 'the very top'. Not surprisingly the chief beneficiaries of her advocacy were musicians or members of the festival staff. This was usually an easy matter for Winifred. For when dealing with servants of the Wagner temple, Hitler's 'principles' became oddly flexible. At the 1937 festival, for example, he chatted in a relaxed way in public with the celebrated singer Max Lorenz and his wife Lotte – even though everyone knew that Lorenz was gay and the woman he had married for appearances' sake was Jewish. The couple survived the war unharmed. Sometimes, however, Tietjen and Winifred also stood up for people who were completely unknown. In some cases the two found out from 'good friends' in senior positions about imminent arrests and were able to warn the people concerned. The conductor Leo Blech and the baritone Herbert Janssen stated after the war that this was how they were able to leave Germany in time. In all this, Winifred was playing a tricky double role, since frequent or too public action against state terror could of course prejudice her own position as well. In 1937, when Goebbels telephoned her at Hitler's request to demand that she dismiss all homosexuals on her staff, Winifred did in fact indicate her willingness to co-operate. 'It's very bad luck on Bayreuth', the minister noted with ill-disguised glee. 'We'll have to take the vacuum-cleaner to them. Spoke to Frau Wagner. She is very upset about it. But she sees that things can't go on as they are.'

> Regarding my dealings with people, I never let the Party tell me what to do. I always kept up my relationships with Jewish friends or those married to Jews and as far as it was in my power I helped Jews who were completely unknown either to them or to me.
>
> *Winifred Wagner*

During the years of peace, from 1933 to 1939, Hitler was a regular guest at the Bayreuth festivals. In 1936 performances were suspended for the duration of the Berlin Olympics, specially so that the dictator could attend both events. From that year on, during the opera season, Hitler occupied 'Siegfried Wagner House', an annexe on the left-hand side of Wahnfried, which had by now been extended. At his request, Winifred had put the building at his disposal and he moved in bag and baggage, along with bodyguards, personal servants and his vegetarian cook. The opera-loving Reich Chancellor continued to insist that whenever he sat down to a meal in Bayreuth, a member of the Wagner family should join him.

For his entourage, who were far from sharing the Führer's obsession with Wagner, these must have been trying days. His photographer, Heinrich Hoffmann, later gave this account: 'For Hitler the festival meant recuperation – and so he thought he was also giving his retinue a treat, by inviting them to Bayreuth for a week or more. He paid for their tickets out of his own pocket. But not everyone greeted Hitler's invitation with unalloyed joy. Many would have preferred to go up into the mountains or down to the sea, instead of sitting in a stifling auditorium every day, listening to Wagner. Those who were obliged to sit with Hitler – dressed in uniform or dinner-jacket – in the Wagner family box, could be forgiven for taking forty winks in the often unbearable heat. To be on the safe side, they watched out for each other, and a swift jab in the ribs was called for at the first hint of a snore.' Goebbels himself was responsible for a witticism about the days when the Third Reich was governed from Bayreuth: '"Wahnfried" and "*Wahnsinn*" (lunacy) both begin with the same syllable!'

In the evenings, after a performance, Hitler used to sit by the fireside with Winifred – and later with her children as well – and hold forth until the early hours of the morning. The relationship between the lady of the house and Tietjen no longer seemed to worry him, particularly as he scarcely ever saw the director face to face, and Winifred's enthusiasm for her 'Wolf' was in no way diminished. 'She was besotted with him', Tietjen scoffed, even after the war. The fact that the festival nights often took place in the heat of high summer did not prevent Hitler from making sure there were always some logs flaming in the grate for his fireside chats.

At home we never discussed politics at all.
Winifred Wagner, interview with Hans Jürgen Syberberg, 1975

Accounts differ as to what was discussed by the firelight. Winifred later claimed that never a word was spoken about politics, and that Hitler's interest in Bayreuth was purely musical. Her son Wolfgang who on several occasions was 'allowed' to sit in on the conversation, confirms 'Wolf's' extravagant disquisitions on Wagner: he was 'an intense Wagnerian, you couldn't accuse him of ignorance' but remembers also the political monologues. In these Hitler frequently attempted to justify brutal and violent political measures by making historical comparisons: 'He always took the view that when Charlemagne slaughtered the Saxons, that was a political act.' Wolfgang's sister Friedelind remembers another telling statement that Hitler made shortly before the outbreak of war. 'Uncle Wolf' turned to her mother and said: 'I hope you realise that in the next war the first bomb will fall on the Festspielhaus and the second on Wahnfried.'

However, as long as the 'temple buildings' of the Wagner-cult remained intact the high priestess maintained her position as a friend of the Reich. She dined with Mussolini at the Reich Chancellery, acted as hostess at a reception for 'creative artists' at the House of German Art in Munich, and practised her English mother-tongue at tea with the British Foreign Secretary, Anthony Eden. Furthermore, the 'great lady' and the Führer regularly reaffirmed their mutual admiration with expensive presents. One day, for example, an elegant Benz limousine was found standing in the driveway at Wahnfried; and on Hitler's fiftieth birthday Winifred arranged for presentation to the Führer of some of her father-in-law's treasured papers. They were the manuscript draft of *Rienzi* and original scores of *Das Rheingold* and *Die Walküre*, as well as a sketch for *Die Götterdämmerung*. According to eye-witnesses, these presents moved the recipient more than anything that day. In addition Winifred demonstrated her devotion by having Bayreuth decked out as if for a national holiday. There are photographs of the Festspielhaus on that day, 20 April 1939, when 'Wolf' was celebrating his important birthday in distant Berlin with a massive military parade. A vast portrait of Hitler decorates the frontage of the theatre, which is surrounded by a forest of swastika flags.

*

The festival that followed in the late summer of 1939 was already overshadowed by the dark clouds of war. The last performance of *Tristan und Isolde* had to be given with an understudy, because the French singer Germaine Lubin had left Germany the night before for fear of internment. Many of the visitors also left in a great hurry. The mood of impending doom in *Die Götterdämmerung* (Twilight of the Gods) seemed to spread beyond the stage and into the audience. In the course of the festival Winifred Wagner tried her hand as a peace-maker and made efforts to arrange a meeting between Hitler and the British ambassador, Henderson, who was also in Bayreuth. But after the war she reported that her patron simply had no further interest in negotiations. If Henderson should turn up in his box, her old friend informed her brusquely, he would leave Bayreuth there and then.

> Every one of us regretted the outbreak of war. Every National Socialist, too. I mean, we certainly weren't fanatical war-mongers.
> *Winifred Wagner, interview with Hans Jürgen Syberberg, 1975*
>
> For her, the war was the most terrible thing that could have happened.
> *Wolfgang Wagner*

The outbreak of war hit Winifred where she was most sensitive – her family. True, her eldest son Wieland was one of twenty-five chosen 'pillars of the future', to be ready when the 'final victory' was won, and as such was exempt from war service. However, Wolfgang was fighting at the front in Poland. Hardly a week had passed since the outbreak of war when a terrible message came by phone: her son Wolfgang had fallen 'for *Führer, Volk und Vaterland*'. Fortunately this report proved to be premature – Wolfgang had only been taken prisoner, but severely wounded, probably by German fire. Nevertheless the shock had affected Winifred deeply. A Wehrmacht aircraft brought her son back to Berlin to recuperate, where his supreme commander, 'Uncle Wolf' from the Bayreuth days, visited him in person and brought flowers to his bedside.

Winifred's daughter Friedelind, always known as 'Mousie', also caused her great concern. Since August 1938 the 'difficult child' had been living in France and Switzerland – for 'political and personal reasons', as she put it. Winifred and Wieland had once followed her to Paris and tried in vain to make her change her mind. But now, in the winter of 1939–40, time was getting short. 'Mousie' had announced her intention to emigrate to America. Thus, at the beginning of February 1940, Winifred travelled to Zürich, determined to fetch her daughter back even at this late stage. Obtaining permission to leave Germany was of course not a problem for a highly placed personage with direct access to the Führer. If we are to believe Friedelind's account, her mother's mission was not so much to keep the family together as to prevent the committing of 'treason'.

In a dramatic confrontation Winifred employed every weapon at her disposal. 'Come home', she implored with a sob in her voice, and told her about Wolfgang's severe injury, which apparently made her brother request urgently to see her again. When none of this seemed to have any effect, she abruptly changed her tone and uttered dire threats. Friedelind later recounted the showdown between her mother and herself. 'If you won't listen, an order will be issued for you to be exterminated, liquidated at the earliest opportunity' – there she was, in a Zürich hotel bedroom, hearing the words 'exterminated' and 'liquidated', straight from the vocabulary of inhumanity, spoken by the director of the Bayreuth Festival. Was this the phraseology of 'Wolf' breaking through, the man who had revealed to her his visions of the future while sitting by the fireside? How fanatical did a mother have to be to threaten her own daughter in such a way?

Winifred's outburst only strengthened her daughter's resolve and she emigrated to the United States. There she managed to survive by taking occasional work and was passed around as an 'exhibit'. In 1944 she set down her Bayreuth experiences, especially those involving Hitler, in a book entitled *Night over Bayreuth*. It is fluently written and was plundered for anecdotes of every kind. For example, we read that Hitler very much wanted to see the young enchantress in *Parsifal* appear stark naked on stage, that he once 'foamed at the mouth' in a fit of rage at the dining-table, and that in a good mood he liked to tell stories about Goebbels and Göring. Both Winifred and her lover Tietjen come out of it remarkably badly as well.

Unfortunately it seems that Friedelind's colourful recollections were enhanced by some poetic licence. Not all her anecdotes stand up to examination. As the US secret service organisation, OSS, observed in a surveillance report: Richard Wagner's granddaughter was 'not very credible, attention-seeking and garrulous'. After the war the majority of her family – including Winifred – naturally dismissed the book as a 'tissue of lies'. Yet it cannot be as simple as that. Friedelind based her book on a detailed diary and after the war many of her descriptions were confirmed by eye-witnesses. For this reason *Night over Bayreuth*, because of its merciless frankness, remains an extremely valuable source, provided it is read with caution. In the case of 'Mousie's conversation with Winifred in Zürich, one has to discount some of the apparently verbatim content, but in essence the domineering mother's terrifying message is thoroughly believable. We can well imagine with what emotions the two parted – Friedelind on her ocean liner to America and Winifred back to the swastika-draped Bayreuth.

> In a manner of speaking, I am the mother of the festival and final court of appeal for every question that arises within such a complex organisation.
>
> *Winifred Wagner, 1940*

At least the other three children caused no worries to their family. Wolfgang, now back on his feet, and Wieland soon brought home respectable brides, married and continued the family line. Their beautiful sister Verena, known as 'Nickel', delighted her mama by marrying into the highest circles. Her new husband was Bodo Lafferentz, an imposing *Oberreichsleiter* (national officer) of *Kraft durch Freude*, the Nazi 'Strength through Joy' organisation, which provided holidays and other salubrious activities for the workers. Lafferentz was responsible for drumming up a suitable audience for the 'wartime festival' at Bayreuth. In fact Winifred had not intended to hold any festivals for the duration of the war – which was only expected to last a year, or two at the very most. During the First World War, too, her late husband had closed the gates to the 'green hill'. But Hitler had other ideas, and without him no important decisions were made in Bayreuth. From now on no more tickets were to be sold to the general public. All costs incurred including artists' fees were paid for out of the *Kraft durch Freude* budget – after deduction of a 17 per cent profit margin, which remained in the Wagners' pocket.

> But one thing that Frau Wagner certainly did – and that is her great service to history – was to bring Bayreuth and National Socialism together.
>
> *Adolf Hitler, March 1942*
>
> We have Winifred Wagner to thank that the legacy of Bayreuth is being carried on.
>
> *Joseph Goebbels, diary, 30 May 1942*

Now, finally, the Wagner festivals were a totally nationalised affair. The audiences, ferried in on special trains, were certainly a strange mixture. 'Deserving compatriots', were now allowed to visit Bayreuth for their edification – and all completely free of charge. As Hitler declared enthusiastically: 'And now, while the war is on, I have been able to do what Wagner always wanted: to enable men and women chosen from the people, soldiers and workers, to attend the festival and pay nothing.' Tietjen, who had been able to have his staff recalled from the battle-front, saw it differently. In 1940 he joked that the novice audiences clearly 'hadn't the faintest clue what was going on'. Then, as time went on, and the visitors were not only clueless, but limbless as well, no-one felt like joking any more. It almost seemed as if the wounded and disabled were being carried to Bayreuth to be cured by Wagner.

In 1940 'Uncle Wolf' came to the festival for the last time. On the way back from his 'lightning victory' over France, he arranged for his special train to stop in Bayreuth and, still exulting in his triumph, watched a performance of *The Twilight of the Gods*. It was his last meeting with Winifred, apart from a brief visit by the 'great lady' to the Führer's train. In the years that followed they only communicated by telephone and telegram. However, her children met the warlord a few more times in Berlin. On those occasions Wieland and Wolfgang were always concerned with a project that was to start 'the year after peace has been concluded': the enlargement of the Festspielhaus.

A few sketches for the plan have survived. What they show is no longer an opera-house of the traditional kind but more of a 'Franconian acropolis' with dozens of wings, colonnades and flat roofs. Like a south German counterpart to the gigantic domed building planned for Berlin, the very size of the new building in Bayreuth was intended to convey the magnificence of its builders. The sketches took as their model the temple complex at Pergamon, in ancient Asia Minor, but even that would have found room on the expanded 'green hill' a dozen times over. The focal point of this megalomania in concrete was to be provided by a dome, large enough to enclose the old Festspielhaus in its entirety, so as to protect it for all time from wind and weather.

*

Wieland and Wolfgang, now both in their twenties, were beginning to lay claim to their future control of the family inheritance. Their visits to 'Wolf' were not only to discuss the planned expansion but already to talk about future productions. For even though Hitler no longer came to Bayreuth, he had not lost his burning enthusiasm for Wagner. The most audacious – and the most insane – of his campaigns, the invasion of the Soviet Union, he named 'Barbarossa', after the historical figure who had also fascinated Wagner. 'Barbarossa', the Italian for 'red-beard', was the medieval emperor Friedrich I, of the Hohenstaufen dynasty. A surviving fragment of an opera entitled *Barbarossa* shows the powerful attraction the emperor exerted on the composer. What intrigued Wagner most of all was the 'grand, barbaric, sublime, indeed divine ignorance of this figure', as he noted in the margin of the fragment.

When the Wehrmacht was driven back from the gates of Moscow in the winter of 1941, or perhaps even earlier, the German generals surrounding the 'greatest military leader of all times' realised that they too had marched eastwards with the 'ignorance' of a Barbarossa, and that their fate could be likened to that of the emperor who had brought such disaster on himself. (Barbarossa led no less than six exhausting expeditions against Italy and finally, in Venice in 1177, fell on his knees before Pope Alexander III and begged absolution. He died by drowning and a legend grew up that he would rise again one day and save Germany in her hour of need. *Tr.*) The continuation of the war after the débâcle outside Moscow could scarcely have any rational justification – particularly as the dictator had now chosen to declare war on the USA, the strongest industrial power in the world.

In those days, irrationality took an ever stronger hold on Hitler. When he listened to Wagner, he explained to his senior officers, it seemed as if he were 'hearing the rhythms of a previous world'. As the outlook of the war became increasingly hopeless, Hitler appeared incapable of distinguishing the real world from his operatic fantasies. Indeed, the consuming flames of the *Götterdämmerung* were being matched, even surpassed, by the horrors of reality. Did not a grand and terrible end beneath the ruins of his capital, like the fate of Rienzi the Roman tribune, seem ever more likely?

*

Meanwhile, management of the festival in a Bayreuth still untouched by war was running into trouble of another kind. Winifred Wagner had her hands full, trying to mediate in a bitter power-struggle between Tietjen and her two sons. The 'Youth of Wahnfried' were jostling for power, but as director of the festival, their mother could not trust her sons to run it independently. Tietjen threatened to withdraw completely, both from the festival and from their relationship. Winifred appealed to 'Wolf' in his distant headquarters, who decided that Wieland and Wolfgang would have to wait until the end of the war, and at least complete their training first. This was a severe blow for the two young men, though apparently it did not lessen their keenness on Hitler and his cause. As late as September 1944 Wieland Wagner still believed in 'ultimate victory', and in a letter expressed the hope that 'the Grail will shine again'. His own son, born in 1943, was loyally christened Wolf-Siegfried – an odd combination of the names of his mentor and his late father. Nor did Wolfgang forget his mighty

Uncle Wolf. For example, he proposed that the choice of the
Wagner opera to be performed for the 'celebration of final
victory', ought to be left to the Führer.

Winifred's loyalty was no less strong than that of her sons. She
did not let her enthusiasm for 'the cause' be clouded by that fact
that all round Bayreuth Germany's cities were collapsing in ruins,
nor by the horrific rumours of extermination camps. Every day
fresh flowers were placed in front of the Führer's portrait in
Wahnfried. On the occasion of the 1943 festival she penned a fiery
peroration for the programme: 'When, of all the operas, we chose
Die Meistersinger von Nürnberg for the 1943 wartime festival, we
did so because of its deep and symbolic significance. For this work
surely demonstrates in an impressive manner the ethnically rooted
creative will of the German people, which the Master has
immortally personified in the character of Hans Sachs, the
Nuremberg shoemaker and folk-poet. In the current struggle with
the destructive spirit of the world conspiracy of plutocrats and
Bolshevists, for the world of western civilisation, this same creative
will gives our soldiers their indomitable strength in battle and their
fanatical belief in the victory of our arms.'

Despite such declarations of loyalty, Winifred Wagner was in
touch less and less often with her friend in the 'Wolf's Lair,'
preoccupied as he was with his crumbling front line. She missed the
high-level socialising and glittering occasions of the 'peaceful' Nazi
years. Instead, she now had to engage in correspondence to refute
allegations that Cosima Wagner had Jewish blood, not to mention
writing a thank-you letter to Heinrich Himmler, the head of the SS,
who had taken time off from committing the greatest mass murder
in history, to send her some 'beautiful yuletide dishes'.

*

It is one of the ironic footnotes to history that the most famous
attempt on Hitler's life, led by Count Claus von Stauffenberg,
happened to have a code-name from the Wagnerian world. The
courageous conspirators in the Wehrmacht used the name
'Valkyrie' to conceal from the SS and Gestapo their elaborate plan
to remove the Nazis from power – once they had succeeded in

killing Hitler. Unfortunately the tyrant survived the attack largely unharmed and was then able to mount his own very personal *Götterdämmerung*, which lasted nine terrible months.

On 20 July 1944, the same day that Count Claus von Stauffenberg placed his bomb under the map-table in the 'Wolf's Lair', *Die Meistersinger* was being performed at Bayreuth – the crowning glory of that last 'wartime festival', with sets designed by the young Wieland Wagner. When Winifred heard about the assassination attempt, she immediately sent several anxious telegrams to her 'Wolf's' headquarters and tried desperately to reach him by telephone. After several hours she did manage to get through to Hitler in person and to congratulate him on his 'salvation'. Yet to her considerable surprise the dictator hardly mentioned the attack but steered the conversation as usual to questions about future productions and about 'Providence'. When being interrogated after the war, Winifred stated that one of his sentences was: 'I hear the wings of the Goddess of Victory rustling.'

Even in the last months of the war, the occupants of Wahnfried were scarcely aware of the desperate struggle for survival in the rest of Germany. 'We lived damned well', remembered Wieland's wife Gertrud – not without a twinge of conscience. Winifred exploited her organisational skills to the full. She sent her staff out to scavenge in the surrounding villages, knowing she could rely on the great respect that the local Franconians still held for her. Her cellar was filled with smoked meats, lard and sugar. They even had freshly ground coffee – an exotic luxury in the last years of the war. That was a Christmas present from Hitler. In October 1944 Winifred's son-in-law Bodo and son Wieland told her about a special assignment they had been given. They were to work alongside prisoners in the Flossenbürg concentration camp on various secret projects, including the prototype for a 'smart bomb'. This was the first direct contact that any of the Wagner clan had had with the terrifying world of the camps. According to Gertrud, the things that Wieland and Bodo described certainly gave Winifred cause for reflection and doubt. But not enough to make her renounce her Nazi faith.

*

As late as 20 April 1945 Winifred Wagner sent birthday greetings to the Führer in his subterranean realm beneath the Reich Chancellery in Berlin. His apocalyptic vision was now becoming reality. He conveyed to his secretaries the obscure desire to hear the *Liebestod* from *Tristan* in his dying hour. But in the fatalistic atmosphere of the bunker nothing more came of it. When the Reich Radio announced Hitler's death, the funeral march from the *Götterdämmerung* was played for the last time. When Winifred heard the news, she was in the Franconian village of Oberwarmensteinach, where she had a summer home. On a visit to Bayreuth she was shocked to discover that refugees had raided the opera-house stores and were now strolling around the streets dressed up as Wotan or Isolde. She was equally offended, if not more so, by the fact that the victorious US Army had commandeered the Festspielhaus – on the grounds that it was 'Hitler's property'. In a strictly legal sense they were wrong, but for the twelve years of the Nazi dictatorship the 'green hill' had been Hitler's spiritual property, through Winifred Wagner's devotion to him. However, she was in no mood to think about that. Instead she complained in her usual unpleasant tone about the 'occupation' of the Bayreuth premises: 'For several weeks the building was turned into a barracks for American blacks', she wrote in 1946 about the use of the Festspielhaus. 'During that time, you can imagine how much damage was done!'

In 1947 Hitler's 'great lady' was charged before a denazification tribunal in Bayreuth with being a 'leading perpetrator and beneficiary' of Nazism, but in the event was only categorised as 'incriminated'. The judges' main finding was that she had 'thrown the weight of one of the most famous names in German culture behind Hitler'. Her assets were confiscated and as a further penalty she was to complete 450 days' community service, working on jobs like cleaning the forecourt of Bayreuth's railway station. However, it never came to that, since a year later the appeal she had lodged was successful. After various statements by victims of Nazism whom Winifred Wagner had helped, she was reclassified merely as 'incriminated to a minor degree'. Winifred then resigned from all her posts, leaving the way free for her sons. Prior to this she had done everything in her power to block all alternative plans for the future of the 'green hill' – such as inviting Friedelind back from America, or even appointing management from outside the family.

From then onward she stayed in the background and did no more than occasionally gather around her some old Wagnerians, as well as former Nazis, in her quiet little sitting-room. Among friends she did little to hide her unreconstructed attitudes, signed her letters '88', the neo-Nazi code for *Heil Hitler*, smirked at the abbreviation 'USA', which she translated as '*Unser Seliger Adolf*' (Our Blessed Adolf), told toe-curling jokes about Jews, and from time to time met up with old friends such as Lina Heydrich, widow of the assassinated head of SS security. However, her sons, who revived the Bayreuth Festival with great success, did her a favour by keeping her views hidden from the public. It is true that she ranted about 'festival crimes', by which she meant Wieland's avant-garde, abstract productions; and sometimes she would listen to performances with her back to the stage – but any eulogies for the 'Wolf' who had so decisively influenced her life she kept to herself. No doubt she realised what great damage her pro-Nazi confessions would cause her sons in postwar, democratic Germany, particularly since Wieland and Wolfgang had themselves once been Hitler's protégés.

She maintained this self-imposed oath of silence until 1975. Had she held on longer, the verdict on her would probably have been different. For Winifred Wagner could not be accused of committing any specifically guilty acts during the Nazi period. True, she was an utterly fanatical believer in Hitler, steeped in the ghastly Nazi ideology, yet she had committed no crime in either the legal or moral sense of the word. Winifred Wagner was not a 'perpetrator'. Nonetheless, she had been an extremely prominent supporter of the dictator, and her collaboration at the highest level helped to make his disastrous project possible. At best, her intervention on behalf of victims of persecution only does a little to lessen her guilt. On the other hand, accusations of this kind can, in varying degrees, be levelled against the majority of Germans of that generation. Hitler did not lack a blindly loyal following. In this respect Winifred Wagner was merely among the first of many. Her exalted status and personal friendship with Hitler make no difference to that.

> There is absolutely no question that my grandmother remained a convinced National Socialist to her dying breath. And most of all it was the fascination with Hitler that she articulated publicly to the very end of her life. It is beyond any doubt that she stood fully behind Hitler.
>
> *Gottfried Wagner*

Not until 1975, three decades after the demise of the would-be Rienzi from Braunau, did Winifred achieve a unique notoriety that was as sad as it was irritating. Persuaded by a film director, Hans Jürgen Syberberg, and by her grandson Gottfried, she gave a lengthy interview in which she laid bare her utterly intransigent commitment to Hitler. Her 'friendship with Wolf', she told the cameras, was something she would 'never deny'. She explained her attitude to his monstrous crimes in memorable words: 'I regret that very deeply. But for me, in my personal relationship with him, it makes no difference. Let's just say that the part of him that I knew I still value today, just as much as I did then. And the Hitler that one must reject completely, is someone who didn't exist in my mind, because I didn't know him in that way. I mean, my whole relationship with him was entirely based on what was personal to us.'

It was a perfect example of suppressing the truth, full of an arrogant naivety that was terrifying to behold. This irrational separation of the likeable private man from the sinister mass murderer, this mental distinction between Jekyll and Hyde, was an immoral, indeed a culpable way of thinking. It probably arose on one hand from Winifred's 'inability to grieve', as her granddaughter Nike Wagner believes, but on the other hand also from a staggering inability to understand. A letter that Winifred wrote around the time of her denazification hearing sheds light on her complete incapacity for coherent thought: 'As a former idealist I am faced with a riddle. How was it possible that all the good things that we in the Movement hoped at the beginning to be able to do for our people and our fatherland, could turn into exactly the opposite and produce excesses of the most terrible kind and with the most horrific effect?' She never came to understand that it was precisely her 'idealism' that provided the breeding-ground for the greatest crimes of the twentieth century. Perhaps she lacked the moral strength, or perhaps she could feel nothing for the victims. Winifred Wagner died aged eighty-three, on 5 March 1980.

CHAPTER FIVE

The Songstress – Zarah Leander

Ninety per cent of the songs I sing are about love. That's because ninety per cent of people think love is more important than politics. I'm convinced of that.

Where does it say that performers, more than other people, have to understand anything about politics? I'm rather glad to have been labelled a 'political ignoramus'.

In films and on the stage I've only ever played one role, in a variety of costumes and in different settings – the role of Zarah Leander.

I wanted to go to Germany and never, ever regretted it. You can't imagine how much I learned in Germany. It was the Germans who shaped my life.

The Ufa Studios gave me a certain brand image and that was how I had to stay.

Politics don't interest me. They're something that men should do if they want to.

I'm 'Leander' – that'll have to do.

Zarah Leander

Zarah was neither a Nazi nor a non-Nazi; she just wanted to make a career for herself.

Douglas Sirk (born Detlef Sierck), film director

The woman hit a spot in the German soul, that wonderfully *kitsch* sentimentality that lies in the heart of all Germans. The *kitsch* films she made were truly appalling.

Will Quadflieg, actor

If you are prominent and are kept employed in a dictatorship, whatever it may call itself, then you have to do what you're told, otherwise you end up in jug. And even being Swedish would not have kept her out of concentration camp. So I know *I* would prefer to sing morale-boosting songs for the troops.

Evelyn Künneke, singer and actress

A very tall, statuesque redhead, with a freckled complexion and an amazingly lovely mouth.

Ilse Werner, singer and actress

My mother had the feeling that now she could achieve what she wanted to achieve, and that was to be really successful abroad. And of course the Ufa Studios were almost as famous as Hollywood. My mother had the chance to go to Hollywood, but she turned it down. She didn't want to be so far from Sweden. She really was as Swedish as can be, and liked to feel that Sweden was just down the road. Better to be in Berlin than far away in Los Angeles.

Göran Forsell, son of Zarah Leander

She was having a difficult time earning money and feeding her family. She wanted more money and that's why she went over to the Nazis. It worked well for her, and her financial situation changed fundamentally. After that she was rich, very rich.

Ingrid Segerstedt-Wiberg, Swedish politician

The curtain opens to reveal the star in a spectacular *mis-en-scène*: a pyramid of female figures rises from the stage, their faces hidden behind feather boas. In the midst of them, like an angel clad in white: the singer Zarah Leander. With the first notes from her deep, husky voice, every corner of the theatre's packed auditorium seems filled with its warm, dark timbre. It seems to get under one's very skin. '*Ich weiss, es wird einmal ein Wunder geschehn, und dann werden tausend Märchen wahr*' (I know one day a miracle will happen, and a thousand fairy-tales will come true), the diva sings with her sibilant 's's and rolled 'r's. The 'divine creature' stands on a pedestal, enveloped by five gigantic feathers and dressed in a long gown trimmed with glittering diamanté – the epitome of 'pure femininity'. '*Ich weiss, so schnell kann keine Liebe vergehn, die so gross ist und so wunderbar*' (No love can ever fade so soon, when it's so great, so wonderful). The music swells and blends with a celestial choir. The singer's face can now be seen in close-up, yet seems far from all earthly concerns: with her eyes raised heavenwards, her gaze enraptured, her cheeks wet with tears, she sings with fervour: '*Und darum wird einmal ein Wunder geschehen, und ich weiss, dass wir uns wieder sehn*' (That's why a miracle will one day happen, and I know we'll meet again).

Like flowers turning their faces towards the sun, the women now unfurl their boas. But closer inspection produces a shock: the faces of the flower-fairies are angular and severe. Here and there we seem to discern a five o'clock shadow. The expression on these faces is serious, one might almost say unhappy. The billowing dresses hang as shapelessly on them as on a coat-stand, the waistbands do not really emphasise any waists. And there seems to be something not quite right about the bosoms; on one of them they sit too high, on the next too low, on a third oddly far apart. As the actor Wolfgang Preiss remembers: 'The problem was finding women for that scene who were just as good-looking, just as tall and if possible just as well-upholstered as Zarah herself, so as to produce an aesthetically balanced ensemble.' He was describing a set-piece from Zarah Leander's most successful film, *Die grosse Liebe* (The Great Love). 'But they couldn't find any – so they just called in some SS men from the *Leibstandarte*, Hitler's personal protection squad. It was like a guards regiment, so they were all the same height. It was an ideal solution really. There was a war on, most of the men had been called up, and no-one else could be found in a hurry. The *Leibstandarte* just had to be detailed off – and that way you were saving the cost of extras. That's how it came about that in this number there is only one woman to be seen and that was Zarah, right in the middle. All the others were men in drag. It was only for the close-ups that they used the faces of pretty girls.'

The SS *Leibstandarte* was Hitler's bodyguard and private army. They had earned a bloody reputation in the 'Night of the Long Knives', when SA chief Ernst Röhm and many more of Hitler's political rivals were liquidated. Later, as an elite unit of the *Waffen-SS*, they became famous, even notorious, for their toughness in battle. This grotesque sidelight from movie history has an almost symbolic importance if we are to understand Zarah Leander. For she always claimed that she was just an artiste and remote from any kind of National Socialist politics. Yet whether she liked it or not, she was the diva of the Third Reich, and as such was not just a part, but actually the leading entertainment personality of a state that was built on injustice. It is simply impossible to regard her as a performer in isolation from Hitler's Reich, for it was that very dictatorship that made her into what she was. The revue number just described sums up the myth that was Zarah Leander. An extraordinarily deep voice – almost a baritone – that went deep under the skin; a star whom the film-makers of the Third Reich brought to the screen and turned into an ethereal, unapproachable goddess. The woman who sang *'Ich weiss, es wird einmal ein Wunder geschehn'* – a song that brought her not only international fame, but also the accusation of being the morale-boosting voice of Nazi wartime propaganda. And finally the film, *Die grosse Liebe*, from which that scene comes. It is a wartime love-story and calls upon German women to sacrifice love in the cause of Germany's victory. Zarah Leander was the highest paid female star in Nazi Germany. Between 1936, when she was put under contract by Ufa, and 1943, when she returned to her native Sweden, she made ten films. Strange that, of all people, a solidly built Swedish woman with flame-red hair and a voice like a man – a mixture of vamp and mother-figure – should become the Third Reich's most successful export and an idol to millions of men and women. A nation lay at her feet. But what was Zarah Leander really: a great artiste or an artificial creation? A 'Nazi siren' or a victim of politics? A rustic innocent or an ambitious careerist? With Zarah Leander, what is myth and what reality?

> I grew up with four brothers, so I got used to dealing
> with men.
>
> *Zarah Leander*

When Zarah Stina Hedberg was a child, no-one would have seen in
her the star that she would later become – least of all her four
brothers, who teased her about her chubbiness, her freckles and her
unruly red hair. She was born on 15 March 1907 in the southern
Swedish town of Karlstadt, the daughter of a music-loving estate
agent father and a strict mother. Although the latter had little time
for the fine arts, Zarah was given piano and violin lessons from the
age of four, and when she was six she played in public for the first
time, in a Chopin competition. However, that was the extent of her
musical training; she never had singing lessons. In any case, as was
usual in those days, Mrs Hedberg had already mapped out a life for
her daughter as a respectable housewife and mother. Zarah attended
high school until 1922 and then spent two years as paid companion
to a woman her mother knew in the Latvian capital, Riga. There she
learned to speak German fluently and in the company of her
employer savoured the cultural life of the city, went to the theatre
and to concerts, and had soon set her heart on a stage career.

> I never had a singing-lesson in my life, never. As a young
> girl I learned to play the piano and violin, but study singing?
> No, I didn't . . . I always had an alto voice, yes, but it was a
> natural voice.
>
> *Zarah Leander*

However, her first venture in this direction was a hopeless failure.
At the audition for the drama school of the Royal Dramatic
Theatre in Stockholm in 1926, Zarah failed to make any impact at
all. But she did fall in love with an engaging young actor named
Nils Leander, the son of a pastor. They married when she was
nineteen, and the penniless couple moved in with Leander's

parents in the provincial backwoods of Sweden. A year later, in 1927, Zarah gave birth to a daughter, Boël, and two years after that a son, Göran. But in 1927 she took the stage for the first time, playing alongside her husband in a musical version of *Snow White*. In Gothenburg in October 1929 she was hired as a singer in the company run by the then famous king of revue, Ernst Rolf; it marked the beginning of her career. By this time her marriage to Nils Leander, who apparently drank a good deal, had already broken down. Zarah left him, and in 1931 their divorce went through.

Her début in the high-profile world of theatre was a success. However, her fee for singing some malicious verses about the press in her first revue was very modest and she was unable to make ends meet. She was determined to improve her circumstances. Bent on making a career and now with some favourable notices in her pocket the young artiste set off to conquer Stockholm. The very same year she secured a part in the New Year revue at the *Folkteater*. With her flame-red hair and her height of 5 foot 9, unusually tall for a woman in those days, she was something of an oddity, but directors were struck by her beauty and not least by her deep contralto voice. With her two children and her mother – her father having died – Zarah moved into a two-bedroomed apartment. For a time she even took in her two school-age brothers. The burden of her family responsibilities, the cramped accommodation and the shortages of those lean years were to be the driving force behind the actions she later took. Zarah was dead set on becoming a star and overcoming her material problems. 'What I lacked in money, I had to make up for in will-power. I had to fight my way to the top. I was like a fiery young mare, who had just broken out from her stall and was galloping off hell-for-leather. Her movements were certainly still awkward, and her neighing laughter was downright coarse, but there was something in her that held audiences in their seats. And the sparks around her hooves were like stardust. A blaze of lights.' As it was to turn out later, neither politics nor morality would divert her from her goal, once she had set her sights on it.

> She was a naturally cheerful person. She had cheerful people
> around her, too. It was really a great time in her life.
>
> *Ilse Werner, singer and actress*

In the years that followed, Zarah performed in numerous revues,
operettas and comedies in Sweden, and went on tour throughout
Scandinavia. This breakthrough was achieved with the help of
Gösta Ekman, Sweden's most famous actor and theatre director.
He had become well known in Germany through playing the title
role in Murnau's film, *Faust*. When Zarah played the heroine in
The Merry Widow in 1931, they celebrated real triumphs together
in Stockholm. Yet Ekman's visions of the future were not to be.
'He wanted to make Zarah Leander not only a star of operetta but
also a tragedienne and an all-round actress', a colleague of Ekman
wrote later. 'The fact that he was unable to carry out these plans
was not his fault, but was due to her being more interested in
financial than artistic success.' In her memoirs Zarah agreed with
this barbed comment, but added: 'What drove me was not simply
the desire for money. I had a pretty clear idea of my limitations.'
Even at the start of her career, Zarah was shrewd and businesslike
enough to recognise that her main asset was not her theatrical
talent, but her voice. As early as 1930 she had signed a recording
contract with the Odeon label. By the time she went to Berlin she
had made sixty records and thus created for herself a constant
source of income.

> Once she was on stage she had complete confidence, but
> backstage she suffered dreadfully from stage-fright. It was so
> bad that she seriously had to be shoved on to the stage and
> had to calm her nerves from a hip-flask.
>
> *Evelyn Künneke, actress and singer*

It was in Sweden that she also made her film début, though it is
true to say that these first forays on to the screen were mostly
rather embarrassing. In *Dante's Mysteries* (1930) she made a brief

appearance as a beautiful young witch and was a smash hit riding around on a broomstick. In a comedy of errors entitled *The Wrong Millionaire* (1931) she was a sophisticated vamp. Her thespian achievements were rather modest, but she certainly opened people's eyes with the deep cleavage she displayed in this film. In her third Swedish film, *The Adultery Game*, made in 1935, she played a successful entertainer and thus more or less acted herself, a role she later perfected at the Ufa Studios in Berlin. However, on her way to the top, it was Vienna that provided a springboard.

*

By now the name Zarah Leander meant something in Scandinavia. When the Danish actor-manager Max Hansen offered her a part in Vienna, in the operetta *Axel at Heaven's Gate*, by Ralph Benatzky, she accepted straight away. After seven years on the stage in Sweden she had the feeling she was marking time. She was ready for new adventures. With her second husband and manager, Vidar Forsell, Leander moved to Austria. The elegant and good-looking Forsell was the son of a theatre director and his own profession was that of editor on a newspaper. They had met when he wanted to write a review about her. The two got married in September 1932. Forsell adopted Zarah's children, gave up his job in journalism and from then on devoted himself exclusively to Zarah's career, which was now beginning to take off in a big way. *Axel at Heaven's Gate* was a huge success and all of Vienna was talking about the unknown Swedish singer. 'She was a knockout', Ilse Werner tells us. 'She was an amazing personality, with that flaming red hair. And she sang with a slight catch in her voice. She was fabulous, a real stunner. She came on stage and – a star was born.' In the operetta Zarah actually played the part of a star, based on Greta Garbo. In the Theater an der Wien, the song to which Zarah gave all she had was meant to be about the 'Divine' star of the story, but seemed to anticipate Zarah's own future development:

> I am a star. A great star with all her moods
> That's what the men say about me, don't they?
> . . .
> A movie star, the envy of a thousand girls.
> A movie star, idol of the present age.
> The smallest town proclaims your fame,
> Your incomparable beauty.
> Movie star, idol of the century!
> Everyone wants to be where you are.
> Yet the harsh spotlight conceals
> My true face from the world
> Deep down in my heart I'm alone.

Her dizzying success at Vienna's Theater an der Wien in 1936 brought Zarah Leander her first contract for a German-language film. Significantly its title was *Première*. Once again Zarah played a revue star, in other words herself. It is true that Zarah is often seen in an unfavourable light in the film (her ample hips prompted the director Geza von Bovary to remark: 'The woman's got a rump like a carthorse'). But the film was a big hit at the box-office and Zarah was fêted as a new discovery. The singer Evelyn Künneke explains her success in this way: 'She had an unusual voice and conveyed an inner strength, a strong charisma and an extraordinary radiance; added to which she had a girlish charm that came from her soul, and something mysterious, which you couldn't describe. People were fascinated.' But not only in Vienna – in Berlin, too, Zarah Leander was attracting attention.

> She chose Germany and never regretted it, because it was in Germany that she had the most fans. And she loved Germany, especially Berlin.
>
> *Brigitte Petterson, Zarah Leander's housekeeper*

At this point in time the German film industry was looking for a star. The Nazis were competing with the much-admired example of Hollywood and had visions of beating the Americans at their own game. But in 1930 Germany's biggest star, Marlene Dietrich, had left her country for Hollywood and – despite many fabulous offers from Goebbels – was never persuaded to return. Ingrid Bergman only made one film in Germany, then also pursued her career in the USA, while another Swedish-born actress, Greta Garbo, was already enjoying overwhelming success there. What the German movie scene lacked was a diva with class, international style and exotic sophistication. It was certainly this 'Garbo complex' that drew attention to Leander, who was so successfully imitating that very star in Vienna.

> At that time, Ufa needed new star material.
> *Douglas Sirk (Detlef Sierck), film director*

> Possibly without being aware of it, she was coldly exploiting the gaps left by talent that the Nazi system had, as elsewhere, ripped out of the film industry.
> *Cornelia Zumkeller, film historian*

'It is our firm belief that film is one of the most modern and far-reaching means of influencing the masses', Hitler's propaganda minister, Joseph Goebbels, once wrote. He saw himself as a 'passionate lover of the art of cinema' and as its protector and patron. Consequently, as soon as Hitler had seized power, Goebbels began poking his fingers into the film industry. The newly established Reich Chamber of Film, which everyone involved in movie-making had to join, was aimed at suppressing undesirable elements and immediately excluded 'non-Aryan' artists. Then the great exodus began: screenwriters like Billy Wilder and Robert Liebmann, directors of the calibre of Fritz Lang and Max Ophüls, the composers Hanns Eisler and Kurt Weill, as well as actors such as Peter Lorre and Conrad Veidt, all went to the USA, leaving painful gaps behind.

> . . . they were looking for a new Garbo. A German Garbo.
> *Zarah Leander in her autobiography*

By the end of the Depression in the early 1930s, only three large German film companies had survived, and despite heavy financial deficits, could still be counted as competitors to Hollywood. These were Tobis, Terra and the Universum Film AG (known as Ufa). In order to gain total control of the film industry, Goebbels set up the Film Credit Bank in 1933, which by 1937 was providing up to 50 per cent of the finance for feature film production. Naturally, this money was reserved only for what appealed to the men in power. 'Art is free', Goebbels had promised, 'though it will have to adapt to specific norms.' A year later a draconian Reich Law on Moving Pictures came into force. It gave powers to 'Reich Film Supervisors' to censor screenplays, propose changes to completed films and to ban films that 'offended National Socialist or artistic sensibilities'. At the same time they awarded a seal of approval to films that were of 'artistic or political value to the state'. In the central office of film supervision the Ministry of Propaganda now had the decisive vote. Goebbels even had a personal say in the casting of films: on the 'A' list were those who enjoyed the particular favour of Hitler and Goebbels, and one name would soon occupy a permanent place there, that of Zarah Leander. The task of finding roles for up-and-coming actresses was one that Goebbels reserved for himself personally. It was known that he liked to 'give them a leg up'. 'Undesirable' actors and actresses were put on a blacklist and could no longer get work.

> She accepted the Nazi regime for what it was, and was grateful to be able to work under it.
>
> *Will Quadflieg, actor*

By 1942 Goebbels had completely nationalised the German film industry and merged all the companies into the Ufa-Film GmbH. A 'Reich Director-General of Film' immediately took responsibility for the artistic content and 'overall intellectual stance' of film production. The post was held by Fritz Hippler, who had demonstrated the level of his aesthetic taste with the unspeakable Nazi hate-film, *The Eternal Jew*. Every form of film-making was now under Goebbels' control. In the Wehrmacht 'propaganda companies' were formed which had the job of documenting the course of the war. Cinema-goers were usually forced to sit through hour-long newsreels or 'cultural' films before they could see the main feature. But back in 1936, when Ufa was looking for a new international star, it was still largely independent – Goebbels did not yet have the final word.

> Zarah was not the type of girl to rest on her laurels; she was too full of ambition and energy.
>
> *Cornelia Zumkeller, film historian*

The first man to spot the new star in Vienna was Carl Froelich, one of Germany's most respected film directors. She was then checked out by Hans Weidemann, vice-president of the Reich Chamber of Film, who was very enthusiastic. Only then did they make Zarah an offer. On 28 October 1936, with the help of her husband, Vidar Forsell, Zarah negotiated a thoroughly acceptable contract with Ufa. Over the next two years Leander was committed to making three films, but could choose the scripts herself. For the two-year period she would receive a sum of 200,000 Reichsmarks, of which 53 per cent would be paid in Swedish currency direct to her account in Stockholm. At the end of two years the fee could be renegotiated. To put this in perspective, the average annual income of a male German worker in 1942 was all of 1,728 Reichsmarks, and for a woman only 1,116 Reichsmarks. Furthermore, under a decree by Hitler in 1938, leading performers could set off 40 per cent of their income against tax, as 'promotional expenses'. Zarah Leander was earning even more than her famous contemporaries Emil Jannings, Hans Albers and Heinz Rühmann.

At the same time Zarah apparently received several offers from Hollywood. The English were interested too. In 1934 she did a screen-test for a British production company, singing a number called 'I've written you a love-song'. But she never heard from them again. There has been a great deal of debate about why

Zarah Leander did not take up any of these offers, but chose Hitler's Reich instead. She herself blamed her decision on her family: 'I got letters on fancy letterheads from famous companies like Pathé, MGM and Ufa, sometimes followed by visits from elegant gentlemen to my dressing-room. But to me the most important thing was that my work should not be too far from home, that is to say from Sweden and the children. After only two weeks in Vienna I was already getting homesick, and it just went on like that. I'd be better off in London than Hollywood, but better still in Berlin – that was what I thought.' Whether any firm contracts from Hollywood were ever on the table, we do not know. In any case, Zarah spoke no English and in the Hollywood film-factory she would have had to start from the very bottom as an unknown Swedish entertainer. As she admitted in an interview on North German Radio in 1974: 'How far would I have got outside Germany? Number ten in America? Nowhere! I wanted to go to Germany, and I never, ever regretted it. You can't imagine how much I learned in Germany. It was the Germans who shaped my life.'

> She wasn't a typical 'Aryan' girl, but a mature woman who already had ideas of becoming rather a 'legend'.
>
> *Ilse Werner, singer and actress*

Before the outbreak of the Second World War, Germany was, despite being a dictatorship, a recognised state with which other countries maintained good relations. For European actors wanting to make a career, one of the first ports of call was the Ufa Studios in Babelsberg, outside Berlin. Ingrid Bergman and Greta Garbo both went there from Sweden to make their first films. But behind all the fine show that Hitler tried to put on for world opinion, with the 1936 Berlin Olympics, there lay a dictatorial state built on injustice, whose crude excesses grew by the day. And Zarah Leander was in a better position than most to know this. Admittedly, in her memoirs she carefully avoids all political questions. It is of course understandable that, faced with the monstrous crimes committed in Hitler's name, the greatest star in the Nazi Reich should in retrospect be willing to be described as a 'political ignoramus'. But even at the start of her career, Leander came into closer contact with politics than she later admitted. As a struggling actress in Sweden, she met the famous Gösta Ekman, and through him got to know the actor, director and script-writer Karl Gerhard. He became besotted with Zarah and regarded her as his protégée. The two formed a deep friendship and worked together closely from 1932 to 1936.

In Sweden Karl Gerhard belonged to the political left and made this quite clear in his satirical lyrics and sketches. One of Sweden's left-wing icons and a staunch opponent of Nazism was the publisher and editor, Torgny Segerstedt, and it was in his house in Gothenburg that artists and intellectuals would meet regularly to discuss the political situation in Europe and especially in Germany. In March 1933 Hitler had passed his Enabling Law, securing all legislative powers for himself, and stifling democracy. People outside Germany anxiously observed the increasing exclusion of Jews, the ban on political parties and the accompanying persecution of all who did not toe the Nazi line. Then came the manipulation of the Reichstag elections and, not least, the passing of the Nuremberg Race Laws in 1935, by which German Jews were robbed of their faith and their rights. Karl Gerhard was often at those Gothenburg meetings – accompanied by Zarah Leander. 'All of us, and especially Karl Gerhard, were strongly opposed to Hitler and the Nazis in general', we are told by the publisher's daughter, Ingrid Segerstedt-Wiberg. So when Zarah Leander decided to go to Berlin, far from being 'politically naïve', she was very familiar with the political situation in Germany, and with the arguments against the Nazi regime. What is more, before 1936 she sang songs written specially for her by Gerhard, songs in which she took up a clear political standpoint – or so her Swedish friends thought at the time. In a summer revue in 1934 at the Folksteater in Stockholm, Zarah sang a song called 'In the Shadow of a Jackboot', which became a popular anti-Nazi hit. It mourns the plight of the Jews and the loss of freedom in Hitler's Reich:

I stand in a jackboot's shadow
Chained to a massive pillar
A relic of Prussian rule
And slavery in ancient Babylon
. . .
For art has a nobility
That rises eternally
Above time and race
It bows not down
Before a soldier's insult
Spirit and joy can be
Banished from a land but not killed
Europe is losing its senses.
The step toward civilisation
Will only be taken
When we step out from
The shadow of Babylon.

'No-one could sing that song as beautifully as she did. That's why we were astonished when she suddenly went off to Berlin', Ingrid Segerstedt-Wiberg recalls. 'At first we didn't understand. We were proud of her, she was the most famous star we had. But then we found out that she had been in contact with Hitler and Goebbels and accepted the situation in the Third Reich. She had changed sides, so to speak – we were bitterly disappointed.'

As a Swede, Zarah came from outside and had no political reservations of any kind. She was just glad that she could somehow make a career for herself.

Will Quadflieg, actor

Yet it was not only in the group around Karl Gerhard that Hitler's regime was discussed at length. Zarah's colleagues at the Theater an der Wien, the Jewish actor and director, Max Hansen, the lyricist Hans Weigel and the author of *Axel at Heaven's Gate*, Paul Morgan, had all been put out of business by the regime for 'racial reasons'. This cannot have escaped her either. Ingrid Segerstedt-Wiberg, today a liberal member of the Swedish parliament, explains the star's indifference in this way: 'Zarah was never stupid. But she had once been very poor and had problems keeping her family. I can understand her frustration; she wanted to earn money. And when she abandoned us and turned to the Nazis, she gained greatly by it, of course. She became rich, very rich.' The argument that Leander herself once put forward in Germany's favour was this: 'In America foreign actors had to pay income tax at 40 per cent, whereas in Germany the government was happy with 4 per cent.' Her son Göran Forsell confirms her financial rapacity: 'She had a very physical relationship with money. She wanted to touch it; she didn't believe in cheques and didn't trust bankers. If someone said "You'll get a cheque for 5,000 marks in payment", she wouldn't take the cheque, she wanted cash.' Zarah Leander grabbed the chance to become the star of one of the most important film empires in the world and to be rewarded royally for it. Her decision was dictated not by conscience but by ambition. Thus she was adopting a political stance, whether she wanted to or not. Since she allowed herself to be promoted as a showpiece of the Nazi regime, she was automatically seen as representing it. After the war, she could hardly be surprised at being reproached for her work under Hitler's dictatorship. As the Germans say, if you stand in the rain, you get wet.

> With the right material and a good director, perhaps we may yet make something of this Leander woman.
> *Joseph Goebbels, diary, 8 February 1937*

> Goebbels exploited her in order to enhance Germany's standing in the occupied regions.
> *Carl-Adam Nykop, Swedish journalist*

Zarah's signing with Ufa caused controversy even in Germany. Representatives of the rival film company, Tobis, had apparently seen her film, *Première*, and had come to the conclusion that the Leander voice was too deep, and that she was too unusual to have star appeal. Even Goebbels' initial reaction was one of profound in-difference: 'Viewed some films this evening, *Première* with Zarah Leander. What's the fuss about? Weidemann won't be able to do anything with her', he wrote on 6 February 1937, and later: 'Looked at Swedish film with Zarah Leander. Her performance is nothing special. I consider the woman very overrated.' But the self-appointed film expert was wrong.

The Ufa Studios were banking on their new discovery. But they still saw her as a rough diamond that needed to be polished into a jewel. The director of her Ufa début, entitled *To New Shores*, was Detlef Sierck, who went on to work in Hollywood as Douglas Sirk. He had this to say about her: 'At that time Ufa needed new star material. They were really looking for a blonde, who was light on her feet, like the star in *The Congress Dances*. I went to Vienna and saw Zarah's show. But she wasn't blonde and nimble. She was rather stolid; she had a face of amazingly classic beauty, above a rather heavy body, which was admittedly both enhanced and concealed by a very flowing gown. I later discovered that she was broad-hipped and heavy, heavy in her voice as well. But that voice, which was really a baritone, I actually found exciting. I had the feeling that here was something remarkable. Well, anything remarkable and strange is always a novelty, of course.'

> Ufa groomed her for stardom and she played that part to perfection. The public threw themselves at her feet. She was their star, because that was how people wanted to see her.
> *Brigitte Petterson, Zarah Leander's housekeeper*

Even before the first scene was shot in Babelsberg, Ufa set about building her up systematically as a diva. The man responsible for creating 'La Leander' was Ufa's promotion chief, Carl Opitz. In order to arouse curiosity and stoke up expectations, he placed reports in the Nazi-controlled press. 'In the autumn and winter of that year, the papers were fed stories about this creature from the Nordic forests', Zarah recalled. At the same time the search went on for the right outfit to suit the star. It was necessary to bring out the Leander beauty and exoticism, and to gloss over her less attractive features. 'The ladies in the dressmaking department inspected me and discovered I was even larger than they had feared, that I had square shoulders, never wore a brassière, and walked on feet that would only appeal to a glove-maker. Everything had to be made specially for me. The make-up artists and wig-makers took a hold of my hair and found that the good Lord must have picked the colour in a fit of absentmindedness. No-one could have deliberately come up with that astonishing shade, somewhere between beetroot and carrot.' Leander's 'problem area' was definitely her ample rear end. However, with deep décolletés and billowing gowns, the costume designers succeeded in drawing attention away from this 'fault'. What the costumier's art could not conceal, Leander hid from the camera by cleverly holding large fans, stoles and handbags in front of her body, or distracting the eye with large hats. Even her height was a problem for some of her leading men in those days. A heart-throb named Willy Birgel, who was to play her lover in her first film, was appalled at first and refused to work with her, because she was taller than he was. To get round the problem, Detlef Sierck had a system of 4-inch high blocks built beside the camera-tracks. 'Then they strolled along side by side, with Willy walking on the blocks. He was embarrassed at first. But Zarah took it all very calmly', Sierck remembered.

> I had the feeling that here was something unusual. It's all in the word 'unusual'. She stayed in your mind.
> *Douglas Sirk (Detlef Sierck), film director*

However, the Leander image was conveyed mainly in the way her face was photographed. The head slightly tilted, the deeply coloured, finely curved lips closed, or with the slightest hint of a smile, gazing upwards with rapturous, far-away eyes, as if into the distance – that was how Leander was presented on posters, publicity stills and in close-ups in all her films. One film critic wrote: 'Zarah Leander – voluptuous, sophisticated and full of erotic promise. Unapproachable and yet inviting, she seems to want to take you away with her on a journey of the imagination. Here is a woman who people look up at on the screen, from their cinema seats. A star who does not want to be touched, who gives the impression of being present and absent at the same time. A portrait that plays with the looks that we know from the cinema, that "lifts" its figures, makes them appear larger than life and brings them near to us.' That inimitable Leander gaze actually had a rather mundane origin. 'She was extremely short-sighted', the singer Evelyn Künneke recalls. 'And when you shine a 1,000-watt lamp in the eyes of a short-sighted person, it creates that look of yearning.' Zarah Leander was built up into a figure that was to be all things to all men: sophisticated *femme fatale*, hypnotic and remote, glamorous and sexy. Similarities with the Greta Garbo image were quite deliberate. 'I was meant to be enthroned on high, unreachable and hence unfathomable', Leander wrote. 'Again it was the ghost of Garbo: enigmatic, untouchable, the mystique and the legend.'

The efforts by Ufa to create the myth of the 'unapproachable Leander' even extended to her private life. Talking about their life in Berlin, her son Göran tells us: 'When we went to a restaurant, we were always given a table in a *chambre separée*, because she couldn't eat with her family in public, without being constantly interrupted.' Even when Leander wanted to go shopping, the owner of the shop was asked by Ufa beforehand to keep the public out. 'Or else we went after closing time to the Kaufhaus des Westens [a big department store]', Forsell remembers. 'Then she could walk around with us children and say: "I'd like to try this on, I'll have that" – it was incredible.'

> The woman was hugely popular. She was known and loved wherever she went.
>
> *Ilse Werner, actress and singer*

The diva image was zealously cultivated. No picture of Leander was released for publication without the personal approval of Opitz, the PR chief. If a photo caught Leander at an unfavourable angle, making her look too portly for example, the outline was retouched before the picture was put on display in cinemas. The master in presenting Leander was the photographer and cameraman Franz Weihmayr, who did the cinematography on nearly all the films she made for Ufa. 'Franz Weihmayr often worked magic with me', Zarah recalled, 'because in reality I was never as beautiful as I looked on the screen. He would spend hours getting the lighting right just for one close-up.' Weihmayr usually filmed Leander from a low angle, so as to magnify her height. He also gave her a good deal of front-lighting. 'In fact that remarkable face remained the same in any light', commented Detlef Sierck. 'You see, it had that flatness that Garbo's face had too, and which is good for the screen; and also a calmness, a lack of nervousness. Well of course, nervousness can make a face enormously interesting. But its opposite, calmness and flatness, can be extraordinarily beautiful on film. Faces like those of Garbo and Ingrid Bergman – many Swedish women are the same – were known as "cow-faces" by us film people. The limpid eyes, which look lovely even in a cow, and the calmness too, exerted a strange fascination on the camera. I felt that you could shoot Leander with any lens at all, with a wide-angle for instance, which distorts everything a little. That face could be pushed about every which way.'

> They carefully built her up, photographed her very well and – with that lovely dark-brown voice of hers – did everything they could to make her a big star.
>
> *Will Quadflieg, actor*

The première of Zarah's first film, *To New Shores*, on 31 August 1937, was staged by Carl Opitz like a state occasion. Zarah Leander remembered it vividly: 'Huge crowds. Long lines of police. Kids with little blue-and-yellow Swedish pennants and flags. Floodlights like at an ice-hockey match. An escort of police motor-cyclists. Behind them a limo with the diva's bodyguard – eight dinner-suits with men in them. Oh, it was magnificent! The premières in the big Berlin cinemas were always fabulously ostentatious. On those evenings the wide streets around the Memorial Church and the Zoo Station where the Ufa Palace and the Gloria Palace cinemas stood, were always thronged with people.' *To New Shores* was a melodrama directed by Detlef Sierck, who created her character, the typical *'femme fatale* who suffered'. In the film, Zarah plays the part of a singer named Gloria Vane, a star of revue on the London stage. Her lover forges a cheque, but she takes the rap and goes to prison. Afterwards, full of yearning, she waits in vain for the faithless man whose place she took. From then on, the portrayal of unrequited passion was part of her standard repertoire.

The two songs, 'I stand in the rain', and 'Yes, Sir', composed by Ralph Benatzky, were perfect for her, and became hits in their own right. In every film she made, the climax always came when the star broke into song. The melodies and lyrics were written specially for her. In order to weave them into a plot in a more-or-less believable way, Zarah usually played the part of a singer, either the star of a revue or musical, or else a film-star with a past as a vocalist, an opera-singer or a 'celebrated' singer of one kind or another. Where the plot did not allow for such a role, as in *Heart of a Queen*, she simply hammed the part of an unhappy queen with a talent for singing. A great actress she was not. Critics later carped that she never really played different roles, only wore different costumes. It is truer to say that all she ever did was play herself. As she wrote in her memoirs: 'I have never been able to get inside the soul, the thoughts, or the feelings of another person. In films and on the stage I have only ever played one role, in a variety of costumes and in different settings – the role of Zarah Leander.'

> In the years from 1933 to 1945 Zarah was the first and only actress who, despite attractive offers from Britain and America, opted for Germany and the Germans, because of her empathy with German audiences.
>
> *Cornelia Zumkeller, film historian*

It is true that *To New Shores* was not a big box-office success, yet the critics applauded dutifully. One Berlin newspaper wrote: 'But above all there is the glory of her voice. It is as intoxicating as a dark, heavy wine. It can sound as powerful as an organ, can seem as translucent as glass, as dense as metal. In that voice there is everything: elation, happiness, life's heady melody and its savage pain. And this voice belongs to Zarah Leander, the great actress, the newly discovered tragedienne of German cinema.' It was hardly to be expected that she would be panned, since under Goebbels film reviews had become 'observations on art'; and critics were obliged to write nothing derogatory, unless they received a specific request from above to do so. A woman named Edeltraud Richter, who was a fan of Leander, can remember even as a child being besotted with her: 'It is impossible to describe the effect she had. I was a little girl sitting in the cinema and the whole screen was filled with Zarah's face. She was so lovely to look at, I could have sat there for days and nights on end. And those songs! I wasn't really interested in the words. It was mainly the sound of her voice. And I wasn't the only one to feel like that. There was a deadly hush in the cinema; everyone listened enthralled.'

The second film Detlef Sierck directed her in, *La Habañera* (1937), was a runaway success. And the song from it, '*Der Wind hat mir ein Lied erzählt*' (The wind told me a story) became a popular hit well beyond the borders of Germany. Incidentally, her leading man in that film, Ferdinand Marian, later played the title role in Veit Harlan's appallingly anti-Semitic film, *The Jew Süss*. After the war, he was banned from working as an actor, and he and his wife committed suicide.

Even Goebbels, who had so far failed to recognise Zarah Leander's charisma, box-office appeal and impact on audiences, now had to admit: 'The commercial successes achieved with her are enormous.' From then on he kept a careful watch on her. Zarah Leander had made a breakthrough in Germany. In the years that followed she would make ten films with Ufa, mostly costume melodramas or lightweight romantic comedies. That is why Leander always rejected accusations of having been the voice of the Nazi regime. She claimed this was anything but true, since she had only acted in romantic movies, not propaganda films. But the fact is that in Hitler's Germany, even melodramas had a clear political function. Out of more than 1,000 feature films made between 1933 and 1945, comedies head the list with 48 per cent, followed by melodramas with 27 per cent. Propaganda films as such only accounted for 14 per cent of total production.

Nonetheless, Goebbels realised that propaganda should not be driven home with a sledge-hammer. Addressing the Reich Chamber of Film in 1937, he said: 'I certainly do not want art to demonstrate its National Socialist character merely by presenting National Socialist symbols and emblems. Generally speaking, an important mark of its effectiveness is that it never appears contrived. The moment people realise that what they are receiving is propaganda, it ceases to be effective.' What he was up to became quite clear once the war had begun. 'At critical moments especially, optimism helps to overcome difficulties and push obstacles aside. No war can ever be won without optimism', he told an annual conference of 'creators of culture'. 'The darker our streets are, the more bright lights we need in our theatres and cinemas. The harder the times, the more radiantly must art rise above them as a comforter of human souls.' Goebbels saw films as 'a means of national education', whose task was to disguise the harsh realities of life. 'Zarah Leander's films followed the same principle as in ancient Rome', says actor Will Quadflieg, who had a part in *Heart of a Queen*. 'Bread and circuses, *panem et circenses*, to keep the masses happy. Films in the Third Reich were a great diversion from all things political. People were lured into the cinema, to keep them from thinking.'

> If you looked a bit more closely at the whole propaganda scene that Herr Goebbels had built up, you could see where it was all coming from. It was quite unambiguous.
>
> *Will Quadflieg, actor*

At first glance it seems odd that of all people a foreigner, a Swedish woman, should rise to be the top entertainer in Hitler's Reich. Yet paradoxically, at a time when almost everything foreign was despised in Germany, it was artists from abroad who enjoyed particular fame and official honours. For one thing, Germany simply did not have any world-class stars of its own, and for another, people liked to see a touch of exoticism and international style, in films at least. Leading film actresses included Marika Rökk from Hungary, and Olga Tchechova, a Russian emigrée; among the most popular vocalists were

Rosita Serrano from Chile, Kristina Söderbaum from Sweden, and the Dutchman Johannes Heesters. Even Goebbels' *grand amour*, Lida Baarova, was a Czech. Zarah was not only a foreign woman, she nearly always played the part of one, a 'stranger in a strange land'. At a time when Nazi propaganda was rousing its people to a war of conquest, Zarah played a London music-hall singer, or a homesick Swedish girl, an American woman, a Hungarian chanteuse, a Russian châtelaine, a Scottish queen, an Italian contralto or a Danish cabaret star. As a 'tragic' heroine she suffered diverse fates in North and South America, Australia, Hungary, Scotland and the Sahara Desert. While Hitler was unleashing the Second World War and the Reich was becoming increasingly isolated from the rest of the world, Leander acted as a safety-valve for the German people. The film historian Karsten Witte once summed it up like this: 'Through Zarah Leander German film-goers could live out their extravagant fantasies about a life of bliss and sensual promise in distant lands. Zarah kept the fire damped down, but she preserved its glow like the promise of a happiness from which audiences at that time had in reality long since been cut off.'

The narrower and more introverted the German world became, the more this dream-factory satisfied the needs of film-goers by projecting distant horizons. More than any other, the film *La Habañera* expressed the desire for what lay out of reach. The heroine, a Swedish woman, falls in love in Puerto Rico with an exotically handsome bullfighter, and longs to live in his country. But no sooner has she settled there than she yearns for the snows of her native land. 'In those days many women had this eternal longing', believes film director Helma Sanders-Brahms. 'But as long as there was a prospect of many more victories, soldiers had the same kind of feelings: onward, onward – and then back to their homeland.'

As audiences saw her, Zarah wasn't simply a great star, she was a bit of the big outside world, and as Nazi domination dragged on, this world was retreating ever further from the Germans.

Cornelia Zumkeller, film historian

Obviously Zarah Leander's screen image was exactly the opposite of
what was promoted in the Third Reich. Her appearance alone was
in striking contrast to the Nazi ideal of the 'German woman', who
was supposed to be blonde and blue-eyed, not to mention chaste
and unspoilt. Any kind of make-up or jewellery was considered
sluttish, and the preferred hairstyle was either long plaits or tight
curls. Smoking was of course frowned upon. According to Joseph
Goebbels: 'A woman's job is to be beautiful and to bring children
into the world.' In contrast to this, Leander's contrived sexiness was
like a blank canvas on which audiences could project their longings,
and the Nazi regime was happy to exploit her for this purpose. As
the actor Wolfgang Preiss explains: 'The blonde German peasant
maiden did not necessarily suit everyone's taste – all that physicality,
and the demand that "you must be tough, hardy and strict with
yourself and with others". Suddenly here was an attractive,
voluptuous woman about whom, though sex might be out of the
question, you could certainly entertain erotic or loving thoughts. A
woman who radiated a certain motherliness, an emotional warmth –
that was her attraction.' Zarah Leander came to be a favourite with
the public, not in spite of but *because* of the way she conflicted with
the Nazi ideal. 'The Nazis meant the word "*rassig*" to mean
"racially pure", a cool, blonde, beautiful, properly behaved Aryan
woman', says Helma Sanders-Brahms. 'But in Zarah's case it didn't;
it meant "racy", that voluptuous personality with a strong hint of
Jewishness, with the big, heavy-lidded eyes, and with that eternal
yearning that comes from deep down. That was the paradox in her
that the Nazis found so fascinating.' There was an excitement in
what was forbidden – even for the top Nazis themselves.

In a dictatorship where orders and obedience, strict morality and
racial ideology set the tone, Zarah Leander represented a continual
overstepping of boundaries. Even her name, Zarah, sounded very like
the Jewish 'Sarah', which under a 1938 decree all Jewish women had
to have stamped on their passports, as a form of racial branding. As
she writes in her memoirs, Goebbels himself once challenged her
about her name, whereupon she retorted: 'And what about *your*
name, Herr Minister – Joseph, isn't it?' Apparently that made him
laugh. She also crossed the boundary between men and women, a
'strangely androgynous creature', from whose voluptuously female

body an almost masculine voice emerged. In her songs, too, she repeatedly dealt with forbidden themes: saucy, liberated, indeed almost lewd lyrics such as 'Can Love be a Sin', 'His name is Waldemar', or 'Don't cry over love, there's more than one man in life', conflicted with the prevailing morality and touched on taboos. Even after the president of the Reich Chamber of Film had banned the singing of English words in popular hits, Zarah went on singing: '*So bin ich, so bleibe ich* – Yes, Sir!' (That's how I am, and I'll stay that way – Yes, Sir!) Most of her performances contained jazzy and exotic elements, as well as musical forms such as the tango, the Cuban *habañera* and the Hungarian *csárdás*, which were certainly not part of the 'traditional German songbook'. But the fact the she sang this music as an 'exotic' woman in some distant part of the world, made it possible for people to live out their emotions without seriously offending against the National Socialist code of morality.

> Her success meant that she became the great decoy, diverting attention from all things political. And from the war itself, which interested us and dominated our lives so much at that time, whether we liked it or not.
>
> *Will Quadflieg, actor*

In her roles, Zarah only *appeared* to be questioning the place of women in National Socialist society. In 1935 Hitler had said: 'Firstly we regard woman as the eternal mother of our people. And secondly we regard her as a companion to her man in his life, in his work and even in battle.' A woman's place, he said, was at home, and ultimately the salvation of Germany depended on 'the devotion with which our women and girls dedicate themselves once more to the family and the notion of motherhood'. By contrast, Zarah always played an independent and usually successful professional woman, who sets her face against the prevailing mores and expects to have excitement and passion in her life. For the women of Germany, who were initially reduced to baby-production, and then thrown into the breach on the home front as the war came nearer, this was balm for the soul and a projection of their own desires.

Yet in every one of her films the finger of caution is always raised: the heroine is usually punished for her supposed independence, and fails in her search for self-realisation through sex. So while the exotic screen star is granted a free-wheeling lifestyle, at the same time fate warns her of the dangers of offending against social norms. What is more, Zarah always played the same type of woman: the woman who loves with a deep passion and then suffers just as deeply, who is prepared to sacrifice her life for her husband or child. By embodying the beauty of suffering, she brought tears to the audience's eyes. People used to say that no-one could look unhappy in such a marvellously attractive way. 'Young girls are particularly sensitive where that's concerned', Edeltraud Richter recalls. 'And in those days, when you had to be so cheerful and on the ball, and weren't allowed to cry, then of course you were sometimes glad of the relief of shedding a few tears. Especially in *The Open Road*, where she dies in the end, we practically died with her and vowed we'd dash back to the next showing, so as to see her alive again.' The heroine's yearning for passion is never fulfilled. When it comes to choosing between the dashing, exotic lover and the ordinary, decent bloke, she decides on the latter, who guarantees her either true love or at least a comfortable life. Yet despite this self-denial and renunciation, she always retains her stature as a 'woman of noble spirit'. As the critic Cornelia Zumkeller puts it today: 'Though Swedish, she personified the German virtues that were drummed into the people by the Nazis, or which are seen as a typical German cliché: courage, loyalty, self-sacrifice and not least the renunciation of pleasure.' Like Bill Clinton and his marijuana, German audiences were able to smoke the Leander drug, but not inhale.

This modest 'rebellion' was entirely in keeping with the ideals of the Nazis, who saw their movement as a modern departure from the ossified bourgeois society of the Kaiser and the Weimar republic. In *Heimat* (Home Town, 1938), one of her most successful films, Leander plays a world-famous singer who, after a career in the United States, returns to her home town in rural Germany. Her father discovers that she once had an affaire with a man who is now director of a bank, and that there is a child from this relationship. He tries to force her into marrying the money-grubbing man she does not love. In the song 'Only love makes a woman lovely', the disgraced heroine, wearing a deep décolletage, tries to defend herself before the outraged ladies of small-town society. However, despite her initial protests, she gives in. But before the wedding can take place, her intended husband – found guilty of fraudulent wheeling and dealing – kills himself. Now she is free to marry the organist, to whom she is bound by true love. 'Here we see the mask torn from a false and hypocritical morality', cried Goebbels with delight over the film.

Heimat was a great success not only in Germany but internationally. The director, Carl Froelich, received the National Film Prize for 1939, and the award for Best Director at the Venice Biennale. The Nazis' stock was rising: Zarah Leander was an international export hit. Goebbels sent the star forty red roses and invited her for a friendly chat at his ministry. 'The sun of his favour rose over Babelsberg', was how Zarah described the hitherto sceptical film minister's message of unreserved approval.

With *Heimat*, her third film, Zarah had fulfilled her contractual obligations for the time being. It was now up to her whether or not she renewed the contract. By now the political situation had become more dangerous. In 1937, while she was shooting *La Habanera* on Teneriffe, the impact of the Spanish Civil War was clear to see: gunboats cruised off the coast and there were armed skirmishes in the ports. In November 1938, only a few months before the shooting of *Heimat* was completed, synagogues were burned down all over Germany. The persecution of the Jewish population was becoming increasingly noticeable, even in the film industry. When Zarah's director on *La Habañera*, Detlef Sierck, had completed filming, he left Germany because the life of his Jewish wife was in danger. They fled to the United States via Switzerland and Holland. He made his name in Hollywood, but it was a new name – Douglas Sirk.

However, Zarah Leander now found herself on the top rung of a steep career ladder and enjoyed being in the limelight: 'Sometimes we children were allowed to go with her to a première', her son Göran recalls. 'There were thousands of people all screaming hysterically in unison: "Zarah, we love you! Zarah, we love you!" – We found it rather weird that our mother could suddenly become an idol who sent people crazy.' Influenced by this heady success, Zarah renewed her contract with Ufa. Not even the outbreak of war on 1 September 1939 could prevent her from continuing to serve the Nazi propaganda machine – even if she did not admit that she was doing so. And in any case, Goebbels had been doing everything he could to hold on to her. In a long conversation on 14 June 1939, he offered her a large new house in the country and endless privileges, in the hope that she would feel at home and feel she was German. Prompted by the outbreak of war, Leander wrote to Ufa that 'my feelings towards Ufa and my German friends have been reinforced even more by recent events'. Goebbels personally attempted to dispel the anxieties of his star. He noted in his diary on 11 January 1940: 'Frau Leander is worried about her children. She fears that Sweden may get drawn into the conflict. I calmed her down a bit. Women are so totally unpolitical.' The Swedish journalist, Carl-Adam Nykop, explains the actions of his compatriot: 'Zarah wanted the money, and perhaps, like so many Swedes, she thought Hitler would win the war, and that staying in Germany would be a good investment for her future.' In the event, the war did affect the rest of her family. Her husband, Vidar Forsell, left Germany to become an officer in the Swedish army reserve. He took their two children, Boël and Göran, with him.

Zarah stayed behind – and profited from the privileges of a superstar, even though in her memoirs she likes to portray herself as a busy bee, with little time for glamour: 'People think that being a star means lying on a chaise-longue, dressed in silk and lace, drinking champagne, eating chocolates and reading trashy novels. In fact, my working week in Berlin was as strictly scheduled as in any workshop or factory. From 5.45 on Monday morning, when my alarm-clock went off, until 3 o'clock on Friday afternoon, I belonged to Ufa. On several evenings a week, filming went on regularly until midnight. And I had to give up quite a few evenings each month to make publicity appearances. When I got up in the morning I gulped down a boiled egg, some bread and butter and a cup of coffee before my driver Herrmann came with the car and dropped me at the studios at 7 on the dot. At 9 a.m. precisely the hooter went for filming to start. At midday we had a half-hour break, and I could thankfully get out of my magnificent, but often enormously hot and heavy costume. There was just enough time to take off all the finery and baubles, grab some lunch and stretch out on the sofa in my dressing-room. Then from 12.30 to 7 p.m., apart from a few minutes off now and then for a cigarette, we filmed non-stop. That was how life went on, day after day, week after week, year after year. It could hardly be described as a magnificent existence.'

However, Goebbels noted in December 1940: 'She enjoys being part of what we are doing.' Indeed, Leander was never so courted, before or since, as when she was the diva of the Third Reich. At first she lived in a house in suburban Grunewald, then in the classy Berlin district of Dahlem. Domestic servants made her life very comfortable, and if she wanted to go for a drive, a chauffeur-driven cream Horch saloon was at her disposal. 'We were spoiled', recalls her son Göran Forsell about their life in Grunewald. 'We had a cook, a governess for us children, a maid, a private riding-instructor, a private gym-teacher and a chauffeur who took us to school – and we were only a family of four. If you think about it today, it's unbelievable.' When time allowed, Zarah liked to go 'shopping' with her actress friend, Grethe Weiser, around the jewellers of the city, or browsing through antique shops looking for fine pieces of furniture for the country estate in Sweden, to which she had treated herself with her earnings and recording royalties.

> It was not that she put on airs and graces. But she had a strong feeling about being the star of the whole business.
>
> *Will Quadflieg, actor*

Her property, near the Swedish town of Norrköping, south of Stockholm, she appropriately named 'Lönö', meaning 'Reward Island'. Actually a 15-acre peninsula, it included private fishing, woodlands, paddocks, and twenty-two islands and skerries. The house had no fewer than thirty-nine rooms on two floors, including a magnificent library. In buying this palatial home Leander was fulfilling the dream of a lifetime; from now on she would regularly spend all her free time from the studios on her estate. Goebbels was most interested in reports of her commuting between the Reich and neutral Sweden, and liked to talk to her about the political situation: 'A little chat with Frau Leander', he wrote in his diary in 1940. 'She is just back from Sweden. Has some very interesting news from over there. Sweden's attitude to us is much more positive than before. They think Britain has no chance of winning. And are no longer sympathetic towards Norway; its independent political existence is no longer considered possible. Interesting insights into the Swedish mentality.' If Zarah Leander was a political informant of Hitler's Minister of Propaganda, it is an unexpected aspect of the diva, who was supposed to be so 'unpolitical'.

Goebbels was an extremely interesting man. He had a great deal of humour and intelligence. Whatever else he did is none of my business.

Zarah Leander, 1974

She pretended to be naïve about politics. She was certainly never naïve.

Ingrid Segerstedt-Wiberg, Swedish politician

She had sold her political morality to the Nazi regime in return for her career. However a life of stardom did no harm to Zarah Leander as a person. Göran Forsell describes her as a 'dream mother' who, whenever possible, took the trouble to see that her children had a sensible upbringing. 'At home she wasn't a prima donna at all but a completely different person', her son tells us. 'She ran around just like anyone would, with no make-up, glasses and freckles, wearing a dressing-gown and with her hair all over the place. When she came home late at night, she woke us up to have fruit salad and said: "Come on, kids, let's sing something."' On Sundays, Forsell recalls, the children went into their mother's bedroom, acted little plays with her, and played piggyback or Monopoly. Even when on the set, Zarah kept her starriness in check. Her colleagues all agree that she was highly disciplined in her work, rarely demanded special treatment, and was a cheerful and amusing person who was good buddies with everyone.

> She certainly knew how to enjoy herself, and could hold her liquor.
>
> *Evelyn Künneke, actress and singer*

Zarah loved big parties and it is said that there were often high old times at her house in Berlin. According to eye-witness reports 'her guest-lists only ever included single men, so that as the only woman in the house she could be sure of maximum attention'. It is said that Zarah was not averse to the occasional fling. An affaire with actor Victor Staal was talked about. And her personal accompanist Michael Jary was pasionately in love with her, so his daughter says. Yet there was never any scandal surrounding Leander's private life. Indeed there was apparently a clause in her contract forbidding her to kick over the traces.

'To say her parties were orgies is quite true, at least where food and drink were concerned', writes a film critic. 'Only the best was served, especially delicacies which had long since ceased to be available on the open market. Alcohol flowed freely but here too only the choicest labels would do. Zarah, who always had to struggle with her figure, left her diet-plan as just that – a plan – and ate enough for three.' Her head for liquor was nothing short of legendary, as Margot Hielscher tells us: 'During the filming of *Heart of a Queen*, Zarah always took a drink from a mug before and after each take. And I once asked her what she was drinking. She replied: "Milk, milk, you all ought to drink lots of milk, so that you stay beautiful." When she was in front of the camera again I picked up the mug and sniffed it. But that wasn't milk, it was whisky.' Zarah's love of the good life certainly did her figure no favours. She had tended to be plump at the best of times and before every film she had to undergo a radical slimming regime. Even so in quite a few of her films it is clear that she has put on weight.

Nor did Ufa spare any expense on her behalf. For her birthday in 1939 they organised a grand reception at her house, as the guest of honour herself writes: 'Wagon-loads of laburnum were brought all the way from sunny Italy to decorate the house. The butler, head-waiter and servants were all put into violet livery, the tables were adorned with lilac orchids and I was also dressed completely in lilac. All the "in" people were invited, and the managing director, Ludwig Klitzsch, the top man in Ufa, headed the film-crowd procession. As a sign of my pulling-power and importance to the German film business, even Goebbels honoured the reception with his presence.' Clearly the Reich Minister of Propaganda stimulated Zarah's theatrical talent. On Sundays, her son tells us, Leander regularly invited a dozen colleagues to lunch at her villa. 'Mother was a brilliant comedienne with a fantastic sense of humour; she could have been a clown. She took particular delight in making fun of Göring and Goebbels. I can still remember how they all roared with laughter when Mum imitated Goebbels.' But it seems she never risked criticising the propaganda minister in public.

*

As an Ufa star, Leander was obliged to make public appearances at premières, film balls, gala evenings and receptions – to please the crowds and flatter prominent Nazi officials. Goebbels liked to surround himself with stars and starlets, and regularly invited Zarah to his country home or his city apartment in Hermann-Göring-Strasse. He was quite often to be seen at the showbiz club, KDDK, on the Unter den Linden avenue, where film people got together. Zarah Leander describes her relationship with Goebbels as that of an employee to the 'boss'. Her opinion of Hitler's firebrand was certainly not unfavourable: 'No-one can claim he was a good-looking man, but when he warmed to a subject he was not without intellectual charm. At moments like that he became eloquent and witty, his dark eyes sparkled and his voice had a warmth and intensity.' She found that Goebbels 'had intelligent views on cinema. As an art form he loved it far too much to misuse it unnecessarily for propaganda. Goebbels was an interesting man. I didn't dislike him. It was only towards the end that he changed. Then he became foolish – and dangerous.'

*

Behind his back, people called Goebbels 'the Babelsberg Buck', and it was said that many a young actress earned his favour on the casting couch. Indeed, we now know that there was scarcely a single Ufa actress who did not have to fend off his advances. Zarah Leander was no exception. She tells us in her memoirs about being invited to a 'party' at his lakeside home in Schwanenwerder, at which she unwittingly found herself alone with Goebbels. 'No-one else is coming', he told her. 'So I thought we could make a cosy evening of it, just the two of us.' As Zarah acidly comments: 'What Goebbels intended with this "private invitation" was as clear as daylight. It was a sleazy seduction scene. And to make matters worse, it had been clumsily set up. A huge lamp with a silk shade threw a yellowish glow over my hands resting on the grand piano. In one corner there was a flickering candle. There were huge vases of flowers everywhere. On the sofa were silk cushions, the size of mattresses. He was playing something by Chopin.' Zarah boasts how she took control of the situation by correcting his piano-playing and cheekily demanding something to eat. 'By now I had learnt that it does these powerful men good to be contradicted, and they rather enjoy it when someone tells them a few home truths.'

As it emerges from her memoirs at least, Zarah enjoyed playing the temperamental star in the company of top Nazis. According to her, she only met Hitler twice: once at a 'reception for entertainers' and the second time at the 1939 première of the film *Song of the Desert*. The latter encounter is cheerfully dismissed by Leander as a bit of light-hearted banter: 'An adjutant came marching up to me and announced: "The Führer and Reich Chancellor would like you, Madame, to join him at his table." Not having had much practice in dealing with dictators, I trot along behind the adjutant with rather mixed feelings. Hitler gets up very politely and I sit down, wondering all the while what on earth I can talk about to someone called Adolf Hitler. So I adopt a tone of friendly interest and with a maternal smile I say: "Tell me, *Herr Reichskanzler*, have you ever tried to do something about your hair?" Hitler gives a start and turns sharply towards me. When he sees that I'm only looking friendly and sympathetic, he smiles at me hesitantly and takes up my conversational gambit with a worried seriousness. He describes in detail his struggle with the errant quiff: "You have no idea all the things I've tried – oil, hair-cream, wax and all sorts of strange concoctions. But nothing helps. The hair keeps falling over my forehead. It's simply hopeless." Then we ate a mouthful or two, and Hitler ordered some champagne.'

The encounter ended, according to Zarah, with her going out on to the terrace to smoke a cigarette, and shortly after that Hitler politely took his leave of her. Zarah Leander described all her meetings with prominent Nazis as amusing incidents, where she disarms the 'gentlemen' with her irreverent repartee. In retrospect, she seems in no way disturbed by the fact that Hitler and his henchmen were responsible for violence and persecution throughout the Reich, for spreading death and destruction all over Europe and for having gone down in history as double-dealing mass murderers. To her Hitler was 'mainly a voice bellowing from the radio – which I immediately switched off, because I'm very sensitive to nasty noises – and an incomprehensible person with a moustache and a quiff, whom I knew from thousands of photos and hundreds of newsreels'. She was admittedly uncomfortable about the Hitler Youth, and forbade her son from having anything to do with it. 'It's out of the question', she told him when he begged her to let him join. 'Boys aren't supposed to march around shouting; they should racket about and play games.'

> She put up a shield around herself. She said: I'm Swedish, what has any of this to do with me? And she was right, in fact. She certainly wasn't a German.
>
> *Cornelia Zumkeller, film historian*

Hitler's attitude towards his diva is not recorded. But we do know that the dictator was a regular film buff. Up to the beginning of the war hardly an evening went by when he did not have one or two films shown in his chancellery residence or at the Berghof. He and Goebbels chose them together. According to Hitler's architect, Albert Speer, the Führer had a weakness for undemanding light comedies and romances. His favourite actresses included Lil Dagover, Olga Tchechova – and Zarah Leander. Spectacular dance numbers, 'with lots of bare legs, were sure to meet with his approval', Speer recalls. However, despite Goebbels' pleas, Hitler refused to appoint Leander a 'state actress'. True, on 21 November 1941, Goebbels writes: 'In this connection I also threw in the name of Leander. The Führer takes the view that of course Frau Leander should also be appointed a state actress, firstly because she is a genuinely great actress and secondly because she has done a great service to the international reputation of German cinema.' However, it seems that Hitler changed his mind. Months later, after the première of *The Great Love*, the Ministry of Propaganda once again sounded out Hitler and gained the impression that Hitler was having second thoughts on account of Zarah Leander's Swedish nationality. In September 1942 Hitler clearly let it be known that he did not wish her to be given the honour.

*

Zarah Leander was not only a cultural advertisement for the Nazi state. She was also the goose that went on laying golden eggs. During the war especially, when other leisure activities were restricted, Germans spent more and more time at the cinema. Thanks to Hitler's campaigns of conquest, Germany's commercial film distribution expanded over almost all of Europe. The number of cinemas in the 'Greater German Area' nearly doubled to 8,600, with a total of 2.8 million seats. In 1943 the German film industry's annual number of cinema visits exceeded the billion mark for the first time. The biggest wartime hits were *Request Concert* starring Ilse Werner, and Zarah Leander in *The Great Love*. German film output naturally benefited from the fact that after Hitler's declaration of war on the USA in December 1941, Hollywood films were finally banned. In the financial year 1942/3 Ufa made a net profit of 155 million Reichsmarks, and in the following year as much as 175 million – but most of this money flowed into arms manufacture, and thus contributed to a prolonging of the war.

All ten films that Zarah made with Ufa were among the top box-office earners of their year. No wonder Goebbels and Ufa did all they could to market their prize product. Both her wardrobe and her public appearances were planned in minute detail. In 1938

she made a launch tour of the Netherlands, about which she writes:
'I was shipped off as a live promotional package to a film première in
Amsterdam. Every minute that I was on public display during my
"state visit" was spoken for and scheduled. I knew in advance that on
arrival at the central station I would be given gardenias, and that I
would be served lobster on the final evening.' Even in France, under
German occupation since June 1940, she was given celebrity
treatment during the 'German Culture Week' in 1941, and handed
out autographs to German soldiers on the Champs Elysées. The
Swedish journalist Carl-Adam Nykop remembers with horror that in
an interview Zarah remarked that Paris had not changed at all under
German occupation, except that instead of tourists you now saw
visitors in uniform. In the same year, when she was in the French
capital to dub the soundtrack of *The Open Road*, she confessed to a
Nazi journalist: 'My strongest impression in Paris was on Sunday,
when they mounted the German guard of honour at the Arc de
Triomphe. It was deeply moving!' Zarah Leander was made an
instrument of National Socialist propaganda – and willingly allowed
it to happen. On many occasions she obeyed Goebbels' orders and
sang at request concerts for the Wehrmacht. And she happily made
herself available to promote collections for the 'Winter Welfare'
organisation.

In spite of having given her full support to the Nazis, Leander
retrospectively distanced herself from any kind of political activity: 'In
the studios, no-one ever talked about politics', she insisted. Broadly
speaking, that is probably true. Most of the artists and performers
who remained in Germany preferred to keep out of day-to-day
events, if only to avoid damaging their own careers. 'We weren't
interested in politics in any way', Wolfgang Preiss assures us. 'We
thought it was marvellous that we could make films, and just
concentrated on that. We had little interest in what the army was
doing near Moscow.' The Babelsberg studios were considered a free
zone, where politics stopped at the front door. 'In those studios even
Zarah Leander was remote from what was going on in the streets,
and to that extent it was a world of its own', the director Helma
Sanders-Brahms believes. 'The studios were fitted with insulated
walls, and even while Berlin was being bombed, they went on filming
those monstrous tear-jerkers. When the actors went in front of the

cameras, they were soundproofed in the truest sense of the word.' The Ufa actress Ilse Werner even cherishes the blissful illusion that 'we were one big family and we all stuck together'.

Yet behind the façade of elaborate pretence lay a spreading morass of fear and indifference. For not even the self-obsessed stars of Ufa could prevent the excesses of the dictatorship from invading the studios. 'At best, politics were discussed in whispers', Margot Hielscher stated in an interview. 'But then you never knew who was listening. It could be extremely dangerous, and the fear of being denounced was great.' 'We all had the enemy breathing down our neck,' says Will Quadflieg. 'Nobody dared speak their mind honestly, except among a few friends. We actors were fellow-travellers in a depressing but understandable way. Because of course we all wanted to survive the war.'

Even when certain colleagues were forced to disappear abroad for 'racial' or political reasons, they were dismissed by many as 'isolated cases'. However, one instance of persecution and humiliation did cause great dismay in film circles: from 1937 onwards, Joachim Gottschalk, one of the most popular actors in the Third Reich, was increasingly harassed and then blacklisted by Goebbels, because he refused to divorce his Jewish wife. 'If this man thinks he can pocket wads of money making German films during the day and then go to bed with his Jewish tart at night, then to hell with him', Goebbels is said to have ranted. On 5 November 1941, Gottschalk gassed himself, together with his wife and child, in their apartment. 'Only a few had the courage to be as true to their convictions as Gottschalk was', Will Quadflieg comments on the suicide. 'We were all shocked to the core when we heard about it, but then we thought to ourselves: Well, what about me, where do *I* stand? Do I go along with it all and not put up a fight?'

*

Once the war started the situation deteriorated. Goebbels was absolutely determined not to let artists get away with any more 'political bad behaviour'. His first wartime victim was the director Herbert Selpin. In the summer of 1942 Selpin was hired to direct *Titanic*, a film designed to demonstrate British incompetence. The director was known to have a short temper, and on the set he began making derogatory remarks about the war and the Wehrmacht; he was denounced by his script-writer and made to explain himself before Goebbels. Because Selpin did not immediately withdraw his 'statements undermining the military effort', Goebbels had him arrested in his office and imprisoned. The next morning he was found hanged in his cell. 'Typical of these film types', Goebbels is reported as saying. 'First they shoot their mouth off and criticise Führer and Reich, then they deny everything. But when they're bowled out, their courage deserts them and they have the poor taste to hang themselves by their braces.' For the benefit of the studios, Goebbels announced that Selpin had 'seriously violated war morale, by vilely slandering and insulting German officers and men serving at the front'. But rumour had it that Selpin had been murdered by the Gestapo.

The longer the war lasted, the more threatening the atmosphere became. Goebbels now did not shrink from ordering executions: in August 1943 the actor Karl John was condemned to death by the People's Court for 'voicing defeatist views' – in other words telling jokes against the Führer. Then in 1944 it was the turn of the PR chiefs of Terra and Ufa, Erich Knauf and Richard Düwell. But by this time Zarah Leander had long since returned permanently to Sweden.

Yet news of persecutions beyond her immediate circle must have come to her attention. Unlike others, her frequent visits gave her access to foreign newspapers. As early as the end of 1941 reports of the horrors of the Holocaust had filtered through to Britain. In May 1942 Jewish labour union officials passed information from the Polish underground to the British press. The BBC broadcast detailed reports and on 7 June the *Daily Telegraph* wrote: 'More than 700,000 Polish Jews have been slaughtered in the greatest massacres in world history.' The article also mentioned specially modified trucks being used by the Nazis as mobile gas chambers. In the west the public were learning more and about the Holocaust. On 7 December 1942 Hitler's adversaries issued a public declaration: the USA, Britain, Soviet Russia and the governments-in-exile of eight German-occupied states condemned the Germans 'in the strongest terms of bestial methods of extermination'.

> No, she wouldn't have been risking her career. Not at all. She
> could definitely have done something, if she'd wanted to.
>
> *Will Quadflieg, actor*

In her memoirs Zarah made the self-serving excuse that she had
always stayed in touch with one persecuted minority – homosexuals.
'I kept up those friendships even during the war and for that reason
was once summoned by the head of Ufa. He warned me not to go
around with homosexuals. But I stubbornly refused to be told what
to do where that was concerned. It was for me to choose the friends
I saw in my free time. 'It could lead to terrible complications', the
Ufa boss went on. 'Fine, I'll have to put up with that', I said. "As a
Swede I have a different attitude to yours. I have always believed
that homosexuals are human beings like the rest of us. And think
how many great figures in human history have been homosexual!
Nonetheless they enjoyed the respect, devotion, love and admiration
of the people who knew them. My Swedish morality tells me that
we shouldn't ride on our high horse, we shouldn't point the finger
at those people who live differently."'

The regrettable fact is that Zarah Leander did not lift a finger to
help homosexuals. From a male homosexual population of some 2
million, between 1939 and 1945 alone an estimated 50,000 were
imprisoned or sent to concentration camps. But the real figure is
probably much higher, since not all the gay inmates were identified
with the 'pink triangle'. A larger number were classified as criminals,
child abusers, sexual offenders or anti-social elements in general. As
early as 1930 the Nazi Party newspaper, *Völkischer Beobachter*, wrote
that 'all the malevolent urges of the Jewish soul' come together in
homosexuality, and that these would be soon be punished as the
'most serious of crimes, to be punished by exile or the rope'. After
the murder of Ernst Röhm, leader of the SA storm-troopers, whose
homosexuality was admittedly only a pretext for liquidating the
entire senior ranks of the SA, the criminal prosecution of
homosexuals became more severe. In 1938 the number of
convictions reached 8,500 and only began to decline gradually when
the war started. Instead, from 1940 onwards, Heinrich Himmler

ordered that any homosexual who had had relations with more than one partner should be sent to the concentration camp without trial. In 1941, homosexual activity between members of the SS was made punishable by death.

Even Zarah Leander's longest-serving lyric-writer, Bruno Balz, fell foul of the Gestapo. The writer of hits such as 'The wind told me a story', 'Perhaps', 'Can love be a sin?', 'A lovely lady tells you', 'His name is Waldemar' and 'You must never give me red roses again', was denounced in 1941. He spent three weeks in the Gestapo dungeons in Prinz-Albrecht-Strasse. Apparently it was the composer Michael Jary who obtained his release, on the grounds that he needed Balz for the next Leander film. As for Zarah herself, either she knew nothing about the arrest of her friend and favourite lyricist, or if she did, she did not react in any way. Incidentally, it was after his brief imprisonment that Bruno Balz is said to have had the idea for his song, 'Davon geht die Welt nicht unter' (It's not the end of the world). If that is so, then the song was really intended to give encouragement to persecuted homosexuals, and was not the patriotic morale-booster it was later claimed to be. The actor Gary Philipp, who was put into a concentration camp for being both a Jew and a homosexual, adds this story: 'In the camp, when we inmates got together, we sang this song and hoped a miracle would happen, that the war would end and we would be rescued. It was a comfort to us.' Looked at from this angle, other songs such as 'Can love be a sin?', with which Zarah Leander sang her way into the hearts of the top Nazis, were in fact anthems for persecuted homosexuals. It is a phenomenon that helps to explain the Leander success-story. In a song like 'I know one day a miracle will happen' everyone could read a positive message for their own personal lives. It could equally be understood as a love-song, a morale-booster for those in the field or on the home front, or as an encouragement for the persecuted. Zarah Leander belonged to everyone.

It is of course easy to reproach people in hindsight for having simply accepted injustice. Zarah Leander had a favoured position in the Third Reich, good connections with Hitler's henchmen, and as a Swedish woman with a Swedish passport, enjoyed unlimited freedom to leave and re-enter Germany. She had more opportunity than most to take up the cause of persecuted minorities. 'During the war I myself was involved in helping refugees', says Ingrid Segerstedt-Wiberg. 'It was no easy task, and for Zarah I fear it would have been well-nigh impossible. You needed a lot of courage for that sort of activity, because at times like that you are always gambling with life or death.' Yet to Zarah Leander her career was more important – particularly as this had not fallen into her lap.

> She allowed herself to be taken over by the Nazis. She didn't keep her distance.
> *Ingrid Segerstedt-Wiberg, Swedish politician*

> Zarah Leander was only interested in earning a lot of money.
> *Carl-Adam Nykop, Swedish journalist*

Not long after the runaway success of *Home Town*, there followed one 'turkey' after another. *The Blue Fox*, directed by Viktor Tourjansky in 1938, was an insipid romantic comedy. The only notable thing about the film was Zarah's song, 'Can Love be a sin?' Another film, *Night of the Enchanted Ball*, was at best a modest success. This romance was premièred on the eve of the Second World War, two weeks before Hitler's assault on Poland. In it Leander plays the composer Tchaikovsky's devoted mistress, who forgoes her love for the sake of his career. Apart from the fact that once again Zarah was magnificent in her suffering, the only memorable thing in the film was the song 'Don't ever cry over love'. The peak of overblown tastelessness was reached with *The Song of the Desert*, released only a few months later, on 17 November 1939. Despite having a chance to ride a camel in the film, even Zarah Leander was embarrassed by it in retrospect: 'With sand between my toes and in my teeth, I appear in the story without explanation or motivation, as the celebrated singer Grace Collins. It was so-o *bad*!' Despite its strongly anti-British flavour, the film was such a stinker that 'even German audiences stayed away. *Song of the Desert* was a total flop. It was withdrawn after a few days. At that particular moment, this was extremely awkward for me, since my two previous films had not been successful either.'

Whether such débâcles were so 'awkward' for Zarah that she
had to fear for her job is debatable. It was only a short time later
that her most expensive film reached the screen, and also marked
the low point of her career. *The Heart of a Queen*, a pretentious
costume drama directed by Carl Froelich, told the story of Mary
Queen of Scots. With rather too many extra pounds around her
midriff, which not even the lavish costumes could conceal,
Leander moved awkwardly though the badly directed scenes. Even
with her ballads, inserted quite gratuitously into the action, the
singing royal heroine failed to make an impact. The film was a
failure. Two weeks after its opening on 1 November 1940, the
Luftwaffe chief Hermann Göring, in a mindless fit of rage over his
defeat in the Battle of Britain, sent his bombers to reduce the city
of Coventry to ashes. The British hit back with a series of
devastating air-raids on German cities.

After her three disastrous films Zarah Leander might well have
disappeared from the screen without trace, had not a new director,
Rolf Hansen, helped her to restore her reputation. His very first
production with Leander, *The Open Road* (1941), was a huge
success. But their second collaboration, *Die Grosse Liebe* (The Great
Love), outstripped them all and was the climax of her career. At the
same time, it was her only film that in retrospect has been described
as a 'propaganda potboiler' and brought her the charge of being a
'Nazi siren'. In it Zarah plays a music-hall singer, who meets a young
Luftwaffe officer during an air raid. For both of them it is love at first
sight, and they spend the night together. However, wedding-bells
and a happy ending are delayed by the war. The flyer is repeatedly
sent to the front and then volunteers to serve in the Russian
campaign. Hanna, the singer, resents this. However, when he is lying
wounded in a field-hospital, she understands that in these times of
war, military loyalty takes priority and that it is a woman's duty to set
her personal desires on one side.

> She had to do what was written in the script and what the
> director told her. And of course the director got his
> instructions from the Ministry of Propaganda.
>
> *Evelyn Künneke, actress and singer*

Die Grosse Liebe bears the unmistakable fingerprints of the Ministry of Propaganda and is the only Leander film which reflected the experience of ordinary Germans, albeit in an idealised way. For the first time the diva had descended from her Olympian heights and mixed with the common people. In the film we see her riding on the subway, just as most Germans had to do at a time when petrol was in short supply. When there is an air-raid warning the occupants of the apartment block gather in the cellars. But whereas in reality the atmosphere under ground was one of mortal fear, horror and suffocating confinement, the mood in the film is cheerful, even exuberant. The householders sit cosily drinking coffee together, and when the 'all-clear' is heard, a boy whose games are interrupted groans: 'Oh, it *would* have to be now.' More of a picnic than a bombing raid. In the interests of realism Goebbels personally made a change to one scene: the couple are celebrating their engagement at home with friends, when the fiancé is summoned to the front line. Actor Wolfgang Preiss takes up the story: 'The week's shooting was always delivered to Doctor Goebbels on Saturday, and he looked at the "rushes". He then observed – and remember, this was the third year of the war – "German women don't live like that". So we had to re-shoot the scene, with a smaller apartment, fewer guests and less champagne, but more German *Sekt* instead.' In place of a feminine flowered dress, in the Goebbels version Zarah had to wear a severe white jacket and skirt, presumably modelled on the plain uniform of a German soldier.

In this film Zarah Leander was presented as a paragon of the feminine virtues that were in demand on the home front. In the story, the celebrated vocalist gives up her exciting and independent life and transforms herself into the long-suffering officer's wife, who finds fulfilment in her role as a spouse, but nonetheless bows to military imperatives. As a propaganda message, it was chiefly aimed at women. In 1942, with the start of the summer offensive on the Russian front, there was scarcely a family in Germany that did not have at least one son, brother or father serving in the field. For almost every German woman the pain of separation felt by the singer Hanna Holberg was only too familiar. The film's 'happy ending' gave them the hope that their waiting would be rewarded, and that their loved ones too would return to them when victory was won – perhaps 'a miracle' would indeed happen.

At the same time the film promoted the ideal of the 'soldierly husband', whose first duty is the defence of the fatherland and only then to his family. Nevertheless, the love that can lead to marital bliss only when peace comes, helps him to live through the war. As we learn from former members of the armed services, Zarah Leander succeeded in raising the morale of the men fighting at the front. One war veteran recalls with warmth how 'we soldiers were stuck in the mud in Russia. We often heard Zarah's voice on the radio, and it gave us all comfort and hope again.' True to the Nazi ideal of a woman committed to her country, Hanna the show-singer recognises that her place is looking after the troops, and in a requisitioned château in occupied France she sings 'It's not the end of the world' to an audience of wounded Wehrmacht soldiers. The men, some with SS insignia on their collars, link arms and happily rock to and fro to the waltz. A critic wrote of this scene at the time: 'The cheerful refrain excited the war-invalids in the cinema as much as it did their wounded comrades on the screen.' For the rest of her life Zarah Leander insisted that she had never sung to Wehrmacht soldiers. So we must accept it as an ironic footnote to cinema history that the 'comrades on the screen' were in fact real infantrymen. Wolfgang Preiss explains: 'The theatre in which we shot this scene had between 500 and 800 seats. To save the cost of hiring extras, some soldiers were simply detailed off to fill the auditorium. And when she sang "*Davon geht die Welt nicht unter, sie wird ja noch gebraucht . . .*" (It's not the end of the world, the world will still be needed . . .) – of course that had great propaganda value. The world must go on, we'll need you, and you, and you.'

After the war, the songs 'It's not the end of the world' and 'I know one day a miracle will happen', were put down as Leander's Nazi morale-boosters. The film was premièred on 12 June 1942 – two weeks after the first major British air raid on Cologne had reduced the historic city centre to ruins. On the eastern front the German armies had launched a massive new offensive. But as yet the real catastrophe had not struck; not until six months later did Hitler sacrifice an entire army in a vain attempt to hold Stalingrad, and in Berlin's Palace of Sport Goebbels consigned the nation to 'total war'. At that point in time the songs promised instead the fulfilment of Germany's dreams of being a great power, rather than invoking heroism in the face of destruction. In an interview some years later, Leander defended herself thus: 'What we were trying to say was that peace will return, and people will be able to live normal lives again. But the gentlemen at the top interpreted it as: "A miracle will happen, and we will be masters of the world." But that's not what we meant.' Be that is it may, Goebbels' maxim about 'invisibly effective propaganda' was invoked with resounding success. The film was deemed to be 'of political, artistic and popular value'.

> 'I know one day a miracle will happen' – stuff like that was of course propaganda of the most effective and insidious kind, because everyone was just longing for that miracle.
>
> *Will Quadflieg, actor*

The only quarter from which a complaint about the film was heard was the Wehrmacht High Command, which claimed that a German flight-lieutenant would not go to bed with a lady on the first night of a fleeting acquaintance. However, the Luftwaffe chief, Hermann Göring, swept the criticism aside: 'If a flight-lieutenant doesn't grab a chance like that, he's no flight-lieutenant of mine', the notorious playboy averred. However, the part played by the men of the elite SS unit, *Leibstandarte 'Adolf Hitler'*, in the filming of the number 'I know one day a miracle will happen', certainly does not appear in any official document. It is one of those absurd twists of history that, of all people, those prototypes of Himmler's 'steel-hard Germanic warriors' should take the stage with Zarah Leander in women's clothes and parodying Zarah herself. A story is told with glee by Wolfgang Preiss, who played a Luftwaffe officer in the film. 'I was completely unknown as an actor. One day, when I was dressed as an *Oberstleutnant* (wing-commander), I walked passed the extras' changing-room, and the SS men were there, dressing up in their costumes. Some devil got into me and I bawled: "Atten-*shun*!" They all stood strictly to attention just as they were, in women's dresses, wigs askew, half made-up or in their underwear – it was a grotesque scene. I then said, as naturally as I could: "All right, men. Carry on!" but inside I was killing myself with laughter.'

*

By 1944, against production costs of just over 3 million Reichsmarks, box-office revenues had reached no less than 9.2 million. By 1943, *Die Grosse Liebe* had been seen by 27 million people. Zarah Leander was at the zenith of her success and had become one of the highest-paid stars in Nazi Germany. While in 1937 she was already earning 200,000 Reichsmarks a year, in 1943 alone she earned double that figure. However, the bulk of her income came from her records. 'His name is Waldemar', 'Don't ever cry over love', 'Can love be a sin?' and 'The wind told me a story' were all hits that sold in millions. She recorded many of the numbers in Swedish and French as well as German.

> In Germany, whether someone sang morale-boosting songs, or didn't, was basically not an issue. Under a dictatorship it makes no difference. You are simply forced to do what they demand of you.
>
> *Evelyn Künneke, actress and singer*

By now the war that Hitler had unleashed had long since crossed the borders of Germany itself. From February 1942 the British adopted a strategy of raining terror down on the civilian population. Their declared aim was to 'wear down the morale of the German people' by the saturation bombing of German cities. Early in 1943 the Royal Air Force was joined by the Americans and there was no respite for the beleaguered population. By day US bombers flew precision-bombing sorties, while at night the British laid down carpets of incendiaries and high explosives. Ever since 1940 Berlin itself had been subjected to repeated attacks. In January President Roosevelt of the USA, and Britain's prime minister Winston Churchill, met in Casablanca and agreed to demand Germany's unconditional surrender. Propaganda-inspired rumours now circulated throughout the Reich, that the Allies wanted not only to defeat Germany but also to destroy it and annihilate its population. However, the slogan: 'Our walls may break, but not our spirit!' did not cut any ice with Zarah. She was a Swede and she wanted to go home. In any case, with the disaster of Stalingrad in February 1943, it was becoming increasingly clear that Hitler's Reich was going to lose the war. Goebbels attempted in his notorious, rabble-rousing speech at the Palace of Sport to mobilise the German people for the final struggle: 'You all want total war, don't you?' Zarah's answer was a definite 'No.'

The diva certainly could not complain about lack of comfort. In her villa, which had its own underground air-raid shelter, she could happily let the bombs drop on nearby Berlin. Nonetheless she lived in constant fear that sooner or later a bomb would hit her home too. Life in Hitler's Reich was becoming rather unpleasant for the star. And it was made worse by a further conflict: while making her last film, *Damals* (Way Back When) she came to blows with Goebbels and Ufa for the first time, though admittedly for financial rather than political reasons. Due to the increasing shortage of foreign currency, Ufa refused, in breach of their contract with Leander, to pay 53 per cent of her fee in Swedish crowns, and proposed payment entirely in Reichsmarks. Consumed with rage, the diva stormed off the set and stayed at home for days until Ufa gave in and remitted the crowns.

> She never wanted to become German. She was Swedish and would stay Swedish.
>
> *Göran Forsell, son of Zarah Leander*

From the autumn of 1942, Zarah Leander only spent a little time in Germany, making use of her permanent freedom to travel to Sweden. Her last 'brief conversation' with Goebbels, on 28 November 1942, was far from amicable. Goebbels tried to talk her into making more films, and she appeared to agree to this. Goebbels went on to offer the susperstar a mansion in Germany and a handsome pension for life. He asked only one thing in return: that she, Zarah Leander, should adopt German nationality. He must have hoped that in this way he could bind the Swedish diva to the Third Reich for all time. But Zarah was a Swede through and through. 'I refused', she wrote, 'and we parted in a very chilly atmosphere.' She had made up her mind: she would leave Germany for ever. She had already shipped most of her valuables over to Sweden. She now succeeded – or so she boasts in her memoirs – in getting the economics minister, Walther Funk, so drunk that she was able to wangle a permit to export her costly antiques to her Swedish dream-house.

The last time she visited Berlin was on 3 March 1943, for the première of *Way Back When*. The film's director, Rolf Hansen, recalls the occasion: 'At about 11.30 p.m., when it was finally over, we drove out to the Babelsberg studios, where Ufa was giving a party. They produced such amazing drinks and delicacies, you just couldn't believe it was the middle of the war. Later on, Zarah came up and invited me and a few others to her villa in Grunewald, so that she could go on partying with her closest friends. So we drove off, having no idea that by this time the whole of Berlin was being bombed. When we reached Zarah's house, which was a long, low bungalow, the whole kitchen wing was ablaze.' The destruction of her home must have been the last straw that made her turn her back on Germany. In April 1943 Leander finally took up permanent residence in Sweden. Her contract with Ufa ran on until the middle of that year. In the months that followed, Ufa kept on sending screenplay proposals to Sweden, but Zarah turned them all down. She did not want to go on, and in September 1943 she announced to the Swedish press that her contract with Ufa had expired.

She didn't want to stay in Germany any longer. When the first bombs fell, she was afraid. She didn't feel comfortable in Germany any longer. And it wasn't just to do with the bombs.

Göran Forsell, son of Zarah Leander

For many of her German fans Zarah's departure came as a shock. 'It was the writing on the wall', a critic wrote later. 'Amid the rumours that "Zarah Leander has quit" there was a feeling of having been abandoned, and of impending doom. Just as the exhaustion of war was setting in, people had lost their most voluptuous love-object, their universal source of fantasy.' However, the most biting reaction came from the Nazi-controlled press, which claimed that Leander had given interviews in Sweden that were 'hostile to Germany'. Under the headline 'Zarah Leander, a friend of the Jews!', the Nazi paper *Stosstrupp* (Shock-Troop) wrote on 20 July 1944: 'The Swedish film-star Zarah Leander, who made her name in Germany, will appear this autumn in a revue at the Stockholm Circus, directed by the German-hater Gerhard [the same Karl Gerhard with whom Leander had worked closely from 1932 to 1936, *Tr.*]. Gerhard is a well-known 'drawing-room Bolshevist', who uses his touring revue to spread shameless political agitation all over Sweden. Stockholm's communist mouthpiece *Ny Dag* (New Day) publishes an interview with Zarah Leander, in which she admits to being a friend of the Jews, and is happy to leave the decision as to whether she will sing anti-German lyrics entirely to the producer of the revue.' The journal *Political Service for SS and Police*, published by Heinrich Himmler, also contained a malicious and slanderous article in 1944: 'We have seen nothing of that superwoman Zarah Leander for quite some time. 'Can love be a sin?' she sang, and for her it wasn't. Or if it was – and in her case we often got the impression that it was – then she could not have cared less. "Yes, *sir*" – the path to that tart's door was a short and well-trodden one, by all accounts. 'Only love makes a woman lovely' she sang – and basked in fame and fortune. First she wanted to present herself in Germany as a sophisticated woman of the world, then increasingly to squeeze out and replace German women altogether. In the process we made her a big star. Her pictures decorated every bunker, and for many ordinary foot-soldiers she was the epitome of womanhood. Now the Russkies are probably sitting in those same bunkers and can delight in her gleaming smile. We wish them a lot of fun with her! Zarah has vanished. She left us as soon as the fount of eroticism had been drained dry, and enough money had been earned. German women can breathe easy again.'

However, the hate that was building up against Zarah did not prevent the Nazi authorities from continuing to show her films, despite calls from individual departments for her to deposed. A memo from the Reich Director of Film, Hans Hinkel, to Goebbels, was probably decisive. It drew attention to the fact that Leander's export success was after all 'the engine of the whole German film output, whose sales would be undermined by her absence'. For commercial reasons he advised against withdrawing the films either at home or abroad and pointed out that 'in the cinemas of the Reich 500 prints are being shown as re-runs, and will bring in total box-office receipts of 3.5 million Reichsmarks this year. No doubt we can make do without this money, but it will be extraordinarily difficult for the German film industry to supply 500 cinemas with other films.' The films remained on release and Zarah's voice could be heard on radio as well, until January 1945.

> I could not change my political colours, because I had never had any.
>
> *Zarah Leander in her autobiography*

In Sweden, however, an unpleasant surprise was awaiting Zarah. Naively she had believed she would be able to carry on her previous successes without a break. Instead she came up against contempt and rejection. She was accused of having been Hitler's star. However, on the part of many Swedes this reaction was nothing if not hypocritical. For this officially neutral country had from the beginning had an ambiguous relationship with Nazi Germany. Even after Hitler seized power, Swedish artists and writers thought it quite natural to work in Germany. To begin with the Swedes were actually proud that 'their' Zarah Leander had become an international star and was making her name in Hitler's Reich. When her films *Première* and *To New Shores* were shown at the Venice Film Festival, Swedish newspapers reported that 'Zarah Leander is representing Sweden in Venice with an Austrian and a German film'. All Zarah's films were shown to great acclaim in her native country.

After the outbreak of war, Sweden became critically important to Germany as a source of war materials, supplying at least 30 per cent of Germany's iron-ore requirements for the production of weapons and armoured vehicles. In order to secure its 'independence' after the German occupation of Norway and Denmark, and Finland's entry into the war, Sweden went as far as permitting German troop movements across its territory. In return, Sweden received coal and textiles from Germany. It is believed that right up to the end of 1944 gold from the Reichsbank was exchanged in Sweden for foreign currency, even though it had been known since early in 1943 that this gold had been plundered from occupied nations. Like Switzerland, Sweden persuaded the German authorities to mark the passports of Jewish citizens with the letter 'J', so that Jewish refugees could be recognised more easily and turned back at the frontier. Young Swedish men even joined the *Waffen-SS*, served as guards in concentration camps and took part in mass shootings. When Hitler invaded the Soviet Union in June 1941, the Swedish head of state, King Gustav V, sent the warlord a telegram wishing him 'great success in the crushing of Bolshevism'. Not until the end of the 'Thousand Year Reich' began to loom, with the catastrophe at Stalingrad, did the Swedish worm turn. An anti-German attitude began to spread in Sweden, which, officially at least, had never really been present before.

Karl Gerhard, Zarah's friend and patron from the 1930s, did his best to organise a comeback for his prodigal protégée. He decided to book her for one of his shows. But when people got wind of this it provoked a wave of outrage, and the press launched an outright anti-Leander campaign. Carl-Adam Nykop, then editor of a leading illustrated magazine, wrote: 'No self-respecting Swede would keep company with Doctor Goebbels for years on end, and join the clique which tyrannised our Scandinavian neighbours so cruelly and ruthlessly; she would not travel to occupied countries nor receive the homage of representatives of the occupying powers. Not even if the main purpose was to earn money. She might find it convenient to pose as a political innocent and excuse herself that way. But that is no excuse.'

> She had big problems in Sweden, enormous problems,
> because of what she had been doing with the Nazis in
> Germany.
>
> *Evelyn Künneke, actress and singer*

The most vehement protests came from the Association of Danish
and Norwegian Refugees in Sweden. As Nykop recalls: 'They wrote a
letter to Karl Gerhard, in which they made this threat: "If you simply
sweep under the carpet all the things Zarah has been doing in
Germany in these last years of the war, then it will be the end of *your*
career as well."' In order to defuse the tense situation, Karl Gerhard
invited Stockholm's leading citizens to a reception at his home, on
14 July 1944. But a row broke out there. While a few journalists and
colleagues spoke to Zarah, others – as soon as they knew of her
arrival – pointedly walked out of the house. In the face of this
massive opposition, Zarah Leander wrote an open letter to Gerhard
cancelling her agreement to appear in his revue. Deeply hurt and
embittered she withdrew from the hostility to her Lönö estate.

In the five years that followed, the diva transformed herself into
a landowner and busied herself with her fisheries and stock-
breeding, her vegetable garden and housekeeping. For a while she
took in refugees from north-eastern Europe, who had fled across
the Baltic Sea to escape the advancing Russian armies. Financially
Leander had nothing to worry about. Her film earnings and
royalties from her records kept her in luxury. Yet Zarah was only
thirty-six years old when she suddenly fell from the peak of her
fame into complete oblivion. She was an actress and a singer to her
fingertips and she missed her public. Nor was she faring any better
in her private life: her marriage with Vidar Forsell was already in
crisis and her unhappy situation only made matters worse. The
marriage was dissolved in 1946.

*

And yet Zarah Leander did finally succeed in returning to the
limelight, despite all the obstacles that stood in her way. After the

collapse of Hitler's empire the Allies had banned Leander from appearing anywhere in occupied Germany and Austria. But on 13 November 1948 she stood on a German stage once more, in the border city of Saarbrücken. The concert tour of Germany that followed was like a triumphal progress. The Germans had not forgotten 'their Zarah'. In Sweden, too, the diva finally made a successful comeback, in Malmö on 5 August 1949. In the following years she made seven films including *Gabriela*, *Cuba Cabana* and *Ave Maria*, though she was never able to repeat the triumphs she had enjoyed with Ufa. Nonetheless, she continued well into old age, scoring worldwide successes with her Ufa songs, and starring in musicals.

*

Yet this did not mean an end to speculation about her 'political past'. Far from it. During the war the American secret service had observed Zarah's activities with suspicion. However, on 19 December 1942, the Swedish agent-general in the USA, Erik S. Eriksson, calmed American fears with this statement: 'She was certainly not a Nazi sympathiser. I am more than convinced that she is on our side.' After the war a Swedish diplomat even claimed that Leander had been secretly working *against* the Germans and had helped people to escape. In 1951, when Zarah applied for a visa to make a concert tour of the USA, the secret servicemen swung into action again. CIA documents note that, according to an informant, actors were trained as espionage agents under the Third Reich, and Leander had been particularly successful in spying for the *Abwehr*, Germany's military and foreign intelligence service. Even her husband, Vidar Forsell, was accused of having taken large sums of money from Germany to Sweden, in order to purchase real estate there for Germans. Another report made the far-fetched claim that Zarah had worked for the KGB and was part of a Soviet spy-ring. At the time of the anti-communist witch-hunts in the United States such rumours were sufficient: Zarah's visa application was turned down. Instead, she ended up by touring South America. Similar contradictory reports, to the effect that Leander had spied for both the Nazis and for the Soviets, are to be found in the files of the Swedish secret service. However, no evidence that the star engaged in espionage has ever been produced. Fundamentally, the idea that a woman whose eyes were always on her show-business career might have been politically active, is in any case absurd.

> And there was Zarah Leander, the imposing giantess, sensual, self-confident, cosmopolitan and, whenever it was appropriate, not entirely lacking in a ladylike irony.
> *Christa Rotzoll, journalist*

> She was a great personality. When she came on stage or into a room, she was somebody. You cannot *become* a personality; you have to be born one.
> *Ilse Werner, actress and singer*

In Hitler's Germany Zarah Leander was the godlike, supposedly inaccessible diva. However, her swan-song went on for decades and increasingly descended into grotesque self-parody. The matronly figure with a deeply lined face went on appearing on stage in endless 'farewell tours'. She was even willing to entertain on North Sea ferries, where she had to compete with the attractions of the duty-free shop – a living fossil of her former self. If, during the Ufa years her blend of mother-figure and vamp had guaranteed her a gay following, as she grew older she became an iconic 'fag-hag' and to this day drag-artists love imitating her.

> Berliners irreverently called her the 'fairy queen' because she did occasionally sing at a gay club, and she was their darling.
> *Ilse Werner, actress and singer*

In 1978, after the death of her third husband and accompanist, Arne Hülphers, she suffered from a stroke. She died in Stockholm on 23 June 1981. The songs of Zarah Leander live on to this day. She was a fine figure of Swedish womanhood with a splendid voice, which she would doubtless have put at the service of any regime, provided it had offered her enough money. But she was only able to achieve stardom in Nazi Germany; it was the Germans who most appreciated her brand of melancholy yearning, and it was under Hitler's dictatorship that the myth she embodied was in greatest demand. She ignored the political responsibilities of an international star. In her case, to misquote Brecht, mammon came first, and then morality. She herself never claimed to have been anything but a singer. How much of her was myth, how much reality? In her own words: 'I am "Leander". That will have to do.'

> I regret nothing. It is always foolish to regret.
>
> *Zarah Leander*

CHAPTER SIX

THE ADVERSARY – MARLENE DIETRICH

When the Hitler regime called upon me to return to Germany and become the 'reigning queen of the German film industry', the answer I gave them is, I think, known to everyone. What people don't know is that I couldn't resist twisting the knife in the arrogant hearts of those gentlemen.

If there had been no Hitler, I'd have had lots of children – and a home in my own country.

I am German and I understand the Germans. They want a leader. We all want one. The Germans are like that. They wanted their Führer, and they got him.

I am proud of my Berlin sense of humour, which is like no other in the world and has often helped me get through difficult times in my life.

The Germany that existed before Hitler, my homeland, was a country I loved, of course, and my memories of it are beautiful and often melancholy – like all memories.

If they had any spine, the Germans would hate me.

Marlene Dietrich

She loved the culture of Germany, of the Weimar Republic. When things began to change, when this country with its culture and its beauty was transformed into the personification

of ugliness and cruelty, it was very difficult for her to accept it.
She did not turn her back on her homeland, but rather on what
it had become.

Maria Riva, Marlene Dietrich's daughter

She is a pure throwback to the glittering, superficial world of
the twenties and thirties, whose dreams she not only
embodied to absolute perfection, but also devoutly shared:
she was at once the goddess and the creation of that ultimate
western romanticism that came with the spirit of the cinema.

Gunar Ortlepp, journalist

Whatever Marlene Dietrich does is perfect. She is a perfect
actress, a perfect cameraman, and a perfect fashion-designer.

Alfred Hitchcock, film director

In Germany there have only been two superstars: Marlene
Dietrich and Adolf Hitler.

Karel Dirka, film producer

Her beauty was captivating, but cold. She radiated sensuality
and eroticism but they were always tempered by common
sense. Unlike Rita Hayworth or Marilyn Monroe, she was
never the victim.

Helmuth Karasek, journalist and critic

She knew exactly what men wanted from her. And she knew how
to handle it. The 2,000 GIs in the Algiers opera-house could not
make her nervous – she was only vaguely aware of their impatient
shouts, their coarse heckling. With complete self-assurance
Marlene Dietrich stepped on to the stage wearing a tailor-made
US officer's uniform, and in her hand she carried a small suitcase.
The unspectacular entrance disconcerted the excited soldiers for a
moment – but then they were rewarded: the star of the evening
took out of her valise a very transparent gown. She stepped
elegantly behind a screen in the centre of the stage. Seconds later

she emerged in her legendary 'naked dress', a wisp of gossamer sparkling with sequins, which hinted at everything while revealing nothing. In that creation Marlene Dietrich was the epitome of all the women that soldiers in every army yearn for. The apparition spread her arms wide. 'The men let out an animal howl that lasted five or six minutes. They roared and they shrieked. It was fantastic to see it; the boys were totally gone. And Marlene was completely with them. She just stood there and let herself be carried away', recalls Joshua Logan, who was then a fellow-member of the US Army entertainment unit. And then the audience got to hear the first number – the rousing 'See what the boys in the back-room will have'. She knew what to treat the boys to. No-one could be left unmoved by her performance with the 'musical saw'. Marlene sat herself on a chair, pulled her dress high up her thighs and carefully positioned a long flexible wood-saw between her legs. Then, with a violin-bow, she played 'Pagan Love Song'. In the *fin-de-siècle* opera-house of that French colonial city no-one had ever heard *this* version of the old favourite. And most of the young rookies had never seen such a risqué show.

The uniformed men who filled the auditorium on that evening of 11 April 1944 did not mind that the woman up on stage had a German name and a German background. They were thrilled to see this blonde vision singing and dancing, for the first time in front of US troops stationed overseas. Nor did it concern them that top Nazis – the very men they were going into battle against – had once shared their enthusiasm for 'la Dietrich'. Among them was Hitler's henchman Joseph Goebbels. He was spellbound by the potential of this woman, and for a long time had cherished the dream of making her the leading advertisement for German cinema. It was a dream that never became reality: nothing would induce her to let Nazi ideologues turn her into a figurehead. Time and again Hitler and his lackey Goebbels had tried to woo her, but the German diva rejected all such advances. Instead of making mind-numbing junk-movies in Germany as the 'Queen of Ufa', she preferred to put on her shows at the front, before audiences of American soldiers. Her public was dressed in khaki and olive-green, not field-grey. To the GIs the international star was right up close, there on stage in front of them – sexy yet unattainable. To the Nazis she was merely unattainable.

> Marlene Dietrich is no ordinary woman.
> *Joseph von Sternberg, director, in his memoirs*

It was not just with the troops that Dietrich had scored such a resounding success. One after another, men of a very different sort had fallen for her charms: individualists, artists – men to whom uniforms and uniformity were anathema. Joseph von Sternberg was an eccentric Hollywood director who, though American, liked to dress in lace-up boots, riding-britches and a turban. But on a September evening in 1929, when he went into the 'Berliner Theater', he was conventionally dressed in a black dinner-suit – as befitted a visit to the theatre. The play he wanted to see was called *Two Cravats*, and was the box-office hit of the season. On that early autumn night he was one of 1,500 spectators in the packed stalls – and what he saw was a breathtaking show: Dixieland jazz conjured up the world of Chicago gangsters, a cast of fifty danced the Charleston across the stage, Hans Albers shone in the leading role, but von Sternberg's attention was caught by a woman who brought an effortless elegance to the stage – in every scene she performed her songs in excellent English, all the while radiating a languid arrogance. Only minutes after the 28-year-old Marlene Dietrich had first stepped on to the stage, von Sternberg knew that his search was over. He had found his Lola-Lola, the dangerous temptress of the 'Blue Angel'. For Sternberg was not in the Berliner Theater purely for pleasure – he was seeking an actress for his latest project. He was in Germany to make a film based on Heinrich Mann's novel, *Professor Unrat*. But he still lacked the 'ideal Lola' who, as a singer in the 'Blue Angel' night-club, would turn the professor's head.

The Marlene he saw on stage was a child of the 'Roaring Twenties', the era which brought to the world everything we know today as 'popular culture': the latest hits on record and on radio, the films to be seen in cinemas – all that was available everywhere for instant consumption. It represented a huge market for a burgeoning industry and a vast stage for ambitious performers.

> She was a woman whose every action, every performance,
> was acted out as a challenge, a provocation.
>
> *Helmuth Karasek, critic and journalist*

The twenties were 'roaring' all over Europe and America, but most of all in Germany the new decade was ushering in a new age. Ever since November 1918, the nation had been shaken by political and social upheaval. The defeat on the Western Front and the revolution of 9 November brought about the end of the monarchy – and the end of many an illusion of imperial greatness and aristocratic splendour. 'Why must I live through this terrible time? I wanted to have a happy, golden youth. And now this happens. I feel so sorry for the Kaiser and all the others. The mob attacks anyone driving a car. We had invited some ladies for tea; none of them got through, except Countess Gersdorff. And her husband had his plumed helmet torn off by armed soldiers on the Kurfürstendamm. Everywhere you look there are red flags.' A bemused helplessness is expressed in those lines Marlene wrote in her diary, on 9 November 1918, when she was not yet seventeen.

Born on 27 December 1901, Marlene Dietrich's childhood was only 'happy and golden' until 1914. The seminal catastrophe of the twentieth century, the First World War, left neither her nor her family untouched. On 16 June 1916 her stepfather, Eduard von Losch, was killed on the Eastern Front. He had married Marlene's mother Josephine in 1911. Marlene's real father, Lieutenant of Police Louis Erich Otto Dietrich, had already died in 1907. In Marlene's memory the two men in uniform merged into one idealised father-figure. 'My father: a tall, imposing figure, smelling of leather, gleaming boots, a riding-crop, horses. My memory was hazy, unclear.' Her second father, an aristocrat who served in the Kaiser's Grenadier Guards, offered Dietrich's widow and her daughters Elisabeth and Marlene a distinct improvement in their social status. The family of an aristocratic army officer belonged to the elite in the Kaiser's Germany. The atmosphere in their house in the Berlin suburb of Schöneberg was disciplined in the Prussian manner, though by no means narrow-minded. Marlene and her older sister were privileged. With high school and music lessons, afternoon tea-parties, French and English governesses, the upper-class lifestyle of the Wilhelmine era could be sophisticated and luxurious. Yet the children also absorbed Prussian virtues: 'doing one's duty' was a principle of their upbringing. In an interview in 1991 Marlene described the legacy of those years: 'In my childhood I learned to get a grip on myself. I also learned not to bother other people with my own negative emotions.'

> Now it's war! Horrible! On 6 August father went off to the Western Front. Mummy never stops crying.
>
> *Marlene Dietrich, diary, 15 August 1914*

After 1914 the drab daily reality of war made life more difficult. The German population hoped in vain for a swift victory. But instead they had to survive the next few winters on turnips and swedes, and suffered real hunger. The Dietrich family had to live with uncertainty about the fate of their loved ones at the front. All this – and especially the death of her stepfather – cast a shadow over the life of the young Marlene. She became acutely aware that war was no mere adventure.

> Now they are all dead. Father is being buried today. This morning we weren't at school but went to the cemetery to be with Father. They were just digging his grave.
>
> *Marlene Dietrich, diary, June 1916*

Defeat and the revolution of November 1918 changed the life of every German. And everyone reacted in their own way. Many rejected the new social order, and hankered after Germany's former greatness and the values of the past – in the young republic they were the resentful opponents of democracy. Others, more open-minded, took a gamble and went along with the changes. The feeling of resignation turned into a deep sense of irony, which made it easier to come to terms with the sobering realities of the new Germany. What did moral values count for after such a terrible war? People looked for amusement and carried on with their lives. Berlin became a city in which every kind of pleasure was on offer, every sexual proclivity catered for, every drug available, no matter how bad the times seemed to be. Such was the world in which the young Marlene Dietrich grew up. And she recognised it as a world that offered her plenty of opportunities.

> I had a huge row with Mummy, when she said I must be boy-crazy, going out with so many schoolboys . . . I'm always being told to see wickedness in the most harmless things . . . And if I happen to talk to a schoolboy on the train, that makes me 'boy-crazy'. Really, it's all too much.
> *Marlene Dietrich, diary, 4 February 1917*

Marlene Dietrich, the 'girl of good family', set out to make a career as a musician. From 1919 to 1921 she studied violin at the Academy of Music in Weimar. In the early 1920s the city was home to the avant-garde Bauhaus group of architects and artists and had a distinctly Bohemian atmosphere. This, combined with her independent student life, unusual for young women in those days, made the beautiful, daring and desirable Marlene more determined to forge her own individual style. In 1921, back in Berlin, she found her first job – playing the violin as the only female member of a cinema pit-orchestra, accompanying silent films. It was an irony of fate that her remarkably beautiful legs initially caused a hitch in her career – she was fired after a month because her shapely calves and saucily exposed knees were apparently a constant distraction to the male musicians.

Why, she thought, should she not put her obvious effect on men to professional use? Marlene joined a group of night-club dancers, 'Guido Thielscher's Cabaret Girls', and went on tour with them. Instead of being a problem, her legs were now a trump-card in her career – and were to remain so for a very long time. Back in Berlin, she danced in various risqué revues. The stage, the limelight, and male admiration were like an elixir of life to the young woman, but she did not want to spend the rest of her career as a dancer. At the age of twenty, she was not only beautiful and disciplined, but also ambitious – and brazen. That is why she turned up one day for an audition at the drama school of the then legendary Max Reinhardt. After an encouraging start the examiners failed her in her final evaluation. Yet the talented young lady sneaked into Reinhardt's theatrical world through the back door. She took regular singing lessons and private acting instruction from one of the Reinhardt teachers, and spent most of her spare time hanging around Reinhardt's theatres. This enabled her to secure small parts, which brought her into close contact with the great stage-stars of the day. By 1923 she had appeared on stage no less than ninety-two times and had thoroughly honed her theatrical skills.

> Even at the age of sixteen, she knew she wanted to be '*the* Marlene Dietrich'. If she'd stayed in Germany, Fate would still have been on her side. Who knows, she might have become a Leni Riefenstahl.
>
> *Maria Riva, Marlene Dietrich's daughter*

The budding actress had something to offer – and she had the right instinct: the German capital had not only a thriving theatre but also a booming film industry. Marlene asked an uncle with contacts in the movie business to introduce her to some directors. In 1922 she did in fact get a tiny role in a film called *Men Are Like That* – but thought she looked completely unphotogenic: 'Like a potato with hair', was her comment when she saw the film. Nevertheless, the actor Wilhelm Dieterle gave her a part in the film that marked his directing début, *The Man by the Wayside*. Gradually Dietrich became known to the general public and to a number of critics.

It was also in the film business, in 1922, that she met her first great love, Rudi Sieber. He was employed by a film producer to cast minor roles, and decided there and then that Marlene would play a major role in his private life. The good-looking, experienced and charming Rudi did indeed win the heart of the aspiring actress – and they were married on 17 May 1923. Just seven months later, on 13 December 1924, Maria Elisabeth Sieber, Marlene's only child, was born.

Only a few months after the birth, she could tolerate the restrictions of motherhood no longer. With her husband, Marlene threw herself into Berlin's nightlife. By night the supposed 'dream couple' escaped the constraints of daily life – they haunted the bars and night-clubs of the pulsating metropolis, not always together, but with a shared enthusiasm for its loucheness and decadence. Marlene was known as the 'Kurfürstendamm Girl', after Berlin's main entertainment thoroughfare – too pretty and wanton to be taken really seriously as an actress, but too good to be ignored. In 1924 a critic wrote of the 'eloquence of her legs' and admired her 'beautiful, carnal and womanly youthfulness'. The doyen of critics, Alfred Kerr, appreciated Marlene 'for her flesh'. In 1926 she was finally able to combine her image with an acting role. In a play called *Duel at the Lido* she played a man-eating Frenchwoman. Wearing a silk trouser-suit, very daring for its day, she portrayed a modern, audacious and exotic young woman, unencumbered by moral principles. In 1927 she joined the cabaret singer Claire Waldoff in a comic revue called *Word of Mouth*. In this she displayed the quality that would later so fascinate Joseph von Sternberg: the casual elegance with which she moved, and her languid way of putting over a song – in a throwaway manner, with no great voice to help her.

> She is not satisfied merely with being beautiful. She is a realist and even has something of the clown in her.
>
> *Noel Coward, author, director and actor*

However, her film career was in the doldrums; and there was no breakthrough in sight. Her marriage to Rudi Sieber was also suffering under the strain of Berlin's nightlife. Her daughter Maria had many doting relatives, but not a mother who could give up enough time to her. Marlene went on trips abroad. After several stage appearances in Vienna, which led to a love-affair with the Austrian film-star Willi Forst, she returned to Berlin.

Her next engagement there became the talk of the town. In a musical revue called *It's in the Air*, she performed on the 'musical saw' – with legs spread wide she sat on a chair and coaxed a tune out of the flexing steel blade with a violin-bow. That is how the whole of Berlin discovered the loveliest legs in the city. In the local dialect the word for 'legs' rhymes with her name and she became *Marleene, mit die schönen Beene* . . . .

By the time Sternberg came across her in the Berliner Theater, Marlene Dietrich had already appeared in sixteen films – which she later preferred to disown. When, in 1929, she appeared in the show *Two Cravats*, she displayed to the audience and to the Hollywood director all the qualities that later marked her out: a unique blend of vivacity and melancholy, a voice which betrayed a hint of sadness, even resignation; a pose of taking the world as it is, but never allowing herself to be defeated by it.

It was no business of hers to change the world. She was not interested in the workaday politics of the Weimar Republic – and equally uninterested in Hitler and his party, who despised that republic and wanted to throw democracy out of the window. What interested Marlene Dietrich first and foremost was her career. And that really got going in 1930. In Sternberg's film made at the Ufa studios, *Der Blaue Engel* (The Blue Angel), she played Lola-Lola, whose seductive allure made the priggish and unpopular schoolmaster, Raat – played by Emil Jannings – take leave of his senses. His infatuation with the chanteuse, and the company he kept in the 'Blue Angel' night-club, put him beyond the social pale. '*Ich bin von Kopf bis Fuss auf Liebe eingestellt*' (From my head to my feet, I'm ready for love . . .*) sings Lola the seductress, but when the schoolmaster – like a moth drawn to a candle – falls for her, she shows indifference: '*Wenn Motten vebrennen, dafür kann ich nicht.*' (I can't help it if moths burn to death).

> Her eyes have a misty look, like a cow that is calving.
>   *Emil Jannings, Marlene's co-star in* The Blue Angel

In *The Blue Angel*, the newcomer Marlene Dietrich acts the world-famous Emil Jannings clean off the screen. But the board

---

* The song was translated, and recorded by Marlene under the innocuous title 'Falling in Love Again.'

of Ufa, headed by Alfred Hugenberg, the nationalistic German press-baron, were so shocked by the content of the film that they simply failed to appreciate Marlene's talent – they assumed the film would flop and chose not take up any contractual options on the new star. The film's première was cancelled until further notice. However, a representative of Paramount in Berlin saw a preview and cabled Hollywood: 'She is sensational – put her under contract!' Paramount wasted no time. The Americans offered 20,000 marks, and topped any contracts Marlene still had in Berlin. The young German woman was free – and the Hollywood adventure could begin.

> She was one of the those people with whom you have the strange feeling that life is only there for *them*, and that things only happen so that they can take them over and become greater through them.
>
> *Maria Riva, Marlene Dietrich's daughter*

On 1 April 1930 Marlene Dietrich was sitting in the front row of the Gloria Palace cinema on the Kurfürstendamm – not in the uncomfortable 'barber-shop seats' but in one of the places of honour reserved for the stars of the evening. The whole team was gripped by first-night nerves – the cast of *The Blue Angel* squirmed nervously in their seats. Next to Marlene sat her co-star Emil Jannings, the director Joseph von Sternberg and producer Erich Pommer. Finally the closing sequence flickered in the screen and the curtain fell. There was a silence lasting several seconds, then a roar of applause broke out. The audience frantically cheered the leading lady – and Emil Jannings was reduced to a walk-on part.

Marlene was the star of the future. But the film mogul Hugenberg and his cronies – then running the most powerful film company in Europe – could not see what they were missing. In the world they envisaged there was no place for this rising star. The Germany that Hugenberg wanted, and which after 1933 the Nazis created, would usher in a retrograde culture: one that was folksy and nationalistic, bourgeois and bigoted. The German film industry had offered no contract to its greatest talent. Thus the decision to leave Germany or stay was taken away from Marlene as early as 1930.

And so to Hollywood. Only days after the Berlin première of *The Blue Angel* Marlene left for America. Her husband Rudi, who wanted to stay in Berlin with his mistress Tamara and little Maria, raised no objection. Yet Hollywood and Berlin were worlds apart – as Marlene was appalled to discover. Sternberg and the bosses of Paramount had a little surprise in store: they immediately made it clear that, while they were interested in her potential, they were not at all keen on the woman she currently exemplified. They wanted to alter her completely, to meet the requirements of the studio. Joseph von Sternberg was proud of his discovery and began to shape Marlene according to the precepts of the Paramount image-makers. He sent her to a voice coach, to improve her accent; prescribed diets and workouts; and suggested she should have two molars removed in order to make her cheeks more hollow. Make-up and eyebrow-styling rounded off the improvements on nature required by Hollywood. And as a director, von Sternberg knew what could be made of a face with lighting and camera-work.

'Sternberg's lighting and his make-up smoothed away Lola-Lola's rough edges, and the symmetry of the face now seemed to hint at everything: mystery, desire, seductiveness, warmth, vulnerability, world-weariness', writes Marlene's biographer, Steven Bach. The foundations for the Marlene myth had been prepared – now almost anything could be read into it. Marlene Dietrich, the private individual, disappeared behind a mask-like image. 'She had no private side. She was all things to all men – and merciless on herself', a journalist wrote about her. In an interview in 1991, Marlene herself spoke of a 'damaged private life'. In the United States the new image was promoted in advertising campaigns with military precision. Even before she was to be seen in cinemas, posters and full-page newspaper ads announced 'Paramount's new star – Marlene Dietrich'.

> My mother possessed the intelligence to recognise when someone had the right idea about something. As soon as she had taken it on board, it was *her* idea.
> *Maria Riva, Marlene Dietrich's daughter*

Only then was she presented on the screen. In the film *Morocco* she plays Amy Jolie, a world-weary, stateless night-club singer in Paris, who goes out to North Africa and falls unhappily in love with a Foreign Legionnaire – played by Gary Cooper. Dressed in top-hat and tails, she appears as an enigmatic woman who is unable to break free from the *demi-monde* of prostitution and cocaine abuse. In the end she moves on, this time to Buenos Aires, only to go on living the same life there. 'There's a Foreign Legion of women too', the script makes her say – a motto that was not inappropriate to the life she herself would lead. In the United States *Morocco* broke all box-office records – despite the Depression, the cash-registers kept on ringing for Paramount and for the cinema-owners. The *Los Angeles Times* was full of praise: 'Miss Dietrich is a stand-out with her provocative coolness, and she employs a marvellous economy of expression.' In fact she rehearsed every word, every languid gesture, every deep, mysterious look – she left nothing to chance, for beauty, as she knew, was not a random commodity. The Dietrich style was to remain her recipe for success. The recipe – take some Berlin bohemianism and put it through the Hollywood blender – was savoured all over the world. And in her home city they were proud of the Berlin flower that was blooming so magnificently on the other side of the ocean.

> As for myself, it was no sacrifice to leave the land of my birth. I was living in a country that generously took in any stranger in need.
>
> *Marlene Dietrich, 1991*

Marlene did return to Berlin, though only as a visitor. On the flying visit she made in 1931 she was welcomed with open arms by the German metropolis. It was to be the first and last triumph granted to her by her home city. Dietrich in Berlin was a sight everyone wanted to see. All her public appearances turned into riots, the Berliners were thrilled. Yet Marlene kept her gratification within bounds. She confessed to a journalist friend: 'As a small-time actress I had a hard time in Berlin. Being famous now doesn't really make me happy any more. You see, this fame has come rather too late.' And even in Germany, not everyone celebrated her success: spokesmen for the Nazi Party described her films as 'third-rate and corrupting kitsch', and demanded they be banned in German cinemas.

There was criticism in the United States as well: the morally strait-laced American women's organisations called for a boycott of all Dietrich films, because she nearly always played a prostitute in them. And they reproached her on another point: she lived in Hollywood, while her husband and child remained in Germany. In order to save her reputation, Marlene decided to bring her daughter Maria to live with her in the States. Her husband Rudi Sieber settled down with his mistress Tamara in Paris – where he was employed by Paramount to supervise the dubbing of their films. That way Marlene had provided for everyone. No-one would suffer – at least that was how it looked.

> The only miserable thing about my first spell in Hollywood was missing my little child. I had left her with my husband and the nanny in Berlin, because she was too young for such a long journey.
>
> *Marlene Dietrich*

While *Morocco* got Paramount out of the red, her next film, *Dishonoured*, was rather a flop. In it Marlene plays a Viennese prostitute in the First World War, who works for the Austrian secret service as a 'love-spy'. Despite the film's poor reception, von Sternberg persisted in presenting Marlene Dietrich in the same hackneyed roles. The next was in *Shanghai Express*. The film was Sternberg's greatest popular success and was nominated for three Oscars. But the American magazine *Vanity Fair* was less than complimentary: 'Sternberg has swapped his frank and honest style for fashionable game-playing, especially with Dietrich's silk-stockinged legs and lace-clad bottom; and has turned her into the Queen of Tarts.' Sternberg studiously ignored this. In *Blonde Venus* Marlene once again appears as a night-club singer who goes on the streets in order to feed her children and pay for treatment for her sick husband. This film flopped with the public.

Meanwhile in Germany the Nazis were calling for a boycott of the film *Dishonoured*, which they described as 'second-rate Remarque', alluding to *All Quiet on the Western Front*, a brilliant pacifist film based on the novel by exiled author Erich Maria Remarque. Since that had already earned the contempt of the Nazis, to be called a 'second-rate' version of it was a double insult.

*

By 1932 Marlene had reached a crisis point. Audiences were staying away from her films in droves. Things were going badly for Paramount – it was threatened with bankruptcy and the movie business as a whole was suffering from the worldwide economic slump. Times were getting hard for Marlene Dietrich and Joseph von Sternberg; they no longer had any friends at Paramount. The people whom the director and his discovery had brought over from Europe to Hollywood were either fired or sidelined in the company. The 38-year-old Sternberg let it be known that he was through with film-making. He wanted to retire, he said, and devote himself to painting, reading and building a house.

Marlene, too, was taking a long, hard look at her life. She announced her intention of returning to Europe, to try and make a stage career in Berlin and Paris. Yet the German-born actress remained in America – because she was contractually obliged to do so. Paramount did not want to let her go, preferring to pay her a retainer of $4,000 a week. In the end the studio bosses signed her up for a new film, *Song of Songs*. Under the direction of Reuben Mamoulian she was to play – as in her first four American films – a 'girl of easy virtue', in other words a prostitute. Marlene was not particularly thrilled with the part of 'Lily' and failed to appear for important preliminary meetings. When Paramount immediately cancelled her weekly $4,000 allowance, she felt freed from her contractual ties. In December 1932 she was indeed on the point of leaving Hollywood for Europe. The protracted political crisis in Germany held no terrors for her. Surely the Nazis would never become the governing party. Like everyone else, she could not really believe that the most terrible accident in German history was about to occur. Berlin still offered interesting career prospects.

Joseph von Sternberg took the same view. He returned to Berlin where he had occasional meetings with Marlene and dined frequently with the media magnate Alfred Hugenberg. However, this did not produce any concrete projects for Sternberg or Dietrich. What decided the actress's future career was something quite different: her lawyers strongly advised her to fulfil her contract with Paramount. And so, on 3 January 1933, she reported for duty on the set of *Song of Songs* – much against her will since, as she said, she felt she was 'under house-arrest' at Paramount.

Thus, her attention was distracted from Hitler's seizure of power and the profound political changes taking place in Germany, especially as she was now consoling herself with a series of affaires. The men in question – whether concurrently or sequentially, only the diva herself knew – were Maurice Chevalier, who was making a film for Paramount, Reuben Mamoulian, her director, and Brian Aherne, who was playing opposite her in *Song of Songs*.

Von Sternberg, meanwhile, was being made aware of the new political realities in Berlin – on 28 February 1933, on the way to Tempelhof airport, he drove past the blazing Reichstag building. A young Dutch communist named Marinus van der Lubbe was accused of setting fire to the German parliament house, but to this day the presumption is that the Nazis were behind the whole thing. The shock of the Reichstag fire gave Hitler a free hand to take action against the communists and his political opponents in general. President Hindenburg, the head of state, introduced an emergency decree setting aside sections of the constitution and granting far-reaching powers to Hitler as Chancellor. Von Sternberg, who described himself as a 'non-political person', failed to see which way the wind was blowing, and in this he was no different from many other Germans – scarcely anyone took the danger of Nazism seriously. The fact that Alfred Hugenberg, the owner of the Ufa film studios, was financing the Nazis and had been instrumental in securing the chancellorship for Hitler, was of no great interest to Sternberg.

From the other side of the Atlantic, Marlene saw things more clearly. She realised that, whatever happened, she and Sternberg now had no chance of succeeding in Germany. Faced with the 'brownshirt revolution' that her homeland was living through, she sensed that it was unrealistic to plan a film in Germany with an American Jew from Vienna. Her instinct was correct; as early as April 1933 the Nazis deprived several prominent Jewish creative artists of their citizenship. They included the theatre director Max Reinhardt, composer Kurt Weill and author Lion Feuchtwanger. Anyone who did not conform to the Nazi concept of art was under threat. The novelist brothers, Thomas and Heinrich Mann, left-wing writers Bertolt Brecht and Arthur Koestler, and film-makers Fritz Lang and Billy Wilder, as well as a number of modern painters and architects who had created the Bauhaus style, were all suddenly declared 'undesirable'. They and many others emigrated in order to escape further persecution.

On 10 May 1933 the Nazi regime dealt a second blow to German cultural life. Nazi students and activists publicly burned the works of Marx, Freud, Heine, the Mann brothers, Stefan Zweig, Erich Maria Remarque, and hundreds of other writers, both Jewish and non-Jewish, who were condemned as 'degenerate' and outlawed by the brown-shirted Philistines. The failed picture-postcard painter, Adolf Hitler, was now the one who decided what art was of value and what was not. Artists and writers who did not fit his bigoted view of the world were muzzled and exiled, or – as in the case of the anti-military and anti-Nazi journalist Carl von Ossietzky – locked up in a concentration camp in conditions they were not expected to survive.

> We knew nothing about politics, but of course we were anti-Nazi.
>
> *Marlene Dietrich, in an interview with Maximilian Schell, 1982*

Marlene Dietrich was unable to find any redeeming features in the new wielders of power and their cultural policy. In a remarkable way she was free – free of prejudice, free from convention, moulded by the cultural life of Berlin in the Roaring Twenties. At the same time she felt bound by the ideals of her upper-class Prussian upbringing; she despised the vulgar Nazi leader, Adolf Hitler, and his upstart party cronies. Their fatuous talk of a *Volksgemeinschaft*, an 'ethnic German community', left her cold. The company she kept would remain her choice alone. Her attitude was reinforced by her husband Rudi. He could see with his own eyes what was happening in Berlin, and cabled his wife in Santa Monica: 'Situation dreadful . . . bars nearly all closed. Nothing worth seeing at the theatre or cinema. Streets empty. The Jews in our business are all in Paris, Vienna, Prague.'

> He was the one who told her that terrible things were happening in Germany, who said: stay away, stay away. He was much more politically aware than her. He gave her a lot of strength.
>
> *Maria Riva, Dietrich's daughter, on her mother's relationship with her husband Rudi*

The things that went on in Germany after the Nazis seized power had an impact on Hollywood. While the 'land of poets and philosophers' was being culturally impoverished, American civilisation was enriched by Germany's best brains and greatest talents. Yet even in the New World these intellectual giants encountered enormous difficulties. It is true that Hollywood offered plenty of work for film professionals, but many emigrants to the USA were stranded with no prospect of a successful and lucrative career. Only if they were lucky did these still disorientated and often penniless newcomers meet fellow-countrymen in Hollywood, who were generous enough to help them. Marlene Dietrich was one of the 'established' immigrants, along with people like Ernst Lubitsch, Salka Viertel and Lion Feuchtwanger. As she modestly put it: 'Luckily I was in America when the Nazis came to power. That meant that, like everyone in America, I knew about the atrocities and everything that was happening in Germany. I was able to help many of those persecuted to escape, then to arrange accommodation for them and later find them work.' She did not mention that she gave very generous financial assistance to ease the plight of numerous political refugees – and perhaps even saved their lives. This was because the USA adhered strictly to fixed and relatively low immigration quotas and, outside these, only granted visas if applicants could show they had a sponsor, who would guarantee their financial upkeep. Under the pressure of events, Marlene recognised that discipline was the order of the day – from now on her financial security and solvency were more important than artistic vanity or switching studios. It was not only emigrants who were in need of her support. As well as her daughter in the US, she still had family living in Germany – her mother, her sister and brother-in-law, and their son Hasso – who might one day need her financial help as well.

America accepted me when I abandoned Hitler's Germany. One cannot only take – one must also give. It says so in the Bible.

Marlene Dietrich in her memoirs

She was a Mother Teresa, but with gorgeous legs.

Billy Wilder, director

Marlene was confirmed in her pragmatism by the success of the first film she made without Sternberg. The production she so disliked, *Song of Songs*, received extravagant praise in the press. The *New York Times* wrote of her: 'Marlene Dietrich floats through *Song of Songs* with the lyrical grace of an apparition that has been sent from heaven to beautify the moment.' No-one would forget the song Marlene sings in the film, as a prostitute with a cigarette drooping from her lip. It was an erotic come-on that held a promise for every male: 'When it's your birthday, Johnny . . .'

Women of that kind were hardly to the Nazis' taste. Marlene Dietrich was a complete contradiction of their feminine ideal. Her casual playing with gender-roles, her tendency towards the androgynous, her excursions into lesbianism, her preference for men's clothes – all that raised eyebrows, and not only in Germany. But it was for different reasons that Goebbels so resented Dietrich's success. It annoyed him that Germany's only international film-star was celebrating her triumph in Hollywood rather than Berlin. The 'Babelsberg Buck' made sure that caustic comments about her appeared in the press. So the Germans read that they would have to do without Marlene: 'It is rather doubtful whether German audiences will have a chance to see any Marlene Dietrich films, as long as she opts for the dollar.'

At the end of 1933 the government in Berlin issued a regulation whereby 'Aryan film professionals' who lived abroad, other than on temporary contracts, would be banned from working in Germany. The reason given was that they were sabotaging the development of the new culture and were therefore traitors. This came as a shock to Marlene, since she was very anxious to preserve her good name in Germany. That is why, up till then, she had avoided expressing publicly any criticism of the new Reich. On the contrary, she took the trouble to mount a 'damage limitation' exercise, and visited Berlin in March 1934. In the interests of her family in Berlin, she wanted to pour oil on troubled waters. On 14 March the head of the Nazi 'Chamber of Film' announced that Marlene had donated a 'considerable sum' to the welfare fund of his organisation. Yet only two days later the Nazis banned the showing of her film *Song of Songs* in Germany. The Nazi poodles of the press supported their master, Dr Goebbels, and dutifully provided the justification: Marlene Dietrich, they claimed, was 'a German actress who in America particularly enjoys playing tarts. The whole world knows she is German and so gains a completely false and unreal image of Germany.'

When Hitler came to power, I was forced to change my nationality. Otherwise I would never have done so. America accepted me when I had no country of my own, so to speak, and I was grateful for that. I lived there and abided by its laws. I was a good citizen, but deep down I was still German. German in my soul, German in my upbringing.

Marlene Dietrich in her memoirs

The 'tart' now gradually began to burn her bridges. Her visit to Germany in 1934 had clearly shown that she had no future in Hitler's Reich. In any case, she was not prepared to be harnessed to the propaganda bandwagon by a 'grotesque dwarf', as she called Goebbels. She had seen what the Nazis had done to many of the friends she had made in her Bohemian days in Berlin: blacklisting, book-burning, loss of citizenship and orchestrated witch-hunts in the press. As it later emerged, her donation to the German Chamber of Film was a quid pro quo for two concessions that she had extracted from the Nazi authorities: they had granted an exit visa for her husband Rudi to go to America, and had promised that Marlene's passport and identity papers would not suddenly be declared invalid – even as an international star, she was not keen on ending up as a stateless person, deprived of all her rights.

Marlene Dietrich left Germany never guessing that it would be more than ten years before she would see her homeland again. Nevertheless she remained a German – in her soul, and also to her public. On her return voyage to the States on board the liner *Ile de France*, she made friends with the novelist Ernest Hemingway. Though she had just abandoned her native land in a mood of sad resignation, the writer immediately nicknamed her 'the Kraut'. Hemingway's teasing showed that in American eyes she was still one thing above all: a German.

> I'm suddenly missing Berlin, perhaps because it's spring. I think of those late afternoons, driving down the Kurfürstendamm in an open car, and chuckling for no apparent reason. Perhaps it was because we were young and at home there . . .
>
> I fight so hard against oblivion here, against fading away altogether, against that hollow feeling inside. All I do is give and get nothing in return.
>
> *Marlene Dietrich, letter to Max Kolpe, 2 April 1934*

In the years that followed, not even Hollywood could offer her any consolation. Sternberg's film about Catherine the Great, *The Scarlet Empress*, in which she played the title role, was panned by the critics. Journalists began sniping at her and criticised her for putting on airs: 'Dietrich in love' ran a banner headline, and below in smaller type: 'Dietrich's GREAT love is – Dietrich!' Her affaires became a talking-point, as did her 'open' marriage to Rudi Sieber, who was only her husband on paper.

Her one-time patron Sternberg, who had made her into a world-famous sex symbol, saw that they had reached the end of the road they had taken together. What made it worse for him was that Dietrich, who had countless affaires with men – and women – was the one woman he could not possess. She was only his creation in an artistic sense; her love-life was never under his direction. This tension had benefited the many films they made together, yet now it seemed to be turning into a wearying routine. The film *The Devil is a Woman*, which appeared in late 1934, was intended to be a final tribute to Marlene, playing the beautiful but heartless Spanish girl, Conchita, who can only make men unhappy. The film outraged censors, critics and audiences alike. After that, Marlene never again worked with her mentor. Privately she admitted to being depressed about this: 'I've been a disappointment to him. I was never the ideal he was searching for. I tried to do what he wanted, but didn't succeed. He was never really satisfied.' For public consumption she made a diplomatic statement: 'Mr von Sternberg does not want to make any more films for a while. He has numerous interests besides cinema, especially painting. He wants to get some rest and believes that the moment has come for me to go my own way.'

Don't talk to me about that damned woman!
Joseph von Sternberg, director, 1968

Sternberg made everyone's life a misery, but he was particularly nasty to Dietrich.
Cesar Romero, one of Marlene Dietrich's co-stars

The Nazis could not resist commenting on this turn of events. Marlene's daughter Maria Riva tells us that a messenger from the German consulate handed her mother a newspaper editorial which had 'appeared in the leading German newspapers on the personal instructions of Reich Propaganda Minister Dr Joseph Goebbels'. It read: 'A big hand for Marlene Dietrich, who has finally been fired by her Jewish director Joseph von Sternberg. He always cast her as a prostitute or some other shameless woman, but never in a role that was worthy of this great citizen and representative of the Third Reich.' It continued: 'Marlene ought to return to the Fatherland, take up her historic role as leader of the German film industry and no longer allow herself to be misused as a tool of the Hollywood Jews.'

However, Marlene continued to go her own way. She realised she had an image problem. Through Sternberg's productions, she had become stereotyped in the part of the beautiful and glamorous, but also cruel and unattainable woman. One of Hollywood's top directors, Ernst Lubitsch, had plans to change all that. He, too, felt that she had been presented too much as 'Dietrich' and not enough as 'Marlene'. In his films it was 'Marlene' who would once more be centre stage – a beautiful woman with wit and humour, a real human being, not a goddess, nor a demon. In Lubitsch's comedy *Desire*, she plays a jewel-thief; in Paris she meets Tom Bradley, an American played by Gary Cooper, who helps her to escape. *Time* magazine wrote enthusiastically: 'A romantic comedy, full of charm and ingenuity, in which Marlene turns in her best performance since becoming too respectable to show the legs which made her famous in the United States.' Marlene was back in business and her reputation still enabled her to command fabulous fees for every one of her film projects. In 1936 she was paid $200,000 for *The Garden of Allah*, which, according to *Time*, made her the highest-paid woman in the world.

> Enthusiastic reviews flooded in. To handle her fan-mail a whole section was set up just for her legs. Men wanted to place their fortunes at her feet. Celebrities courted her, so as to be seen and photographed with her.
>
> *Joseph von Sternberg, director*

On the quayside in New York harbour sixty monogrammed suitcases were piled high, waiting to be loaded on board the liner *Normandie*, which was to take a very special passenger across the Atlantic. In the middle of July 1936 Marlene Dietrich was once more on her way to Europe – and the press were there in force. 'She brought all the rules of astronomy to a standstill – the earth (and the ship) no longer revolved around the sun, they revolved around her', wrote the women's magazine, *Vogue*. On board, the star occupied the grandest accommodation: a four-room suite had been reserved for her in first class. The pampered guest received very special attention – for instance, the film *Desire* was shown on board in her honour. Every day the diva posed in a different leisure outfit, held court, had herself photographed and basked in her own glory. The court correspondent of *Vogue* was utterly enchanted and penned the following: 'Even the waves of the ocean submitted to Marlene's charm. On the second day, the sea disgraced itself somewhat and the captain said to Miss Dietrich: "A thousand apologies. I will make sure such a thing never happens again."' Whether Neptune actually paid the respect due to the passenger's cult status is not recorded.

The trip on the *Normandie* took Marlene via Le Havre to London. At Victoria Station, too, she was fêted and the huge crowd of fans, eager to catch a glimpse of her, could only be restrained with difficulty by the police. She alighted from the train clad in mink and red velvet – in her public appearances she liked to resemble her glittering screen image. The Dietrich success-story continued: in London that summer the producer Alexander Korda gave her a cheque for over $450,000 (worth about six or seven million dollars in today's terms) to play in his film *Knight without Armour*. She needed the money to pay for her extravagant lifestyle, but also to subsidise her husband Rudi and his mistress in Paris. Furthermore, the politically committed Marlene was still using her income to support numerous German friends and colleagues who, since the Nazis came to power, were living in penurious exile in any country that was still considered safe. There was one aspect of their fate that they shared with Marlene – none of them knew where their home really was.

On 31 July 1936 the Berlin evening paper, *8 Uhr Abendblatt*, ran the headline: 'Marlene insults her homeland' over a story about her appearance in Britain: 'The actress Marlene Dietrich, who arrived in London yesterday, told reporters . . . that she did not intend ever to return to Germany, since she had been too badly treated there. In Germany, she said, she was attacked and her films were hated, because people could not forgive her for leaving Germany, even though it was not her fault. Whether this attempt to glorify herself at the expense of her former homeland will recommend her particularly to the British, is very doubtful.'

> I have always been a fan of Marlene Dietrich and can understand her very well. If at that time I'd had the chance – I was much too young, of course – but if I could have, I would certainly have done what she did.
>
> *Evelyn Künneke, German singer and actress*

In London the superstar Marlene fell in love with the swashbuckling film hero, Douglas Fairbanks Jr. The couple took a whole floor of Claridges hotel. Fairbanks later described Marlene as a 'good, warm-hearted German girl who . . . sometimes had rather unconventional ideas. She knew exactly what mask the public wanted to see, and enjoyed playing the remote and untouchable Venus, who drove men crazy, but there was a maternal side to Marlene as well. There was also the perfectly normal girl, who liked cooking and playing practical jokes. A nice, sweet girl, very talented, very helpful, very intelligent.' According to Fairbanks she was 'a wonderfully unconventional lover, philosopher and friend – and sometimes rather outrageous'.

It was Christmas Eve, 1936, but the seasonal mood could not soften Marlene's heart. Even the appeals of her daughter Maria went unheeded – in her childish way, the twelve-year-old girl tried to explain to her mother that at Christmastime you could not turn any visitor away. But Marlene could – especially if it was an emissary of Reich Propaganda Minister Goebbels. In the lobby of her hotel in London's Mayfair, a German waited all day for an audience with the diva. Marlene was used to gentlemen callers, but any attempts to woo her by members of the self-styled 'master-race' filled her with unease, and were invariably brushed off without ceremony. The envoy from Germany, a film agent named Alexander von der Heyde, offered her his services as a protector against slanderous attacks in Germany. He sent her a note saying: 'I am sitting alone on Christmas Eve in London, where I don't know a soul – even so, I am happy and satisfied, because after six months I have finally managed to see to it that you will receive official justice as an artist, a German and a human being.' Von der Heyde had the backing of Joseph Goebbels. On 22 December, von der Heyde had received a letter from the Reich Controller of Film, which stated: 'On behalf of Reich Minister

Dr Goebbels, I can today inform you that in future no more articles that are detrimental to the good name of Frau Dietrich will appear in the German press.'

> I myself have not been sent to you by the German government, and have no connection with it. I come solely on behalf of and with the full authority of my company. Although I am not here at the behest of the Führer, my director, Herr Fasolt did, before my departure, confer with the highest government authorities and was given the assurance that it would be much welcomed if you were to come and work in Germany.
>
> *Letter from Alexander von der Heyde to Marlene Dietrich,*
> *14 August 1936*

In addition to his chivalrous offer of protection, von der Heyde had something else to interest her – or so he thought. His Christmas present to Marlene was elaborately wrapped. Never had any man – albeit on behalf of another – promised her so much: 'The whole world' would be at her feet, if Marlene returned to Berlin as 'Queen of Ufa'. She would have a free hand: fees, choice of directors and scripts would all be at her discretion. Admittedly there was a catch, as always with Nazi promises: only non-Jews would be allowed to work with her.

Marlene Dietrich, the international star, as German cinema's big name – Goebbels saw how enormously this would enhance the prestige of the Nazi state. Even Hitler seemed to favour the idea. The dictator's verdict on Dietrich was ambiguous, as his major-domo Herbert Döhring recalled in an interview for German TV: 'We screened a lot of American films that were not seen by the general public. He saw Marlene Dietrich in them and always praised her – as an artist, as an actress.' However, the actress's professional qualities and physical attributes could not divert Hitler's mind from the fact that she had turned her back on Germany. 'She often showed her legs, and he always liked looking at legs. But other than that he called her a hyena. He didn't like her because she'd done a bunk', Döhring tells us. Hyena or not, Dietrich was considered the world's most fascinating woman. But how could she ever be persuaded to go over to the Nazis?

'The Führer would like you to come home', was therefore the message the envoy brought with him. But Hitler's Reich had never been home to Marlene. The Berlin that she knew and loved no longer existed. The brightest minds and most inspired artists had left Germany – some because they were Jews, others because they were persecuted for their political beliefs, and many because they refused to conform to the political and artistic ideals that were proclaimed in Hitler's Germany. Marlene knew innumerable exiles, had helped and comforted them, mothered them and cooked for them – she knew where their personal sympathies lay. And this first-hand experience made it easier for her to follow her political instinct. So, when asked by Goebbels' emissary if she would act as a propaganda front-woman for the Nazis, her answer was: 'Never.'

*

For her part Marlene now laid down a marker: on 6 March 1937, in the new City Hall in Los Angeles, she swore allegiance to the flag and constitution of the USA. In a suit of severe cut and a broad-brimmed felt hat she sat chain-smoking in the lobby, nervously awaiting the decisive moment. Then an immigration official named George Ruperich accepted her application for American citizenship. Outside waited a 16-cylinder Cadillac – and the press. Before climbing into the vast limousine, she announced to the waiting journalists: 'I live here, I work here. And America has always been good to me.' But there was no word of criticism against Nazi Germany.

Nevertheless, the German press reacted viciously. Julius Streicher did not miss the chance to carp in his smear-sheet, *Der Stürmer*, that Dietrich had spent so many years among the 'movie-Jews' of Hollywood that she had become 'completely un-German through these Jewish contacts'. A photograph of the City Hall ceremony was captioned: 'Dietrich swears the oath before a shirt-sleeved judge, so that she can betray her Fatherland.' In the USA, too, Hitler had his sympathisers, such as the newspaper magnate

William Randolph Hearst. One Hearst paper attacked Marlene with the bald headline: 'Deserting her Fatherland!'

Marlene Dietrich was now almost an American, though for bureaucratic reasons it would be another two years before she got her American passport. Meanwhile, she suffered more setbacks. The British film *Knight without Armour* was a box-office disaster, as was Ernst Lubitsch's faultless screwball comedy, *Angel*. What followed was a public humiliation for the superstar. The cinema-owners not controlled by the big studios published full-page advertisements in Hollywood's trade papers, in which Marlene Dietrich was described as 'box-office poison'. It was small comfort for her to know she was in good company. The same treatment was meted out to Greta Garbo, Joan Crawford, Katherine Hepburn and even Fred Astaire, all of whose latest films had done poor business. The advertisements and the failures had their effect. Paramount dropped Marlene; she was paid off and lost a part that had been firmly scheduled for her.

*

Marlene fled back to Europe. She spent the summer of 1937 in Venice, licking her wounds. In the Hotel des Bains on the Lido she joined a group of emigrés who foregathered every day. The melancholy ménage even included her husband Rudi, and Joseph von Sternberg – hardly the best company in which to recover from Hollywood. Yet rescue was at hand. The gentleman who came to their table that summer in the *fin-de-siècle* lounge of the Hotel des Bains possessed exquisite manners – when sober. With elaborate formality he asked Marlene for a dance. Dietrich's biographer Steven Bach takes up the story: 'The world's most famous unemployed woman looked into the monocle of the world's best-selling novelist, and his monocle gazed back into the eyes of the Sphinx.' The man with the monocle was Erich Maria Remarque, author of the hugely successful anti-war novel *All Quiet on the Western Front*. Though neither a Jew nor a communist, in 1933 Remarque had been forced by the Nazis to leave Germany. They regarded his pacifism as subversive and considered him a political opponent.

> She's ninety per cent good and ten per cent terribly stupid.
> *Erich Maria Remarque, for a time Marlene Dietrich's lover*

From then on the successful novelist had been living as a gentleman of leisure, drifting from one European resort to the next. Besides beautiful women and fast cars, his greatest weakness was alcohol. Yet Marlene was very taken with this man, whom she had known in her Berlin years and with whom she now shared the fate of an exile. The two fell in love there and then, and went off to live for a time in Paris, the city of love. They decided to go to America together. But unfortunately there was still an awkward problem. Marlene had come to Europe on her German passport. Although she had sworn the oath of allegiance to the US constitution in a blaze of publicity, the formalities of obtaining citizenship were taking time. Meanwhile, her German passport had expired. So in November 1937, not knowing what to expect, Marlene was forced to go cap in hand to the German embassy in Paris.

The reception committee awaiting her in the Lion's Den was rather overpowering. The ambassador, Count Johannes von Welczek, stood to receive her, flanked by four high-ranking diplomats who had taken up positions behind their chairs. They gave Marlene a hard time, and said that her statements to the press had harmed the reputation of the Reich. She replied coolly that she was not responsible for the gossip that appeared in the newspapers and reminded the gentlemen that she was 'German through and through'. She threatened to take legal action against anyone who claimed otherwise. In the end, von Welczek agreed that her passport would, of course, be renewed, but said he had a special message to pass on: 'Do not become an American; come back to Germany!' If she did, a triumphant reception would be made ready for her in Berlin. Marlene politely referred to her previous collaboration with Joseph von Sternberg: 'Were you to invite him to make a film in Germany, I would certainly be willing to work there.' The diplomats maintained an icy silence. Marlene went for the jugular: 'Do I take that to mean you don't want Herr von Sternberg to make a film in your country, because he's a Jew?'

The ambassador replied with a miserable lie: 'You have been poisoned by American propaganda – in Germany there is no such thing as anti-Semitism', to which Marlene retorted: 'Well, that's *wonderful*! I'll wait until you have made the necessary arrangements with Herr von Sternberg. And I hope the German press changes its tune regarding Herr von Sternberg and myself.' Ambassdor von Welczek, ever the diplomat, attempted to save the situation: 'A word from the Führer and everything will be carried out in accordance with your wishes, as soon as you return.' Marlene received her renewed documents the very next day. As she recalled years later in her memoirs: 'It seems as though that dreadful man in Berlin liked me . . .'

*

History does not relate what the Paris diplomats reported to Berlin, but they clearly tried to present their conduct in a good light. Thus the absurd scene in the German embassy was interpreted by the Ministry of Propaganda as a successful opening of negotiations with Dietrich. On 7 November 1937 Goebbels made this entry in his diary: 'At our embassy in Paris Marlene Dietrich made a formal statement against her slanderers, emphasising that she is German and intends to remain so. She really ought to appear in a Hilpert production at the Deutsches Theater. I will now take her under my wing.'

A little later he made the next move. He despatched Heinz Hilpert, a man who had worked with Marlene in Berlin in the 1920s, and whom she liked and respected. He was now Artistic Director of the Deutsches Theater, and Marlene received him with diplomatic courtesy. Goebbels' envoy took that as an indication that he should send a positive report back to Berlin. Dietrich had declared herself willing, he announced, to return to Berlin as soon as her contracts in Hollywood permitted. Goebbels noted in his diary for 12 November: 'Hilpert has been to Paris. Marlene Dietrich cannot appear in Berlin until a year from now. But she stands firmly on Germany's side.' Exactly a week later we read in his diary: 'I'm going to have her rehabilitated in the press!'

Marlene's excuse that she had pressing commitments in

Hollywood was not strictly honest – there wasn't a booking on the horizon. Just the same, Marlene remained much in demand, especially for photo-calls. At parties and premières all eyes were on the world's most desirable woman, dressed in extravagant gowns and glowing with emeralds and rubies. In those circles she was unbeatable and always a popular guest. Yet in the glitzy world of Hollywood, where events in Europe aroused little interest, there was one thing that made her an exception: the developments in Europe alarmed her and affected her personally. A European war would put her own family in danger. She was appalled to read and hear the news about the Austrian *Anschluss* and the annexation of the Czech lands of Bohemia and Moravia.

Nevertheless, late in 1938 Marlene decided to travel to Europe. In Switzerland, where her daughter Maria was at boarding-school, she met her family from Berlin. A shadow was cast over the reunion when her brother-in-law, Georg Will, brought the name of Goebbels into the conversation. He said he had a message for her from the Reich Minister of Propaganda, to the effect that Marlene's home-coming would mean a great deal to the Führer. Marlene was furious. After the latest events such a step would be even more unthinkable than ever, for on 9 November that year, with the burning of synagogues and the murder of Jews, the Nazis had shown the world their true and hideous face. Marlene had already suffered personally as the victim of a Nazi hate-campaign. Earlier that year in Düsseldorf an exhibition had been organised under the title 'Degenerate Music – The Day of Reckoning'. This was an adjunct to the Munich exhibition of 'Degenerate Art' and was directed against the supposed Jewish influence in music. The songs Marlene sang, such as 'Falling in love again', which were by Jewish composers, were featured in the exhibition and branded as 'degenerate'.

At their meeting in Switzerland Marlene put great pressure on her family to turn their back on Germany. But her mother, Josephine von Losch, did not want to leave Berlin, nor the clock-factory she had inherited and was now running. As Marlene said goodbye to her family in Lausanne, none of them guessed that by the time they met again, the fire-storms of the Second World War would have blazed across Europe.

Obviously Marlene became anti-German, and she was right to be.
Leni Riefenstahl, director

From Lausanne Dietrich travelled to Paris. There she met Jean Gabin, the greatest star of French cinema. They did not begin an affaire – yet, as Marlene had commitments in America. In June 1939 she re-crossed the Atlantic in order to receive her US citizenship papers in Los Angeles. At a ceremony where she was one of 200 new Americans, the judge made a speech that included this warning: 'We must be on our guard against any kind of propaganda that attempts to play off one class, race or religious community against another. Events overseas have given ample proof of the tragic consequences of the propaganda of hate.' Wise words, yet over the past few years Marlene Dietrich had impressively shown that she had no need of such warnings.

If she needed advice it was more to do with her film career. A producer named Walter Wanger made a proposal that annoyed her at first: it meant she would once more have to change her image. He suggested a part in a western. Marlene needed time to think about it. With the ink hardly dry on her American passport she travelled back to Europe that same summer. In Paris she met up with Remarque, von Sternberg, her daughter Maria and other members of the Dietrich entourage, with whom she then moved on to Cap d'Antibes. At this sophisticated resort on the Côte d'Azur she met Joseph Kennedy, the US ambassador to Britain, who was holidaying there with his family. Joe Kennedy's friendly attitude towards the Third Reich was rather a sore point, but it did not prevent Marlene from flirting and dancing with his two charming and good-looking sons, Joe Junior and Jack (as the future president was familiarly known). This dance on the edge of the European volcano, in the fateful summer of 1939, had its more *outré* aspects: while her lover Erich Maria Remarque – whom she treated worse than all her other admirers – drowned his fear of failure in large quantities of calvados every evening, Marlene flung herself into an affaire with a woman – just for a change. The lady in question was Canadian whisky heiress Jo Carstairs, whose yacht lay at anchor off Villefranche-sur-Mer.

Her beauty is so apparent, it is unnecessary to speak of it; and so I bow, not to her beauty, but to her goodness. She illuminates you like the light on a wave in a turbulent sea; a transparent wave that comes from afar and, like a gift, brings us its light, its voice and its foaming crest; it brings them to the very shore on which we stand.

Jean Cocteau, French author, playwright and director

In the South of France she decided that she would indeed make the proposed western. The top producer at Universal Studios, a Hungarian named Joe Pasternak, dreamed up the film with a German-Jewish scriptwriter, Felix Joachimson (aka Jackson), the ex-Berliner Friedrich Hollaender, and the former German citizen Marlene Dietrich, who would play a saloon chanteuse. For such a quintessentially American genre as the western, this was a remarkably un-American team. But in the fantasy-world of the Hollywood studios, this symbiotic relationship with European exiles was highly productive. However, in the real world things looked very different. The nations of Europe were poised to plunge into another armed conflict. The situation in the Old World was about to explode.

Dietrich and her retinue abandoned the European powder-keg at 5 minutes to twelve. On 1 September Marlene was on board a liner in mid-ocean when the news came through that in the early hours of the morning the German Wehrmacht had launched an attack on Poland. Marlene was torn in two directions: one part of her life was in the safety of the USA, but the other was drawn back to Germany and an uncertain fate. She was an American on her way home, far away from the war, but her mother, sister and brother-in-law were trapped in Berlin.

If she was tormented with anxiety, she did not show it. With discipline and professionalism she tackled the job of re-launching her career with the western, *Destry Rides Again*. She played Frenchy, the cigarette-rolling saloon singer, opposite James Stewart, who had just achieved stardom in *Mr Smith Goes to Washington*. Once more Marlene had to sing, and Hollaender wrote several songs for her including the up-beat number 'See what the boys in the back-room will have', a title that would remain with Marlene for the rest of her stage career. Marlene demonstrated her talent for comedy and once again – at last – revealed the limbs that had made her famous. Dancing on the bar she threw up her legs just as she had done in those smoky Berlin night-clubs of the 1920s. In *Destry Rides Again* we see the Marlene who had already turned men's heads as Lola-Lola in *The Blue Angel. Destry* was a huge success and it transformed Marlene from 'box-office poison' into an aphrodisiac.

Her next leading man was John Wayne in *Seven Sinners*. She plays 'Bijou', a floozie with a heart of gold and a great sense of humour; and in a night-club called 'Seven Sinners' on a Pacific island, she turns the head of John Wayne's US Navy lieutenant. It was un-demanding entertainment and went down big with the public. Marlene's biographer Steven Bach sums up her recipe for success: 'Bijou was the character that defined Marlene for the next ten years: tough but not impersonal, seductive but funny, a realist with brains and a sense of humour.'

Those were exactly the qualities that could help people, psychologically speaking, to survive the world conflagration more or less unharmed: qualities that would be in great demand over the years to come, even in America. In December 1941 the Japanese bombed the US naval base at Pearl Harbor, in Hawaii. This surprise attack thrust the United States into war with Japan. Then on 12 December 1941 Germany declared war on the USA – Marlene's old homeland and her new one finally faced each other as enemies.

In sun-soaked Hollywood the rich and the beautiful could take refuge from the reality of war and amuse themselves in endless ways. But for Dietrich that was not the answer. She wanted to play a part in bringing the war to an end, with her new American homeland on the winning side. But how could a screen goddess contribute to the USA's war-effort? Hollywood had the answer. On the day Hitler declared war on America, the stars in sunny California mobilised as well. The 'Hollywood Victory Committee' was founded in Los Angeles – with the actors' section chaired by Clark Gable. The task of the committee's female members quickly became clear; they would promote the sale of Victory Bonds.

In the battle for sales Marlene stood in the very front line. She made radio broadcasts and travelled across the States four times. The US Treasury nominated her the best bond-saleswoman in Hollywood. She exploited her popularity to sell bonds at huge events, and at gigs in bars and clubs she used her sex-appeal to goad men into buying war-bonds. As her biographer Steven Bach relates: 'She sat on the laps of inebriated investors and prevented them from leaving, while Treasury officials rang a bank information-centre that was manned round the clock, to make sure the cheques wouldn't bounce.' Dietrich's patriotic deployment of her body in sleazy bars went a little too far for the most senior patriot of all. One evening while she was working in Washington, President Franklin D. Roosevelt summoned her by phone to the White House, where he gave her a fatherly talking-to: 'I've heard about all the things you are doing to sell war-bonds. We're very grateful to you for that, but I forbid you to perform these salacious acrobatics. From now on you must not appear in any more night-clubs. That's an order.' The diva, daughter of a Prussian officer, knew this tone of voice and respected it. She obeyed.

Marlene extended her war-effort in other directions. With the comedians Groucho Marx and the Ritz Brothers she toured the country visiting military bases and hospitals. The comedians provided the gags while Marlene added a dash of sex and sang 'The man's in the navy' from the film *Seven Sinners*. If the servicemen in the audience wore khaki the lyrics could easily be changed to 'The man's in the army'. But whether such niceties were noticed by the GIs, when confronted by the Hollywood goddess in the flesh, is open to doubt.

Marlene was only just over forty, and this wartime duty offered her a new artistic opportunity. Never, since her early days in Berlin, had she stood on stage and drawn on the full range of her skills in live performance. This new activity diverted her attention from the fact that cinema-goers were now looking to a younger generation of female stars – Lana Turner, Rita Hayworth, Hedy Lamarr and Betty Grable were at the starting-tape, ready to put the favourites of the 1930s out to grass. There were scarcely any parts in Hollywood for actresses 'of a certain age'. Either you had to be young, or else old enough to play the mothers of youthful heroines. Even before the war

Marlene looked at this quite realistically. As she told a journalist, who eagerly took down every word: 'A film-star's career lasts only as long as her youth, and on the screen your youth fades far more quickly than on the stage. On the stage you can fool an audience, but not on the screen.'

The war played an important part in Marlene Dietrich's life. Her biographer Steven Bach explains it like this: 'She entered the history of that war, just as the war was an important part of her own history. It signified a turning-point and at the same time a climax, as well as a premonition of things to come. Marlene could take stock of her past and at the same time – without any help from others – build a new personality for the future which, though still distant, would certainly not be restricted to Hollywood.'

Her whole career, indeed her entire life, is like a magnificently unfolding melodrama that follows the peculiar laws of those good old, weirdly flickering silent movies – from the fairy-story of her discovery by the brilliant image-maker Joseph von Sternberg, right up to the whispered rumours surrounding the legendary lover, whose collection of toy-boys and sapphic sirens shattered even the notoriously lax moral standards of Hollywood.

Gunnar Ortlepp, journalist

In Hollywood new faces kept on arriving from Europe. In the summer of 1940, as a reaction to Hitler's defeat of France, a number of French film-stars moved to America. Marlene spoke perfect French and felt that the newcomers – among them actor Jean Gabin and director Jean Renoir – would enrich the American film industry. But Marlene's old friend Gabin was unknown in Hollywood: the usually self-reliant Frenchman needed comforting, and he got that from Marlene. 'I loved mothering him by day and by night', she confessed later. The comforting turned into romance and he finally became the love of her life. Together they moved into a house in Brentwood, California. But the famous 'tough guy' was not completely happy – he wanted Marlene all to himself, but had to share her with a circle of admirers. And then there were all the servicemen, whom she fascinated – by this time she had added conjuring-tricks to her singing, in the 'Wonder Show', which Orson Welles organised in a tent on LA's Cahuenga Boulevard. Gabin went to see it every night. As he said in an interview years later: 'When she stepped on to the stage in that dress – she really took quite a risk with it – and with that knowing look, she simply knocked everyone sideways. The soldiers went crazy.'

Gabin was insanely jealous. He beat Marlene up whenever his suspicions drove him into a fury. But the movie hero had other reasons to be unhappy. He was not accepted in America, and felt ill at ease there. What is more, his conscience was troubling him. He did not want to act, he wanted to fight – in the ranks of de Gaulle's Free French Forces against Hitler's Wehrmacht. In the spring of 1943 the Free French accepted the 39-year-old Jean Gabin as a volunteer. Marlene went with him to the naval dockyard at Norfolk, Virginia. On a foggy night he said goodbye to her on the quayside and went off to war – sailing on a tanker to North Africa. In a film this scene would probably have seemed absurdly sentimental, but in that war it was a real and harrowing experience that was repeated ten thousand times over.

*

The pain of parting strengthened Marlene's determination to get closer to the war, and to the men who were fighting it out. She wanted to go into the field herself – as an entertainer and welfare-worker for the United Services Organisation (USO). The USO brought together almost all the voluntary associations and organisations in America, in order to make life more bearable for US servicemen wherever they were based and fighting: with canteens, libraries and entertainment facilities. Marlene now asked the USO to send her overseas. She had even devised her own show involving musicians, comedians and girl vocalists.

There was no money to be made with the USO – people worked on a voluntary basis. For this reason Marlene had to go on accepting film roles. In order to finance the rest of 'her' war, she played in MGM's *Kismet*. Filmed in Technicolor, she was a lady of the harem, with her legs painted gold. Clad in gold lamé and wispy material, the

Baghdad sex-bomb reclined languorously and toyed with a bunch of grapes under an artificially starlit studio sky. The public came in droves to see Marlene's worst-ever Hollywood film. The giant banner for the film spanned the whole width of Broadway and showed just one thing: Marlene's provocatively gilded legs.

This was not the worst recommendation for her work in forces' welfare. The Dietrich legs were legendary. Now she was going to swing them for the boys who had to serve their country. Nowhere could the soldiers get so close to those legs as in the 'Hollywood Canteen'. For GIs passing through or stationed in Los Angeles the USO offered R and R on Hollywood Boulevard, in a vast dance-hall with live entertainment. The top swing orchestras and most popular vocalists appeared there every night. Female stars turned up in person to dance with the servicemen. The whole thing was sponsored by MCA, the Music Corporation of America, and by Hollywood 'greats' such as Bette Davis. Before being sent overseas, Marlene worked in the Hollywood Canteen every evening. She danced with GIs who were 'young enough to be her sons, and old enough not to want to be'. She served them coffee, milkshakes and doughnuts and generally made herself useful – when necessary, she even wielded a broom or cracked eggs into the pan.

Yet this somewhat symbolic contribution to the war, made by the stars of Hollywood, was not enough for Marlene. She wanted to make a clean break with her past life and join the war against Hitler. She auctioned all her possessions and left Hollywood, declaring: 'I need money so that my family can have something to live on while I'm away.'

The easy life of the in-crowd irritated her – she could see that it had nothing to do with the reality of war. And this war was closer to her than to many others. After all, her mother and most of her family were living in Berlin, which by now was being subjected to ever more frequent Allied air raids. Marlene's nephew Hasso was serving in the Wehrmacht, while the great, but unhappy, love of her life, Jean Gabin, was with the Free French in North Africa.

'I'm not going to sit here, working away quietly, and let the war pass me by', she announced. Paradoxically, she now began to wonder whether she had been right in refusing to be Adolf Hitler's 'Queen of Ufa'. Would that have given her access to him? In her supreme self-confidence she imagined she might even have been able to influence him. As she later mused: 'I sometimes wonder if perhaps I was the only person in the world who could have prevented the war and saved millions of lives. I will always be haunted by the thought that perhaps I could have talked him out of it.' Talk Hitler out of starting the war and slaughtering the Jews? Marlene, the international star, fluctuated between extreme pretension and deep self-doubt.

> I felt partly to blame for the war that Hitler had caused. I wanted to help in ending the war as soon as possible. That was my only desire.
>
> *Marlene Dietrich in her memoirs*

Now she wanted to influence the course of history in a more modest way. She joined a USO entertainment company assigned to overseas duties. In New York she rehearsed with a specially assembled troupe. The night-club comedian Danny Thomas was hired as compère, and he and Marlene worked on gags together, then there were singers and musical jacks-of-all-trades who could play any instrument from banjo to piano-accordion. Marlene was the star of the ensemble, Her legs were considered a valuable asset in the field of forces' welfare, and her vocals could get any hall swinging. A special treat for the exclusively male audiences would be her renditions on the musical saw. In February 1944 the troupe toured barracks and military hospitals in the States – and generally raised the temperature of the audiences to boiling-point. On 4 April 1944 she was given her orders to cross the Atlantic. She had already exchanged the rather drab USO outfit for a tailor-made officer's uniform and practical army kit. Her flight took her via Greenland and the Azores to Casablanca, and then on to Algiers.

> We brought a little pleasure and entertainment into the grim life of the American frontline soldiers, who to me were the greatest heroes because it wasn't their country or their own soil that they had to defend.
>
> *Marlene Dietrich, 1991*

For the 43-year-old Marlene, her triumph as a forces' entertainer in the Algiers Opera House on 11 April 1944 was the start of an entirely new period in her life. She described her front-line activity in North Africa and Europe as 'the most important thing I have ever done'. Her work was not unknown to the German troops either. After the première a new song was added to her programme – an English version of the German song 'Lili Marlene'. The number was a favourite with both sides fighting in the Western Desert and then in Europe. The evergreen had been made popular by Lale Andersen, whose recording of it had been played on German forces radio-stations. But after the defeat at Stalingrad they never played it again. Instead Marlene now sang the song on Allied stations – and for many Wehrmacht men this was reason enough to tune in secretly to the 'enemy transmitters'.

But the reality of war was very different from its portrayal in sentimental songs – as Marlene was soon to find out. 'I go into a tent. It is pretty dark inside, really gloomy, and then a beam of light enters and cuts through the darkness . . . A terrible silence . . . A nurse sits motionless, waiting in case she is needed, but nothing moves. Then you see the rows of beds. In them lie young men, either asleep or unconscious. Beside each bed stands a tall pole from which hangs a glass container – it contains blood. The only movement in the tent, the only sound anywhere, is the gurgling of blood, the only colour in the entire tent is the red of blood. You stand there and life is running from the containers into those boys. You see it running, you hear it . . .' They are not Marlene's words but those of a reporter from *Vogue*. He well describes the feeling of helplessness that nonetheless strengthened Marlene's determination to continue doing her duty at the front, to make her contribution to the war.

> It upset me that she was performing for American soldiers, while our men were bleeding to death here. I never stopped to think that she *had* to do it, because of course she had already taken up American citizenship. And that's why people made out that I called her a traitor. But I swear to you that I never said or even thought that.
>
> *Evelyn Künneke, German singer and actress*

In spring 1944 Marlene fetched up on the Italian front – she did shows in Naples, then went on to Sardinia, Corsica and finally back to the Allied landing-beaches at Anzio. Here, the US Army was in the process of breaking out from the beach-head they had fought so hard to hold. At Anzio, Marlene stepped between piles of shells, long rows of fuel-cans and other military supplies. 'We put on our shows four or five times a day, usually out of doors, in good weather or bad. We performed on the backs of trucks – two side by side made a workable stage. When it started to rain, we just kept on playing, for as long as the soldiers could stand it.' She was singing for the support-troops, who made it possible for the fighting forces to push the front northward towards Rome. On 4 June 1944 Marlene was with the Americans as they marched triumphantly into the 'free city' of Rome, which the Germans had left undefended. But then she caught pneumonia and was sent to a military hospital in Bari to recover. There, in her delirium she imagined the horrors of war. She was in a place that 'echoed with the screams of burning bodies, as though a herd of cattle were being slaughtered', she recounted later. Eventually, she received an allocation of penicillin, which was strictly rationed and normally unavailable to civilians. The antibiotic was intended exclusively for saving the lives of wounded Allied soldiers.

In the summer of that year Marlene was ordered back to New York, since she was needed for new assignments. With the Allied landings in Normandy on 6 June a new front had been opened against Nazi Germany. It was on this western front that the most potent propaganda weapons were now to be deployed. The 'Forces Radio Calais', run by the British, needed brightening up. There was no shortage of news broadcasts, but on the music side it required help from the Americans. The US secret service organisation, OSS, took up the challenge: 'Our job was to produce with great style the best that American popular music had to offer, and also to write lyrics in German, that would catch the ear of the enemy.' The lyricist originally picked for this was none other than Bertolt Brecht, but he was rejected firstly because of his 'communist tendencies' and secondly for being too avant-garde. The man they did hire was the Viennese night-club satirist Lothar Metzl, who had emigrated to America and was now serving as a private in the US Army. His witty and biting German lyrics, combined with first-rate American band arrangements, were recorded on 78rpm discs in New York. For example, to the tune of 'Californ-I-ay', Metzl effectively rubbished all the leading Nazis:

> *Denn im schönen, im Vierten Reich*
> *Wird kein Goebbels mehr lügen*
> *Kein Funk mehr betrügen*
> *Kein Hitler mehr brüllen*
> *Kein Himmler mehr killen*
> *Kein Schirach befehlen*
> *Kein Ribbentrop stehlen*
> *Kein Rosenberg schnaufen*
> *Kein Ley sich besaufen . . .* *

The numbers were sung by emigré German vocalists, though the names of Herta Glatz and Greta Keller paled in comparison to the star of the group, Marlene Dietrich. She was the only one who knew that their instructions had come from the OSS. From the autumn of 1944 the specially recorded German discs were played on Forces Radio West, which by then had replaced the Calais station.

Marlene gave herself up completely to her new assignment. In public she almost always wore uniform and in the States argued for greater involvement and commitment to victory – she still had the impression that the average American, far removed from the real war, was pretty indifferent to it. 'People here must realise that what we're doing here isn't enough', she told an interviewer. And she, as a former German citizen, publicly praised the American servicemen who were seeing action overseas: 'It isn't so hard to be brave when you are defending your native soil.' But the GIs were 'men fighting alone in a foreign country. They are having their eyes and brains shot out of their heads, their bodies mutilated,

* In the lovely Fourth Reich, there'll be / no more lying from Goebbels, / No Funk to embezzle, no Hitler to bellow / No Himmler to murder, no Schirach to order / No Ribbentrop robbing, no Rosenberg rasping / And no more Ley getting drunk

their skin burned off them, because they've been ordered to. They are bearing the pain and the injuries, just as if they were fighting and dying for their own homeland.' Yet they were waging war against Marlene's homeland, and like Marlene they were fighting against Hitler and Nazism.

At the end of August 1944 Paris was liberated by the Allies and the Free French – and no sooner did this happen than one self-appointed war-hero launched into a non-stop and highly alcoholic victory celebration at the Ritz hotel, in the rue Cambon. Ernest Hemingway, war-correspondent for *Colliers* magazine, was enjoying himself. As an American civilian in the wake of the US Army he assumed the right to demolish the Ritz's stocks of wine. The notorious boozer, macho writer and sometime army auxiliary, was in his element – this was the kind of war that suited him. He was billeted at the Ritz with his mistress Mary Walsh, a *Time* correspondent.

> Even if she had nothing else but her voice, she could break hearts with it.
>
> *Ernest Hemingway, novelist, 1952*

That September Hemingway's old girlfriend Marlene Dietrich – 'the Kraut' – also stayed for a time at the same luxury hotel. The journalist Mary Walsh could see that Hemingway's self-indulgent approach to war really did not interest her. She wanted to start work again, for the soldiers who had to fight this war to the end. 'She was a businesswoman who concerned herself with every detail of her programme, from transport to accommodation, from the size of the stage and the hall to the lighting and the microphones.' As a writer, Hemingway saw the war as a backdrop for masculine fantasies, whereas Marlene had a job to do. She wanted to play her part in the victory. For her it was a serious matter as well as being a way out of the dead-end that was Hollywood. Her daughter Maria, who was then twenty and also working in army welfare, later wrote about her mother's commitment in the Second World War: 'It was the best role she ever played. She earned laurels for her heroic courage, collected medals and commendations, and was honoured and respected. As a Prussian, she was in her element; her German soul, with its rather macabre kind of sentimentality, absorbed the tragedy of the war . . . The officer's daughter had found her true calling, she was playing the part of the brave soldier.'

*

Talking about the way the 'goddess of the front' saw herself, Maria Riva writes: 'When Dietrich talked about her touring, you would think that she was actually serving in the army, that she had spent at least four years overseas, had been under constant fire and was in permanent danger of being killed or, worse still, being taken prisoner by Nazis bent on revenge. Everyone who listened to her was convinced that she had come to believe this herself.' Yet, for all the retrospective strictures of her daughter, who has quite rightly corrected a number of myths, there is one thing which cannot be in any doubt: of all the Hollywood stars, Marlene spent the most time with the troops overseas – and was the most popular. Not only with the troops but with some prominent generals. For instance, in Paris she got to know the 37-year-old General James M. Gavin. Commanding the famous 82nd Airborne Division, he was the youngest general in the US Army. His military skill and hero-status, combined with good looks and perfect manners, made him irresistible to Marlene. After an evening at the Ritz bar with Hemingway and Mary Walsh, a liaison began between the movie-star and the soldier, which had to be handled with the greatest discretion. Not many generals got as close to Marlene as Gavin did, though they all tried. She got on well with General Patton. According to Marlene, he told her: 'If you get taken prisoner, you'll probably be roped in for propaganda and forced to make radio broadcasts, like you've been doing for us.' Then, says Marlene, he presented her with a small revolver, and ordered her to 'shoot a few of the sons-of-bitches, before givin' yerself up!' Another of Marlene's biographers, Donald Spoto, has his own theory about her penchant for romantic heroes in uniform: 'In a certain way she rediscovered in the generals her own uniformed father and step-father, those unapproachable Prussian officers, who had once withheld their love from her.' When asked once, half jokingly, whether she had ever slept with General Dwight D. Eisenhower, the Allied Supreme Commander, she replied coquettishly: 'How could I have done? He was never at the front.'

*

The fronts in north-west Europe moved relentlessly forward – through Belgium and the southern Netherlands to the very borders of the German Reich. There the Allies came up against the *Westwall* defence line and German troops that had re-grouped after months of retreat. For the Wehrmacht it was a matter of defending Germany's native soil, and this they did with great determination. On 21 October 1944 Aachen was the first major German city to fall to the Americans. But then the front became bogged down. Supply problems prevented the Allies from advancing further, and the onset of winter turned the war into a grim struggle over individual villages and hilltops in the Eifel and Ardennes ranges. In the middle of December the Wehrmacht tried once more to turn the tables. Hitler's Ardennes offensive, the 'Battle of the Bulge', inflicted severe losses on the Allies and caused chaos and panic behind the lines in the newly liberated Belgium and France. Not until the end of December did the Americans beat off the attack.

Through this winter war Marlene Dietrich went on playing her courageous and disciplined role – a Prussian woman in American uniform. In flattened villages and cold, rat-infested ruins shows were improvised day after day. For Marlene, washing was no more than a lick and a promise; quick changes and performances in chilly halls were a matter of routine, as were chilblains, lice and diarrhoea. The diva liked to be seen as battle-hardened and dressed accordingly in authentic woollen army trousers, brown pullover and a fleece-lined flying-jacket. Yet on the stage she was a creature from another world. In a sequin-covered wisp of a dress she spread her legs around the 'musical saw' and sang her songs. She swapped corny jokes with her crew and with teeth chattering went through her repertoire from end to end and back again. The men loved her for coming to visit them and conveying the illusion of normality and being at home.

In the winter of 1944–5 she busked her way through Belgium, southern Holland and France. Then suddenly she was back in Germany – for the first time in over ten years. Her first impression was shattering. Arriving in Stolberg, a few miles east of Aachen, she saw it had been totally destroyed. For two long months the Americans and Germans had faced each other and fought over the small industrial town. For weeks the front line ran right through Stolberg. What Marlene saw there was total devastation. Her laconic comment to the American journalist Frank Conniff was: 'I hate to see all these ruins, but I believe Germany deserves everything that's happening now.'

> I loathe violence in any form. And I weep for the victims.
>   *Marlene Dietrich in her memoirs*

Lieutenant Arnold Horwell was baffled – the horror-camp of Bergen-Belsen, which he and his unit were supposed to clear, was the last place in the world he expected to meet a living, breathing film-star. Yet suddenly there she was in front of him – a blonde woman in an American officer's uniform. 'That face, those legs', the British officer kept thinking: there was no doubt that he knew the lady. Marlene Dietrich, screen star and legend, had breezed into his office with a nondescript German woman in tow, whose name turned out to be Elisabeth Will. Dietrich had come to discuss an awkward matter: her sister Elisabeth and her brother-in-law, Georg Will, had been picked up in the vicinity of the Bergen-Belsen camp. Marlene had been hundreds of miles south of there, in Munich, when the news reached her, but she knew the two would need her help. It quickly emerged that her relatives had certainly not been inmates of the camp, where shortly before the end of the war 13,000 prisoners had died of typhus, dysentery or simply exhaustion. Closer examination by the occupying forces revealed that Georg and Elisabeth Will had been running a cinema and canteen for the Wehrmacht. These were located in the barracks of the Bergen tank-training school, very close to the concentration camp. The physical proximity, their contact with the SS guards and knowledge of the horrors of the camp, placed the Wills dangerously close, in moral terms, to the Nazi murderers. This family involvement was clearly very unwelcome to the international star; nonetheless she put up a spirited defence of her relatives, whom she had last met before the war.

She needed to win the goodwill of Arnold Horwell – so it was fortunate that they were both Berliners. Horwell was a German Jew who had emigrated to England in 1939 and later joined the British Army. They hit it off immediately. Having fought her own battle against Hitler, Marlene knew what approach to adopt, and was lucky to have run into one of her fans. They swapped stories from the Berlin of happier days; the actress's concentrated charm and presentation of her autograph melted the heart of the occupying officer. There was no evidence that the Wills had committed any crime, and what Marlene asked was hardly an impossibility. She wanted her relatives to be inoculated against the life-threatening typhus that was sweeping through the area, and also to be allowed to keep their service accommodation. In addition she asked Horwell not to make a big noise about the matter – if possible, it should be kept out of the press. The British officer was happy to do her this favour, though he was surprised to see in books and articles published after the war, the uncontested assertion that Marlene's sister had been 'in a concentration camp'. Years later, when Elisabeth Will began to fantasise publicly about the 'integrity of the Third Reich', Dietrich distanced herself from her, and finally denied that she had ever had a sister.

*

In the summer of 1945 Marlene Dietrich returned to America. But she no longer felt really happy there. 'I came to a country that had not suffered in the war, that did not know what their servicemen had been through over there on foreign soil. My hate of the "carefree Americans" dates from that time.' She was finished, too, with the world that called itself Hollywood. Dietrich clung to her wartime memories and celebrated victory with the returning GIs, but very soon a stale feeling set in, the feeling of no longer being needed.

Europe, on the other hand, was a chapter she had not yet closed. In July 1945 the US Army took over the western sector of the German capital from the Soviets and in September a friendly American officer tracked down Marlene's mother. Marlene, who was living in Paris with Jean Gabin at the time, flew in a military aircraft to the ruins of Berlin. The photographers were already waiting for her at Tempelhof airport. They wanted to capture for the world the heart-warming reunion of mother and daughter, and show that even an international star has a private life. When Marlene stepped from the plane in the uniform of an American officer, and was at last able to embrace her mother, she hoped that the war was finally at an end for her. She arranged makeshift accommodation for her mother, who had been bombed out of her home.

Meanwhile Marlene lived the privileged life of an American occupier. She had unlimited coffee, cigarettes and alcohol to offer the old friends who, one by one, found their way to her door. Yet the Berlin that she had preserved in her memory was no more. Many of her friends and acquaintances who had remained in Germany avoided any discussion of the Nazi years. They disguised their shame with defiance, self-pityingly bemoaned the present and conveniently forgot their own involvement in the past.

> Marlene Dietrich was the voice that defeated the bellowing of Hitler.
>
> *Karin Wieland, journalist*

The postwar Germans were not only forgetful, they were also vindictive – at least towards the woman who at an early stage had decided to defy Hitler and never made any secret of the fact. Her work for the Allied cause was resented and there was even talk of treason. Her public appearances in American uniform struck many Germans as a provocation.

Marlene Dietrich was only too happy to accept an offer by the US Army to work in France. She was in Biarritz in November 1945 when news reached her that her mother had died of a heart-attack at the age of sixty-nine. Marlene went to Berlin for her funeral. After that there was nothing left to tie her to Germany, except memories. 'The Germany that existed before Hitler, my homeland, was a country I loved, of course, and my memories of it are beautiful and often melancholy – like all memories', she confessed. Yet she also wrote: 'The tears I once shed for Germany have dried.'

All of German literature is rooted in me – from Goethe right up to Rilke, with whom I now spend every day and many nights. The magic never fades.

Marlene Dietrich, 1991

It would be fifteen years before Marlene Dietrich made another appearance in Germany. On 30 April 1960 the Governing Mayor of West Berlin, Willi Brandt, greeted the woman he had personally invited to his divided city. They had something in common. Because both had gone into exile in order to oppose Nazism, they now faced the hostility of self-styled patriots, who still had difficulty in separating the idea of Germany from that of National Socialism. However, official Berlin was cordially disposed towards her. In the Town Hall of Schöneberg, her home district, her visit was recorded for posterity in the city's Golden Book.

German is my mother-tongue. I am a German and will remain a German, whatever certain offensive newspapermen may say.

Marlene Dietrich in her memoirs

Her stage appearance at the Titania Palace on 3 May 1960 was overshadowed by placards reading 'Marlene Go Home' and even by a bomb-threat. Nearly a quarter of the 1,800 seats in the auditorium were empty. Those who did come saw the new postwar Marlene, the international star celebrating her success as a singer of sophisticated cabaret songs and ballads. In one song Dietrich explained her own position: 'I don't know who I belong to; the sun and the stars belong to everyone – but I guess I only belong to myself.' And at the end of her show she stretched out an affectionate musical hand to the Berliners: '*Ich hab noch einen Koffer in Berlin*', she sang. 'I've always kept a suitcase in Berlin.' The audience cheered – and Willi

Brandt cheered the loudest. Her performance was rewarded by no less than eighteen curtain-calls. For the first time in her career the diva was reduced to giving encores. The people of Berlin and their lost daughter 'Marleneken' had got back together again – in a way.

> Everything she does is perfect.
>
> *Peter Bogdanovich, director*

Dietrich took on various film parts and continued to perform as a singer until 1975. Yet she was increasingly becoming a parody of her old stage personality. With her whole body encased in an elastic stocking, she tried to maintain the illusion of a perfect figure. People called her 'the world's most beautiful grandmother', though this merely drove the ageing diva into making embarrassing stage appearances. Even during her performances Marlene drowned her inhibitions with whisky and champagne. A series of falls on stage brought her career to an end. After years of undignified denials of her true age, she withdrew from public life suddenly and completely. 'I've been photographed to death', was her final comment. From now on her aim in life was *not* to be filmed or photographed. Fifteen years of solitude in a Paris apartment was the last luxury she afforded herself. For decades she had wanted to please other people; now she would do what *she* pleased. She drew the curtains and vanished from sight. Only the legend remained.

> 'Where have all the flowers gone?' Only a woman as *un*sentimental as her can put over such a sentimental song.
>
> *Helmuth Karasek, journalist and critic*

Marlene Dietrich died in Paris on 9 May 1992. At her express request she was buried in Berlin beside her mother. Marlene caused controversy in Berlin until well into the 1990s. There was a debate about whether it was appropriate to name a square or street after her. In the end a square, Marlene-Dietrich-Platz, was created in the newly built Sony Center. The honour was well deserved, though she did not need it. For as Germany's greatest film-star of the twentieth century she would never be forgotten. Her fame would abide and grow because she had stood up against a man who blackened world history as the greatest criminal of the twentieth century. Marlene Dietrich decided to oppose Adolf Hitler at a time when many believed in him or still did not take him seriously. He seduced Germans without number. Yet Marlene, the eternal screen seductress, showed him – and the German people – the limits of temptation. When asked why she had resisted Hitler, her answer was a very Prussian one: 'Out of a sense of decency!'

> She was a legend.
>
> *Maria Riva, Marlene Dietrich's daughter*
>
>
> She is a myth.
>
> *André Malraux, French politician and author*

INDEX